TIME BASED MANUFACTURING

TIME BASED MANUFACTURING

Joseph A. Bockerstette
Richard L. Shell

McGraw-Hill, Inc.

New York San Francisco Washington, D.C. Auckland Bogotá
Caracas Lisbon London Madrid
Mexico City Milan Montreal New Delhi
San Juan Singapore
Sydney Tokyo Toronto

Institute of Industrial Engineers
Industrial Engineering and Management Press
Norcross, Georgia

99 98 97 96 95 94 93   7 6 5 4 3 2 1

Figure 3-11 is reprinted by permission of the American Supplier Institute, Inc. of Dearborn, Michigan (U.S.A.).

Table 1-1 is reprinted with the permission of The Free Press, a Division of Macmillan, Inc. from *Competing Against Time: How Time-Based Competition is Reshaping Global Markets* by George Stalk, Jr. and Thomas M. Hout. Copyright © 1990 by The Free Press.

Figure 4-2 is reprinted by permission of the publisher: Prentice Hall/A Division of Simon & Schuster, Englewood Cliffs, NJ from *Competitive Manufacturing* by Hal Mather, © 1988.

Figures 10-1 and 10-2 are reproduced with permission of McGraw-Hill, Inc. from Shell, R. 1992. "Measurement of low-quantity work." In *Maynard's Industrial Engineering Handbook, Fourth ed.* New York: McGraw-Hill, Inc.

Additional copies may be obtained by contacting:
Institute of Industrial Engineers
Customer Service
25 Technology Park/Atlanta
Norcross, Georgia 30092 USA
(404) 449-0460 phone
(404) 263-8532 fax

Quantity discounts available.

Bockerstette, Joseph A., date
    Time based manufacturing / Joseph A. Bockerstette, Richard L. Shell.
      p.   cm.
    Includes bibliographical references and index.
    ISBN 0-89806-126-1
    1. Production management. 2. Industrial management. I. Shell, Richard L.,
    1934- . II. Title.
    TS155.B55 1993
    658.5--dc20   92-41480

Contents

Preface

MANUFACTURING remains a vital part of the American and worldwide economies. Its contribution to producing wealth and providing jobs within those economies is clear to most everyone. Over many decades, the manufacturing sector has not just provided jobs, but jobs that pay excellent wages, salaries, and fringe benefits. The economic impact of manufacturing has been and continues to be a highly desirable part of the quality of life for our society.

It is painfully well known that U.S. manufacturing has declined during recent years. The reasons supporting this decline are complex: foreign competition, new technologies used elsewhere, refusal of workers and management to adopt needed changes, and the overall inability of U.S.-based manufacturers to make timely responses to customer demands. These demands have included more product variety, higher quality levels, lower costs, and shortened response times between order and delivery.

Restructuring, downsizing, shrinking overhead, and the general reduction of labor are, in most cases, moves in the right direction. Some companies have closed entire manufacturing facilities permanently or relocated them off-shore in search of lower labor cost, less environmental, safety and health regulations, and exemption from U.S. and other taxes.

The question is, "Has reduction and relocation of U.S. manufacturing facilities been done for the right reason or reasons and in the correct manner?" The best position for providing customer service while still maintaining profitability may not be to downsize with the same manufacturing philosophy or to relocate the plant off-shore. The key for success is innovation that is strategically implemented. Time-based manufacturing is a way of producing products that can make a U.S.-located plant competitive in a world-class market and satisfy customer requirements while maintaining profitability. Time-based manufacturing is innovative and will produce successful results. Nothing worthwhile comes easy, however. The design, development, implementation, and ongoing operation of

TBM has an impact on every part of the business, on all employees from hourly to the CEO, on suppliers, and on customers—in short, it requires a lot of hard work.

This book is a composite of our years of consulting experience. Many individuals and client firms have influenced the thinking that underlies the book's development. Much of the material comes from our work with client organizations. In every instance we have maintained strict confidentiality, which prevents naming those people who have made substantial contributions to this book.

We wish to thank our many friends and acquaintances from the business world and the academic community who have influenced and shaped our views and the examples discussed in this book. Our experience has been greatly enriched by the association with these many individuals. Their friendship is valued and deeply appreciated. Special thanks to Maura Reeves, Senior Editor at Industrial Engineering and Management Press, for her encouragement and assistance; and to Patti Cox, University of Cincinnati, and Patti Bostic, Maureen Kirley, and Amy Rudolph, Coopers & Lybrand, for their tireless efforts to produce the manuscript. The *Bible* in Proverbs 3:13 best states our wishes for the readers of this book: "Happy are those who find wisdom, and those who get understanding."

Joseph A. Bockerstette
Richard L. Shell

A New Manufacturing Paradigm   1

TIME-BASED manufacturing (TBM) is a new industry paradigm for the development, production, and delivery of products and services. The word *paradigm* comes from the Greek word *paradeigma*, meaning pattern. As defined by Joel Barker, a paradigm is a set of rules and regulations that does two things: first, it establishes or defines boundaries; and second, it tells how to behave inside the boundaries in order to be successful (Barker 1992). A paradigm is the way each of us perceives and understands the world to be—our frame of reference.

Companies, just like individuals, have paradigms. These paradigms represent the way things are done around here. They come from the organization structure, management systems, procedures and methods employed, decision making style, and reward systems. Paradigms make up a company's culture, through the formal and informal network of what people believe to be true and the values that are important. Paradigms form powerful interlocks within a company that either strengthen or weaken its ability to compete.

When practicing within a given paradigm, all input that is inconsistent with that paradigm's rules will tend to be filtered out by people within the organization as invalid, unbelievable, or simply wrong. This is the paradigm effect. Because of this, only incremental improvements are possible within an established paradigm. Breakthrough improvements, not five percent or ten percent, but fifty percent or more, require shifting to a new

1

organization paradigm. Stephen R. Covey explains the power of a paradigm shift and gives examples of how almost every significant breakthrough comes first through a break with tradition and established paradigms. "Paradigms are powerful because they create the lens through which we see the world. The power of a paradigm shift is the essential power of quantum change, whether that shift is an instantaneous or a slow and deliberate process" (Covey 1989). Time-based manufacturing is a paradigm shift that redefines the role of manufacturing. It introduces new rules that use time compression as the newest and most powerful source of sustainable competitive advantage.

TIME-BASED MANUFACTURING—WHAT IS IT?

No organization can affect a paradigm shift without a vision. A vision is not a mission statement or a company's goals. Goals have start and finish times and are usually task oriented. A vision is an expression of the organization's basic values and must focus on satisfying the customer. The vision should be a reflection of all employees within the organization. Each individual should have input to the formulation of the vision and believe that his or her thoughts and actions are an important part of the organization. The need for vision is critical: where there is no vision, the business will ultimately perish.

Time-based manufacturing provides organization vision for a complete redesign of the business for continual cycle time reduction and quality improvement. It begins with understanding the customer's requirements for products and services and ends with delivering high-quality products and services as specified by the customer with value-based pricing. The focus on reducing the total time cycle from identifying specific customer demand to delivery and billing is depicted in Figure 1-1.

Time-based manufacturing is a collection of concepts, tools and techniques, and management practice that gives a company quick response capability in designing, producing, and delivering products and services to customers.

Concepts for TBM include the following:
• balance and synchronize supply to demand
• make only what the customer needs when needed
• do only the right activities right the first time
• eliminate waste
• constantly improve reliability and capability

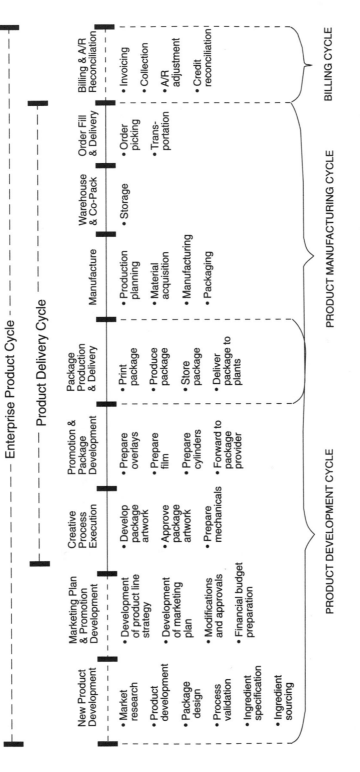

Figure 1-1. Example cycle analysis for consumer goods manufacturing.

Tools and techniques for TBM include the following:
• process mapping
• pull systems
• customer demand loading
• statistical process control
• total productive maintenance
• seven basic quality tools

Management practice for TBM includes the following:
• product-based organization design
• continuous improvement teams
• group rewards
• new performance measures
• customer and supplier partnerships

Conceptually, TBM applies to all manufacturing businesses; however, there are differences in the development, implementation, and operation of TBM depending on the type of business, e.g., process (continuous flow), repetitive (assembly), and discrete (job shop). These differences are demonstrated through the case studies in Chapters 12, 13, and 14.

HISTORICAL PERSPECTIVE

Most elements of TBM are not new. Many individuals have shaped TBM as it has evolved to the present. It is a selective, integrated composite of work that began more than two centuries ago. The classic book, *The Wealth of Nations* (Smith 1776), defined the early concepts concerning the division of labor and line balancing in manufacturing. Adam Smith observed that several persons, each manufacturing a steel pin, produced far fewer pins during a work period than did the same number of persons working together as specialists on assigned elemental tasks. This was the first reported progressive manufacturing line.

Frederick W. Taylor generally is viewed as the father of scientific management. Taylor began his work in 1881 while associated with the Midvale Steel Company in Philadelphia, Pennsylvania. After twelve years, a system had evolved based upon the task idea. Taylor proposed that management plan the work of each employee at least one day in advance, and that each worker receive complete written instructions describing the task in detail and noting the job method to use in completing it. Each job was to have a fixed standard time set by experts performing time studies. This time was based upon the pace of a first-rate worker who, after being instructed, could do the work regularly. In the timing process, Taylor advocated breaking up the work assignment into small divisions of effort known as "elements." Taylor timed these elements individually, and used their collective values to determine the allowed time of the task (Niebel 1988).

In June 1903, Taylor, presented his famous paper, "Shop Management," at the Saratoga, New York meeting of the American Society of Mechanical Engineers. In that paper he gave the main elements of scientific management as follows:

1. the use of time study, with the tools and methods for properly making it
2. functional, or divided, foremanship, with its superiority to the old-fashioned single foreman
3. the standardization of all tools used in the plant, and the acts or movements of workers for each class of work
4. the desirability of a planning room or department
5. the exception principle in management
6. the use of slide rules and similar timesaving implements
7. instruction cards for the worker
8. the task idea in management, accompanied by a large bonus for the successful performance of the task
9. the differential rate
10. mnemonic systems for classifying manufactured products and manufacturing tools
11. a routing system
12. a modern cost system

In addition to his contributions in scientific management, Taylor discovered the Taylor-White process of heat treatment for tool steel and developed the Taylor equation for metal cutting. Although not as well known as his engineering contributions, Taylor was the U.S. tennis doubles champion in 1881 (Niebel 1988).

Frank B. Gilbreth founded the modern motion study technique. This technique is the study of the body motions used in performing an operation, with the thought of improving the operations by eliminating unnecessary motions and simplifying necessary motions, and then establishing the most favorable motion sequence for maximum efficiency.

Gilbreth originally introduced his ideas and philosophies (a paradigm shift) into the bricklayer's trade. After introducing method improvements through motion study and operator training, he increased the average number of bricks laid to 350 per manhour. Before Gilbreth's studies, 120 bricks per manhour was considered a satisfactory rate of performance.

Gilbreth and his wife, Lillian, were responsible for industry's recognition of the importance of the minute study of body motions. Through this study, the Gilbreths learned to increase production, reduce fatigue, and instruct operators in the best method of performing an operation.

Frank and Lillian Gilbreth also developed the moving-picture technique for studying motions, which since has been applied broadly. In industry, this technique is known as micromotion study. However, the study of movements through the aid of slow motion moving pictures is by no means confined to industrial applications. For many years, the sports world has found it invaluable as a training tool to show the development of technique, form, and skill (Niebel 1988).

Henry Ford was truly a TBM visionary and far ahead of his time. He recognized a tremendous market opportunity for low-cost transportation and developed the world's most efficient and timely system for producing cars. The fully integrated River Rouge plant in Detroit, Michigan, produced a single product: the Model T Ford. In the 1920s, boats carrying iron ore docked at the plant and unloaded. Ore was smelted and processed into steel that was forged into engine blocks and springs and axles. These parts were machined, sent to the assembly plant, and assembled into cars. According to published reports, this process required only about 81 hours (Ford 1926).

The limitations of Ford's thinking centered on the fact that he created a highly specialized focused factory without flexibility. Ford produced a single product without variation. However, product variety at the time was not a strong customer requirement. Ford believed, and correctly so, that the customer's main interest was for low-cost, dependable transportation. Ford's view of the importance of product variety at the time can be illustrated by his famous saying, "The customer can have the car in any color, as long as it's black."

These innovators were joined by early industrial engineers, who performed work that helped to develop many of the elements of TBM. The activities of work simplification and methods engineering were focused on reducing work, balancing sequential operations, increasing output per unit of time, and reducing unit cost. This approach asked probing questions about the process or function, such as: Can this work be eliminated, combined, simplified, or improved? The goal of work simplification and methods engineering was to minimize the work content of each operation and to link productive operations. Early industrial engineers worked to eliminate defects in design specifications; improve inefficient methods of manufacture; attack poor supervisory methods including poor planning, scheduling, instruction, and training; and address worker deficiencies, including working at less than a normal pace and reducing excessive nonproductive time. These early efforts, used inside the new manufacturing paradigm, helped shape the approach used today to establish the TBM company.

In the late 1970s, Toyota Motor Company developed a system with both speed and flexibility for responding to market changes. According to a paper presented in Tokyo, Toyota implemented cycle time reduction as a reaction to a business crisis (Ohno 1982). The manufacturing division of Toyota reacted to a chain of events that began with a crisis in sales and marketing and moved to manufacturing. The crisis grew out of a need for product-line variety and the need to produce and deliver vehicles quickly.

To succeed in the economic environment of post-war Japan, Toyota needed diversified, small-quantity production. Although it had the capacity to produce about one thousand vehicles per month, the market demanded that Toyota spread this production over a wide mix of products including four-ton trucks, one-ton trucks, small passenger cars, etc. American methods for low-cost mass production could not satisfy Toyota's needs; that is, a rigid focused factory would not do. A simple transfer of the Ford Model T assembly techniques was not Toyota's answer. To compete in the fiercely competitive Japanese market and, ultimately, in global markets, they needed flexibility.

Toyota addressed the complexity problem through a direct, frontal attack. The solution was remarkably simple. Ohno hypothesized that equipment changeover times were wasteful and directly caused long production runs and inflexibility. By eliminating the changeover waste, Toyota could substantially lower the cost of variety. Changeover-time reduction was the key because it made smaller batch sizes economical, thereby solving the complexity problem caused by added variety. Fast changeover, in turn, became the catalyst for lead-time reduction that provided quick response capability to fluctuations in market demand. Taiichi Ohno ultimately extended these reduced changeover times into the Toyota Production System, the predecessor to the Just-In-Time (JIT) systems that are widespread today. This step was merely the first in the full implementation of JIT. Ohno has said, "Ideal Just-In-Time production is only a dream unless setup time (changeover) is reduced" (Blackburn 1991).

The origins of changeover-time reduction date to the work done by Shigeo Shingo, a colleague of Ohno's. The work Shingo started in 1950 has developed into a precise, scientific system for reducing changeover times. The Single Minute Exchange of Die (SMED) System outlines a procedure that has produced dramatic time reductions in hundreds of cases (Shingo

1985). While working toward the goal of reducing die changes to under one minute, Shingo discovered a procedure that can be applied to all changeovers. Using his approach, companies can typically reduce changeovers by seventy-five percent or more. Shingo's work has had a profound effect on the time compression paradigm and has led the way toward further improvements in waste reduction, quality, and the systematic approach to problem solving.

THE RAPIDLY EXPANDING USE OF TIME AS A COMPETITIVE WEAPON

The term "time-based competition" originated with George Stalk, Jr. and his associates at the Boston Consulting Group. They viewed time-based competition as an extension of JIT concepts applied to every part of the product delivery cycle beginning with product research and ending with distribution (Abegglen and Stalk 1985).

Since the early 1980s, several firms have developed and implemented time compression throughout their product delivery cycles. These efforts have delivered remarkable results by focusing their organizations on responsiveness. Each company in Table 1-1 has used its quick response advantage to grow at least three times faster than other companies in the same industry and with profits that exceed their industry averages by two times (Stalk and Hout 1990). Four of the U.S. companies we have observed experienced dramatic improvements in business performance elements, including space requirements, quality, cost, and capacity (see Table 1-2).

Table 1-1. Time-based competitors (estimated performance). (Stalk and Hout 1990)

Company	Business	Response Difference (%)	Growth Advantage vs. Average Competitor	Profit Advantage vs. Average Competitor
Wal-Mart	Discount stores	80	3X	2X
Atlas Door	Industrial doors	66	3X	5X
Ralph Wilson Plastics	Decorative laminates	75	3X	4X
Thomasville	Furniture	70	4X	2X
Citicorp	Mortgages	85	33X	N/A

Table 1-2. Improvement of four U.S. companies following implementation of TBM.

Improvement Areas	Percentage Improvement	
	Range	Typical
Manufacturing lead time	83-92	85
Inventory		
• Raw	35-73	50
• Work in process	65-85	80
• Finished goods	50-90	70
Changeover time	50-90	67
Space reduction	50-80	50
Cost of quality	20-30	25
Cost of material	5-15	7
Additional capacity	20-50	30

Northern Telecom competes on time. Several years ago, management discovered that all elements vital to their long-term competitiveness had one characteristic in common: time. Operations improvements translated into reducing time in individual processes. Northern Telecom manufactures products in about one-half the time it took a few years ago. Inventory and overhead have dropped, quality has improved, and overall customer satisfaction has steadily risen (Merrills 1989).

Today's new time-based competitors have an expanded pattern for corporate success. The traditional pattern has been to provide the most value for the least cost. The expanded pattern is to provide the most value for the least cost with the quickest response. These new-generation competitors use flexible factories and operations to respond rapidly to their customers' needs by expanding variety without added cost and by increasing the rate of innovation. A company that builds its strategy on this paradigm is proving to be a far more powerful competitor than one with a traditional strategy based on low wages, scale, or focus. These older, cost-based strategies require managers to do whatever is necessary to drive costs down, for example, moving production to a low-wage country, combining old plants to gain economies of scale, or focusing labor cost reduction down to the lowest level of activities. Such tactics reduce costs but at the expense of responsiveness to customer needs—a dangerous exposure. In contrast, strategies based on the cycle of flexible manufacturing, rapid response, expanding variety, and increasing innovation arc time based. Factories are close to the customers they serve. Organization structures are designed and managed to enable quick decisions and fast responses, rather than low costs and control. Time-based competitors concentrate their efforts on reducing and eliminating delays and on using their response advantages to attract the most profitable customers (Stalk and Hout 1990).

REQUIREMENTS FOR SUCCESSFUL TBM

The TBM organization must synchronize manufacturing, engineering, and other support functions dynamically with marketing, sales, and customers. This means quick response to customers with a variety of products that meet customers' requirements. Time and speed are the key requirements of this manufacturing philosophy; in fact, time is the key to comprehending the wider application of JIT principles. As a time-compression process, the principles of JIT become portable to a higher level. They generalize to the entire organization and the broader value-delivery chain. Just-in-time principles apply to the new product introduction process, to customer service, to logistics and distribution, and even to service industries in which inventories are nonexistent (Blackburn 1991).

Several years ago Benson Shapiro asked the provocative question, Can marketing and manufacturing coexist? Shapiro observed that, in most industrial organizations, the manufacturing and marketing divisions do not act in harmony and, in fact, engage in frequent minor skirmishes and occasional pitched battles. The reason for this long-festering conflict is obvious. Traditionally, marketing and manufacturing have opposing objectives (see Figure 1-2). Marketing typically is rewarded on sales volume and sets its sights on maximizing customer demand. Manufacturing, on the other hand, is measured on cost performance and therefore pursues a cost-reduction objective throughout its production systems (Shapiro 1977). In stark contrast to this old way of doing business, the single most important element of TBM is the cross-discipline integration of marketing and manufacturing in solving organization problems and better serving the customer.

At its most basic level, TBM is the compression of the cycle time to procure, produce, and deliver a product that meets the customer's needs. Henry Ford said it best: "The time element in manufacturing stretches from the moment raw material is separated from the earth to the moment when finished product is delivered to the ultimate consumer" (Ford 1926). The

---

THE MARKETING/MANUFACTURING CONFLICT

Marketing Perspective	Manufacturing Perspective
• Deals and promotions to create more sales is always better	• Stable production volume and schedules
• Over forecast to be sure to have product	* If marketing would only forecast better
• Price wins	• Managing capacity wins
• Do whatever it takes to get sale	• The plant can't do the impossible
• High product variety (24 colors are better than 2)	• Low product variety
• Immediate delivery	• Longer lead times to maximize efficiencies
• Feature rich products	• Simplified products

Figure 1-2. Marketing versus manufacturing objectives.

typical cycle time, or lead time, of this business process is dramatically longer than the actual value-added time put in making and delivering the product (see Figure 1-3). It is important to identify what adds value and to work toward eliminating nonvalue-added time. Value-added time is the time spent directly on activities that develop, produce, convert, and deliver products to the customer. All other time is nonvalue added. In our experience, before implementing TBM almost all companies have value-added time ratios to total cycle time of less than five percent, and many ratios are less than one percent. Where the total cycle time is higher than the value-added time, a manufacturing organization directly carries excess costs in the form of inventory, overhead, and manufacturing expense. These excess costs, in turn, lower company profitability.

RELATIONSHIP TO BUSINESS SUCCESS

Satisfying the customer while realizing an acceptable profit is the key to long-term success. The primary driver to achieving customer satisfaction in successful TBM operations is shorter lead time. The advantages resulting from reduced lead times include:
• lower costs, less waste, and less obsolescence
• greater flexibility to respond to change
• closely linked organization priorities to customer's needs
• improved service, quality, and reliability
• substantially accelerated supply system improvements.

The overall TBM relationship to business success is illustrated in Figure 1-4.

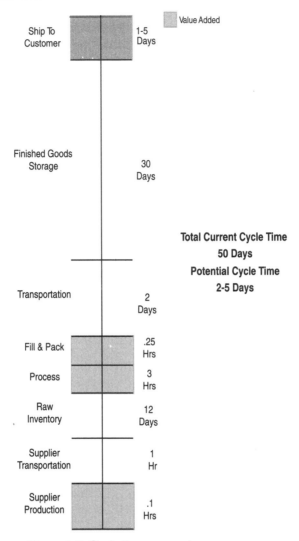

Figure 1-3. Cycle time comparison.

CHARACTERISTICS OF A TBM COMPETITOR

The time-based manufacturer's objective is to build into the organization a sustainable competitive advantage. The following outline summarizes the major characteristics of a TBM competitor.

Vision
• inclusion of time compression within the organization's basic values
• focus on customer satisfaction
• understood by all individuals in the organization

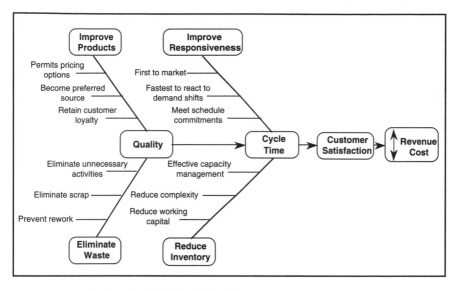

Figure 1-4. TBM relationship to business success.

Customers
• well defined and understood quality requirements
• seeing and meeting the end user's needs
• linked to major customers to support their competitive advantage

Products
• driven by customer feedback
• short development cycles
• variety without proliferation
• robust quality

People
• organization design based on work flow
• multiskilled work force
• lowest-level decision making
• team-based management
• cross-discipline problem solving

Supply System
• balanced and synchronized
• high-velocity product flow
• highly flexible equipment and systems
• capable and reliable processes

Vendors
- clearly understood quality specifications and capabilities
- long-term partnerships
- extension of inhouse capabilities
- joint problem solving

Information
- accurate and reliable
- key real-time information available
- streamlined and meaningful

Performance Management
- group rewards
- time-based measures
- focused on the vital few
- trended using statistics
- process improvement oriented

REFERENCES

Abegglen, J. and G. Stalk, Jr. 1985. *Kaisha, the Japanese Corporation.* New York: Basic Books.

Barker, J. 1992. *Future Edge.* New York: William Morrow and Co.

Blackburn, J. D., ed. 1991. *Time Based Competition.* Homewood, IL: Business One Irwin.

Covey, S. R. 1989. *The Seven Habits of Highly Effective People.* New York: Simon & Schuster.

Ford, H. 1926. *Today and Tomorrow.* Garden City, NY: Doubleday Page & Co.

Merrills, R. 1989. How Northern Telecom competes on time. *Harvard Business Review.* July-August: 108-14.

Niebel, B. W. 1988. *Motion and Time Study.* Eighth ed. Homewood, IL: Irwin.

Ohno, T. 1982. The origin of Toyota production system and kanban system. *Proceedings of the International Conference on Productivity and Quality Improvement.* Tokyo.

Shapiro, B. P. 1977. Can marketing and manufacturing coexist? *Harvard Business Review.* September-October: 105-14.

Shingo, S. 1985. *A Revolution in Manufacturing: The SMED System.* Cambridge, MA: Productivity Press.

Smith, A. 1776. *The Wealth of Nations.* Oxford, England: Clarendon Press.

Stalk, G. Jr., and T. M. Hout. 1990. *Competing Against Time.* New York: The Free Press.

The Product Supply System *2*

THE power of time-based manufacturing (TBM) comes from understanding and managing the product supply system (PSS). The PSS is the link between a business, its supplier firms, and the internal processes necessary to support customer requirements. The total supply chain with both external and internal components must be recognized (Figure 2-1). In its purest sense, the PSS begins with basic raw materials and ends with the delivery of a finished product to the ultimate consumer.

It is important to identify what is organizationally necessary to manage the PSS. Understanding the product and business process flows in the total supply system is necessary for organizing and improving the PSS. In addition, the overall organization design choices made to support the PSS are critical components for compressing PSS cycle times.

DESIGNING THE ORGANIZATION FOR TBM PERFORMANCE

In general, an organization is a social invention developed to accomplish things otherwise not possible. An organization takes a variety of people, knowledge, materials, and equipment and gives them structure and purpose to become an interrelated effective unit with common goals (Martin and Shell 1988). All organizations are perfectly designed to achieve the results they get (Hanna 1988). This means that leaders can move their organizations toward producing the quick response behavior they desire by redesigning their organizations' structure to directly support time-com-

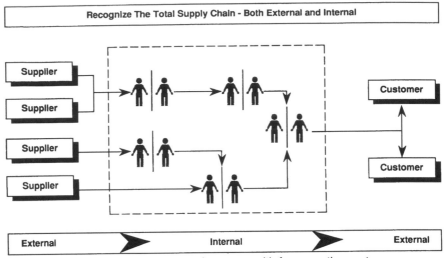

Figure 2-1.The product supply system with focus on the customer.

pressed product flows and business processes. The organization's results are actually the bottom line of all conscious (and unconscious) design choices that are implemented.

The need for a customer-focused, product-based organization design is paramount to achieving TBM goals. The problem seen in many companies is that they are organizationally incapable of carrying out strategies they have developed. While products and work flows move horizontally across the supply chain, organizational functions traditionally are structured along vertical lines. These organizational boundaries contribute to increased cycle times and other TBM barriers. These vertical silos exist where problem solving expertise is deep within a functional discipline or specialty but nonexistent across horizontal flows. Over the past twenty years or so, strategic thinking and planning has far outdistanced organizational capabilities to execute positive change (Bartlett and Ghoshal 1990). Adapting to a PSS-based organization design begins to address these shortcomings.

Three major components are necessary to design the TBM organization. They are:

1. creating a customer/product-based organization structure
2. establishing closer relationships with key customers and suppliers
3. using employee involvement to overcome resistance to change.

CREATING A CUSTOMER/PRODUCT-BASED ORGANIZATIONAL STRUCTURE

The TBM organizational structure should provide for an entrepreneurial spirit that is flexible, innovative, and market responsive. The traditional manufacturing organization is illustrated in Figure 2-2. In it, natural organization boundaries separate suppliers, operations, and sales and marketing. In this scenario, how could the major supplier possibly know customer requirements? More probably, employees involved with these operations do not clearly understand customer requirements. What are the odds that a fabrication department worker has ever seen or talked with a customer?

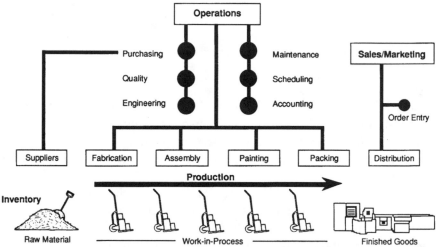

Figure 2-2. Traditional manufacturing organization.

The TBM organization is designed to facilitate individuals and groups working together to complete assignments and effectively integrate human resources, computer-based systems, and advanced technologies. The TBM organizational structure, also called the PSS organization, is illustrated in Figure 2-3. This structure is a focused alignment of all elements of the supply chain around major customer/product groupings. Through this organization alignment, there is a direct facilitation of communications, group problem solving, and supply chain teamwork to meet the end users' needs. This design can substantially shorten throughput time for major projects and products. The traditional practice of sequentially accomplishing work activities is no longer acceptable. For example, moving new product development step-by-step through progressive stages with little contact among involved groups will no longer produce acceptable and

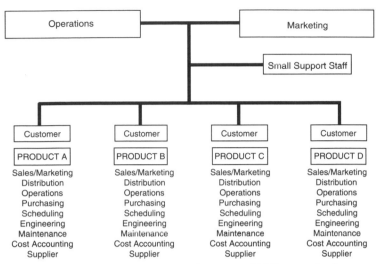

Figure 2-3. The product supply system (PSS) organization.

timely results. The need for simultaneous activities is critical for quick reaction capability; this can be accomplished by integrating key individuals with critical skills across traditional organization boundaries. The PSS organization should be based on common product groups and customers (Martin and Shell 1988).

In late 1987, Procter & Gamble (P&G) created the category management system. The company was divided into thirty-nine product categories, with twenty-six category managers (some have more than one category). Brand managers report to the category manager, who is like a small business CEO with total profit-and-loss responsibility. When new products are being developed, the category manager forms a small team consisting of the brand manager plus individuals from sales, finance, and manufacturing. Included in the team is a new product supply manager who reports to the category manager. The product supply manager has broad responsibility over every aspect of engineering, purchasing, manufacturing, and distribution (Dumaine 1989).

The P&G form of product supply management is ideally suited for TBM. The throughput time from the start of product engineering to customer delivery can be shortened greatly. John Smale, former CEO of P&G put it this way: "I have the growing conviction that the product supply concept is perhaps the single most important thing that can influence our profit performance over the next several years" (Dumaine 1989).

ESTABLISHING CLOSER RELATIONSHIPS WITH KEY CUSTOMERS AND SUPPLIERS

Creating close relationships with customers and suppliers is not new. Sales and marketing organizations for decades have maintained close contact with key customers. Likewise, purchasing and material managers for many years have maintained close relationships with key suppliers. What *is* new is that TBM requires a dynamic understanding of customer requirements and then matches key vendor capabilities, along with internal supply capability, to satisfy that demand — thus forming the product supply system.

Team-based organization design produces excellent results when closely integrated with the customer. In one reported example, an employee team learned about poor service and quality problems. Late deliveries had forced the customer to increase inventories and risked shutting down their plant operations. These customer problems were solved using a multidisciplinary team that had knowledge and experience in each area where the problems were originating (Sirkin and Stalk 1990).

A Procter & Gamble (P&G) reorganization to better accommodate the needs of Wal-Mart represents another example of getting closer to key customers. A team of a dozen or so P&G employees work only with Wal-Mart. A just-in-time ordering and delivery system for Pampers and Luvs diapers is in place. When diapers run low in a store, a computer sends an order by satellite to a P&G plant, which then ships directly to the desired store location. Knowing the dynamic requirements of the customer and being able to quickly satisfy those requirements is a win-win situation for both customer and supplier (Dumaine 1989).

USING EMPLOYEE INVOLVEMENT TO OVERCOME RESISTANCE TO CHANGE

Implementing TBM requires considerable change. By definition, any alteration in the established way of doing things is considered change, and adopting TBM requires change on a large scale. This has been previously defined as nonroutine, nonincremental, and discontinued change, which alters the overall orientation of the organization (Tichy 1983). Large-scale change will always be met with considerable resistance. Acknowledging resistance to change and understanding methods for reducing this resistance are critical to successfully implementing TBM.

Considerable attention has been directed toward proper ways of introducing change to overcome resistance. Many of these techniques have proven value in the professional environment. Often, fear of loss in status, security, or destruction of social relationships is imagined by employees in the middle of change. In these cases, introducing employee participation into the change process can be vital to reducing resistance. Using team-based leadership is helpful for managers in these kinds of situations. Resistance to change can be reduced if the manager can sell through participation the idea that employees and the business will be better off as a result of making the change. Unless the forces for acceptance are clearly greater than those for resistance, the probability of employees resisting the change is high. The magnitude and direction of these forces are determined by several important variables including the manager, organizational climate, work group attitudes, employee value systems, and the change itself. The manager often can use participation among the work group to have a favorable impact on enough of these variables so the employees perceive that a net gain will result from making the change. If the manager is successful with participation, then the forces favoring the change will exceed the forces against the change and resistance will be alleviated as a managerial problem (Martin and Shell 1988).

The process of gaining employee acceptance often involves creating a we attitude in making changes. This attitude can result from employee involvement through team-based management. Ideally, employees should feel that they contribute to the substance of the change. This is not as difficult as it may at first sound because managerially promoted changes are usually desirable for the organization; as the organization benefits, more rewards are available to work teams and the individual employee (Martin and Shell 1988).

Numerous examples of group and team building have appeared in the literature (Dumaine 1989; Sirkin and Stalk 1990). Work groups and cross-discipline teams make it easier for everyone to focus on problems that matter to customers.

THE FUTURE OF TBM ORGANIZATIONS

In the future, more company employees will be knowledge workers with some technical specialty. There will be fewer workers with low skill, and fewer managers. The TBM organization will be information based. Drucker believes the typical large business twenty years in the future will have less than half the levels of management of its counterpart today, and no more than a third of the managers. The organizational structure of a large business in the future is more likely to resemble a hospital or a symphony than today's manufacturing company (Drucker 1988).

John F. Welch Jr., CEO of General Electric, believes a corporation is doomed without the virtues he calls "speed, simplicity, and self-confidence." To obtain these, Welch has mounted a radical assault on the canons of modern management: "We've got to take out the boss element." Twenty-first-century managers will forgo their old powers—planning, organizing, implementing, and measuring—for new duties: counseling groups, providing resources for groups, and helping groups think for themselves. According to Welch, "We're going to win on our ideas, not by whips and chains" (Stewart 1991).

Clearly, organizations in the future will continue to undergo changing and restructuring. Achieving TBM requires teamwork and overall organizational streamlining for effectiveness.

USING PROCESS MAPPING TO DEFINE THE PSS

Defining and understanding the PSS is essential to beginning TBM. Process mapping is a technique that assists in understanding and improving business processes in the entire product continuum. In it, flowcharts are created using a storyboard process. The level of complexity or simplicity can be developed to suit the required amount of detail. Processes are characterized by:
• inputs provided by suppliers
• a value-added conversion process
• outputs received by customers

It is important to remember that people work processes to add value. A series of processes linked together creates the overall PSS. If inputs and processes are improved and controlled at each step along the PSS, then better end results follow.

Determining the process flow for the "as is" process is the starting point for identifying and improving the PSS. Figure 2-4 depicts the major steps required for mapping the "as is" process. The process map includes the identification of sequences, physical move distances, flow patterns, material handling, and people usage. A flow is analyzed to create facility and equipment layouts; event sequence flows, such as product families or representative products, manufacturing, and paperwork; and physical and information flows throughout the PSS.

Data sources for the process map include facilities, plant, or industrial engineering; routings or operations sheets; the materials resource planning (MRP) system; previous studies; and visual observation and interviews. The most common time-wasting activities that cause extended cycle times and ineffectiveness throughout the PSS are given in Figure 2-5.

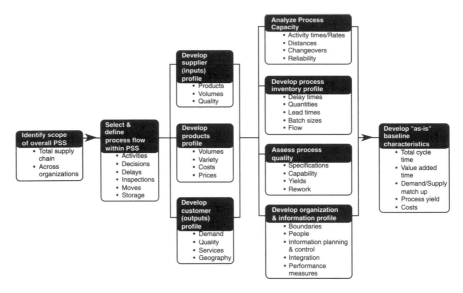

Figure 2-4. Mapping the "as-is" process.

Material and information are both important process inputs. Material flow can be constrained by lack of information, affecting quality and time. Information delays are commonly caused by approval policies (multiple approval signatures), organization boundaries (handoff meetings), and calendar-driven practices (e.g., weekly computer updates).

Standard flow chart symbols are depicted in Figure 2-6. An example event sequence flowchart for a furniture manufacturer is shown in Figure 2-7 and is related to the physical flow as shown in Figure 2-8. Several axioms are useful in studying processes.

- A process rarely works the way people think it will. Process mapping is valuable because it shows what really happens in a process flow. This requires getting close to the people at the source of the work and listening intently to their input.

- Mapping a process initially raises more questions than it answers because new processes must be learned and, inevitably, inconsistencies surface between activities. Taking time to clearly develop activity and operational definitions, and then gaining group consensus on their meaning, can become a breakthrough opportunity for process improvement.

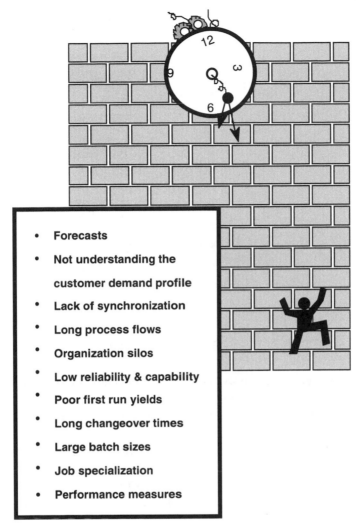

Figure 2-5. PSS barriers to cycle time compression.

- Processes are usually full of data but rarely contain meaningful information. This often results in the need for additional collection of important data to develop the necessary "as-is" process characteristics. This should be done by the people working in the process, using their own methods wherever possible.

- Every process has different characteristics that drive lead times, costs, and quality. Focusing in on the key process drivers quickly saves a substantial amount of time and money in the process improvement effort.

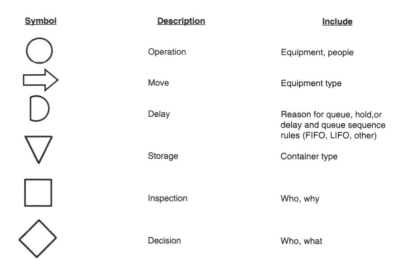

Symbol	Description	Include
◯	Operation	Equipment, people
⇨	Move	Equipment type
D	Delay	Reason for queue, hold,or delay and queue sequence rules (FIFO, LIFO, other)
▽	Storage	Container type
☐	Inspection	Who, why
◇	Decision	Who, what

Figure 2-6. Standard flowchart symbols.

PROCESS REENGINEERING

Process reengineering is applying the breakthrough improvement paradigm to process improvement. The keys to process reengineering are discontinuous thinking and recognizing and breaking away from the outdated rules and fundamental assumptions that underlie present operations. Unless incorrect rules are changed, the results are like rearranging the deck chairs on the Titanic. Breakthroughs in performance cannot be achieved by cutting fat or automating existing processes. Rather, old assumptions and old rules that made the business underperform in the first place must be challenged.

Every business is replete with implicit rules left over from earlier decades: "Customers don't repair their own equipment;" "Local warehouses are necessary for good service;" "Merchandising decisions are made at headquarters." These rules of work design are based on assumptions about technology, people, and organizational goals that no longer hold. The contemporary repertoire of available information technologies is vast and quickly expanding. Quality, innovation, and service are now more important than cost, growth, and control. A large portion of the population is educated and capable of assuming responsibility, and workers cherish their autonomy and expect to have a say in how the business is run (Hammer 1990).

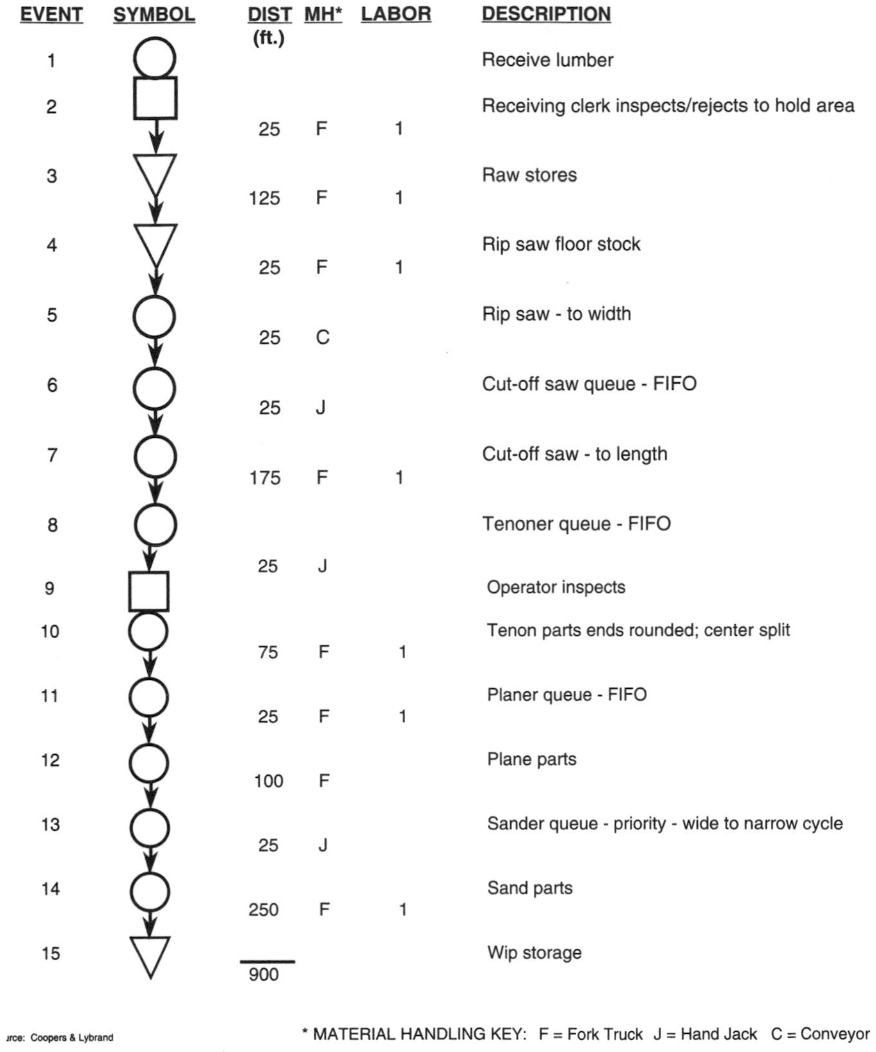

EVENT	SYMBOL	DIST (ft.)	MH*	LABOR	DESCRIPTION
1	○				Receive lumber
2	□	25	F	1	Receiving clerk inspects/rejects to hold area
3	▽	125	F	1	Raw stores
4	▽	25	F	1	Rip saw floor stock
5	○	25	C		Rip saw - to width
6	○	25	J		Cut-off saw queue - FIFO
7	○	175	F	1	Cut-off saw - to length
8	○	25	J		Tenoner queue - FIFO
9	□				Operator inspects
10	○	75	F	1	Tenon parts ends rounded; center split
11	○	25	F	1	Planer queue - FIFO
12	○	100	F		Plane parts
13	○	25	J		Sander queue - priority - wide to narrow cycle
14	○	250	F	1	Sand parts
15	▽	900			Wip storage

rce: Coopers & Lybrand * MATERIAL HANDLING KEY: F = Fork Truck J = Hand Jack C = Conveyor

Figure 2-7. Event sequence flowchart. (Coopers & Lybrand 1987)

Reengineering requires new rules tailored to the competitive environment. Summaries of some reengineering principles follow (Hammer 1990):

1. Organize around outcomes, not tasks. If possible, one person should perform all the steps in a process.
2. Have those who use the output of the process perform the process. This usually means having multifunction capability throughout the organization.

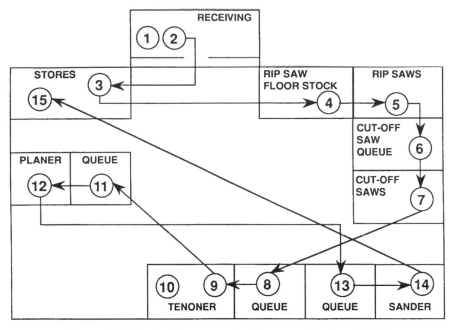

Figure 2-8. Physical flow example. (Coopers & Lybrand 1987)

3. Subsume information-processing work into the real work that produces the information. This suggests decentralizing the computer system.
4. Treat geographically dispersed resources as though they were centralized. The key here is to use decentralized databases, telecommunications networks, and standardized processing to realize the benefits of scale and coordination while maintaining the benefits of flexibility and customer service.
5. Link parallel activities instead of integrating their results. This principle is most useful for product and manufacturing tooling development.
6. Put the decision point where the work is performed and build control into the process. The benefit is the reduction of several management layers. The remaining managers work on exceptions.
7. Capture information once and at the source. This is possible in firms that have on-line database capability.

REFERENCES

Bartlett, C. A. and S. Ghoshal. 1990. Matrix management: not a structure, a frame of mind. *Harvard Business Review.* July-August: 138-45.

Coopers & Lybrand. 1987. *Just In Time Improvement Program, Diagnostic and Conceptual Design Methodology.* New York: Coopers & Lybrand.

Drucker, P. F. 1988. The coming of the new organization. *Harvard Business Review.* January-February: 45-53.

Dumaine, B. 1989. Marketing rules. *Fortune.* November 6: 35-48.

Hammer, M. 1990. Reengineering work: don't automate, obliterate. *Harvard Business Review.* July-August: 104-11.

Hanna, D. P. 1988. *Designing Organizations for High Performance.* Cambridge, MA: Addison-Wesley.

Martin, D. D. and R. L. Shell. 1988. *Management of Professionals.* New York: Marcel Dekker.

Sirkin, H. and G. Stalk Jr. 1990. Fix the process not the problem. *Harvard Business Review.* July-August: 26-33.

Stewart, T. A. 1991. GE keeps those ideas coming. *Fortune.* August 12: 41-47.

Tichy, N. M. 1983. *Managing Strategic Change.* New York: John Wiley & Sons.

The Customer Holds the Key to Competitive Advantage   3

A customer is an individual or group who buys or uses the products, services, or both produced by a company. It is common these days to talk about the internal customer, i.e., the user of the output of a single process, as being the important "customer" to the preceding component of the supply chain. In fact, most businesses can benefit by improving the interface and responsiveness to internal customer needs. Looking only at this narrow view, however, misses a major point in the new time-based manufacturing (TBM) paradigm. That point is simply this: the overall product supply system (PSS) customer is the end consumer (Figure 3-1). Everyone else in the PSS is both a supplier and customer of a product on its way to the consumer. Therefore, understanding the end consumer's need can provide the key to a new breakthrough in competitive advantage. In this way, an organization must at least know the customer's customer and how its product is eventually used. The goal of the business should be to identify, understand, and satisfy the customer while earning a profit.

The customer has always been important to the supplier organization. Today, however, with intense domestic and international competition the need for a different consideration of the customer is critical for survival and success. This consideration must include clearly understanding the customer's needs and acting as a value-added servicer to meet those needs; in short, establishing a close interface and actively responding to change. While interim customers are important to the PSS, the end user is the only true customer and holds the key to competitive advantage.

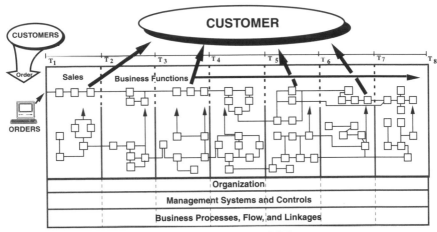

Figure 3-1. The end user is the PSS customer.

As more companies implement TBM, it will become increasingly difficult for their competitors to obtain new customers. The reason will be the drive of these supplier companies to develop partnerships with their customers. Also, customers will seek to improve supplier relations on a long-term basis. These relationships will serve to lock out competitors, as the time and cost required to manage multiple partnerships will exceed the benefits. As the potential new customer base shrinks, considerable effort and cost will be needed to capture preferred customers. While it has always been easier to retain existing customers than to recruit new ones, partnerships with high-quality customers may become the most valuable asset of a business.

CUSTOMER VALUE

Customers will gravitate to and do business with the manufacturer who provides the highest value. Value from the customer's perspective comes from an optimum balance of product quality, customer service, cost, and response times. The price customers will pay for products is directly related to the perceived value of a supplier in relation to the competition.

This section presents a framework for analyzing and applying the above four customer value factors. First the value provided to customers should be developed so that it can be understood; then that understanding should be applied to the fundamental pricing strategies.

Product price (P) equals perceived product value (V), which is expressed in the functional relationship:

$$P = V = f\left(\frac{Q,S}{C,T}\right)$$

where

Q = quality of the product (including product features)

S = completeness of customer service

C = costs incurred to design, produce, and deliver products and services (assumes cost is directly passed through to customer in price)

T = time required to deliver customer orders, respond to requests for quote, provide support services, etc.

UNDERSTANDING THE RELATIONSHIP

The value relationship is an excellent way to present the linkage between value and the four key variables. It is not intended to be used as a mathematical equation, but as a means to explain the impact of the variables on value and ultimately on selling price and profit. In other words, the price that can be charged for products or services is directly proportional to the perceived value of the product to the customer. The perceived value is a function of the four variables.

Quality and customer service directly affect the value of a company's product. These two variables make up the "numerator" of the relationship. The higher the quality and the level of customer service, within the customer's relevant range, the more valuable the product is to the success of the customer. Most businesses will pay a premium (defined here as being higher than the competition) price for higher value and service.

Cost and time to deliver products are inversely proportional to the value. These two variables make up the "denominator" of the equation. The higher the cost of the product, the less value the customer perceives it is receiving. (This assumes that the price is at or above costs.) The relationship indicates that the cost (and resulting price) can be lowered to encourage the customer to buy the product. However, most suppliers raise the price to cover their increased production costs, which would only further discourage customers from purchasing the product.

There are two elements to the "time to deliver" variable. The first is the time to deliver customer orders. The longer customers have to wait for delivery of the order, the less inclined they are to pay a higher (premium) price. In fact, longer lead times more likely require a price discount, especially where the customer has other acceptable alternatives. Second, long lead times to introduce new products usually mean that the company is not first to market and cannot capture the premium price that goes to first-to-market products. In both cases, long lead times indicate excess costs in the PSS. The normal reaction is to recover these costs in pricing. The price-value relationship presents a contrary picture. The customer must wait for the product so it usually is viewed as less valuable, resulting in customers being willing to pay less for the product, or not buy it at all.

The remainder of this section discusses in further detail the role of the four variables in the price-value relationship.

Quality. The quality of a product as compared to competition has an impact on product value. Generally, customers are willing to pay higher prices when they perceive the product quality to be higher. Additionally, the higher the change in perceived quality, the higher the change in market share. Higher perceived quality also corresponds to higher company return on investment (ROI).

Two avenues can be taken to enhance perceived quality. One is to implement total quality management (TQM) techniques to ensure that PSS processes are capable of producing quality products. The other is to enhance the product/company image through advertising and promotion, so that the market recognizes the company as a quality supplier. Companies that try going down the second path without traveling the first do not succeed in the long run.

Customer Service. Customer service encompasses all the nonproduct activities that occur from doing business with the customer. As quality has become less of a differentiating competitive factor, customer service has increased in importance in the value relationship. This includes not only the customary sales and customer service activities, but activities such as shipping, credit and collection, and order inquiries. Any interaction with a customer is a customer service activity.

The importance of customer service cannot be overestimated. By now, most managers recognize that time is a precious resource and a key competitive factor. Customers realize this, too. Every interaction with a customer should be conducted with the objective of providing value for every moment spent. Good customer relationships are the natural result of providing value-added customer service.

Costs. Costs are usually the most familiar variable. Not that long ago, if costs went up, so did product prices. Today, the trend is to find ways to reduce costs and lower prices. Customers are looking for suppliers who provide products and services that reduce overall supply chain costs, not just purchase costs.

The spirit of cost-oriented pricing has changed. The formula is no longer "cost + desired margin = targeted price." The "new" equation (which Henry Ford used to price his cars in the 1920s) is "market price – margin = targeted cost." In other words, manufacturers must now focus first on what the market will accept in price, considering all four variables, and then determine the costs at which they must produce.

The methods used to calculate product costs and to measure performance also are changing. Activity-based costing (ABC) is becoming the new cost management approach to provide visibility of value-adding versus nonvalue-adding costs, and the most accurate product costs.

Activity-based costing considers the activities performed to make the product. Most cost accounting systems use direct labor or machine hours from the manufacturing process to apply overhead costs that are allocated to work center overhead rates. However, the real activities to support making a product are usually far more than those listed on a manufacturing routing. Plus, these other activities usually vary widely from one product or service to another. Focusing only on costs based on manufacturing operations usually leads to incorrect strategic product marketing decisions. By understanding the correct product-cost relationships, companies are more likely to price products based on a truer cost picture.

Time. There are two elements to the time variable: lead time to supply a product to the customer for a specific order and the time to develop a product from concept to final market delivery. Reducing lead time on product supply is the strategic objective of the TBM company. Any time beyond the time necessary to add value to the product represents excess costs and waste to both the supplier and the customer. A customer will pay a premium to the supplier who can supply its product faster and more reliably than the competition. A reduction of the time variable also has a positive impact on the other three variables, thereby generating greater proportional value for the effort on improvement.

The manufacturer who can introduce new products or enhance the value of existing products in the shortest time normally will be perceived as the leader in the field and will be the first to market. Many customers will pay a premium for the assurance that they are doing business with a supplier who can respond the quickest to using new technologies and to their unique needs.

One technique to reduce the time to market of new products is concurrent engineering. Concurrent engineering dictates that design engineering and manufacturing engineering work together to develop the product design and the design of the manufacturing process concurrently, rather than in sequence. This reduces the manufacturing start-up time significantly.

SUMMARY
The value a supplier can bring to customers is a function of four primary variables—quality, customer service, costs, and response time. The relative importance to customers of any one or combination of these variables depends on the industry, domestic and foreign competition, and the specific needs of customers. In some cases, the importance will vary from customer to customer. Ultimately, the price that can be received is based on the value perceived by the customer.

UNDERSTANDING THE CUSTOMER

It is not easy to satisfy customers. Because consumer expectations are higher than ever before, companies want, expect, and have been getting better products and service. Getting closer to the customer represents increased effort and costs (e.g., distribution costs for transport and warehousing, sales costs for personal communication, and marketing costs for promotion and advertising). The key is to minimize wasted or unnecessary efforts in this component of the PSS, while realizing positive economic benefits for all parties concerned. This can only be done by focusing on key customers and establishing closer links with the vital few customers important to the strategic success of the organization. Understanding customers requires the ability to answer the following questions:

- How is my product used?

- Who is the customer's customer?

- What products are purchased?

- What is the customer demand profile?

- What is the true quality specification for the customer? For his customer?

- What are the customer's requirements for service: order related, technical, or application?

- Who else does the customer buy from and why?

- How can my organization provide the customer with a competitive advantage in his markets?

During recent years, the retail industry has been aggressive in obtaining additional services from suppliers (Myer 1989). Sophisticated retailers, such as Wal-Mart, The Limited, and Toys "R" Us, reportedly are cutting costs and inventory at suppliers' expense. These retailers have learned to restrict their inventory investment while insisting on high service levels, the lowest possible net purchase price, all allowable discounts, and the most lenient financing terms—usually without any reciprocal benefit to their suppliers. In short, these customers have found ways to get their suppliers to contribute directly to their own bottom lines (Myer 1989).

The TBM organization strives to provide these benefits to the customer through built-in, quick-response organization capabilities. This takes away the "trade-off" mentality of increasing supplier costs for reduced customer costs. The following guidelines are recommended to create ongoing linkages with the customer:
- find ways to help the customer achieve a competitive advantage
- find a customer need/want that the competition cannot satisfy and build the capability to meet that need into the relationship
- establish a menu of service options with unit pricing to permit customer selection
- incorporate incentives into pricing to motivate long-term relationships and mutual gains
- create a TBM relationship that closes out the competition.

The importance of creating a TBM relationship with the customer is perhaps illustrated best by the maturity continuum concept suggested by Stephen R. Covey. We begin life as infants, totally dependent on others; we are directed, nurtured, and sustained by others. Without this nurturing, we would only live for a few hours or a few days at the most. Then gradually, over the ensuing months and years, we become more and more independent—physically, mentally, emotionally, and financially—until eventually we take care of ourselves, becoming inner-directed and self-reliant. As we continue to grow and mature, we become increasingly aware that all of nature is interdependent, that there is an ecological system that governs nature, including society. We further discover that the higher reaches of our nature have to do with our relationships with others—that human life also is interdependent.

On the maturity continuum, dependence is the paradigm of you—you take care of me; you come through for me; you didn't come through; I blame you for the results. Independence is the paradigm of I—I can do it; I am responsible; I am self-reliant; I can choose. Interdependence is the paradigm of we—we can do it; we can cooperate; we can combine our talents and abilities and create something greater together (Covey 1989).

Time-based manufacturing is industrial interdependence. It is the realization of interdependence in the PSS, starting with the end user and reaching back to the lowest-level supplier.

DETERMINING CUSTOMER REQUIREMENTS

Two major elements are useful in determining customer requirements: the customer base line and the customer survey. The customer base line is the structured collection of internal data concerning customers. The structured survey is a collection of information directly from customers.

CUSTOMER BASE LINE DATA

To determine customer requirements, the following questions concerning internal data should be asked.

- What market segments are we serving with our products and services?

- How many customers are we serving and what are their buying patterns?

- Who are our "key" customers?

- How well do we think we are meeting their expectations?

Figure 3-2 depicts an example of customer distribution by product or service families and market segments served. In most cases, the customer categories will be the same as the product or service families. They may differ when the markets served are known to be dramatically different. For example, the product family "motors" could be divided into two customer categories: small and large motors. Figure 3-3 illustrates important statistics to capture for each customer category; Figure 3-4 suggests the need to identify key customers and their estimated impact on annual sales; and Figure 3-5 lists details about individual customers importance in providing responsive, high-quality customer service.

All figures are the number of customers Date:_____	Segments Served									
	A	B	C	D	E					
1. Motors	7				1					8
2. Regulators	6									6
3. Instruments		16	10	24	10					60
4. Controls	6		4	26	34					70
5.										
6.										
TOTALS	19	16	14	50	45					144

Product/Service Families

Figure 3-2. Distribution of customers. (Coopers & Lybrand 1990)

Customer Category _____

	Year:	19XX	19XX	19XX
Number of customers in category		_____	_____	_____
Average annual sales per customer		_____	_____	_____
Average number of orders received per customer		_____	_____	_____
Average value per order		_____	_____	_____
Average percent change in prices over previous year		_____	_____	_____
Percent of orders delivered when requested		_____	_____	_____
Percent of orders delivered when promised		_____	_____	_____
Percent of orders involving a quality rejection		_____	_____	_____

Figure 3-3. Customer category statistics. (Coopers & Lybrand 1990)

Customer Category: _____   Date: _____

List the top customers in order of greatest to least average annual sales.
(Note: These ___ customers represent ___ % of the annual sales for this customer category)

List up to six "desired" customers who are currently customers of competitors, and their estimated impact on annual sales.

Figure 3-4. Key customers. (Coopers & Lybrand 1990)

Customer Category _____			
Customer Name _____ **Location** _____			
		Year	
	19XX	19XX	19XX
Annual revenue of customer	_____	_____	_____
Sales to customer	_____	_____	_____
Number of orders received	_____	_____	_____
Average number of units per order	_____	_____	_____
Average value per order	_____	_____	_____
Average unit price	_____	_____	_____
Average delivery lead time - desired (days)	_____	_____	_____
Average delivery lead time - quoted (days)	_____	_____	_____
Average delivery lead time - actual (days)	_____	_____	_____
Percent of orders delivered when requested	_____	_____	_____
Percent of orders delivered when promised	_____	_____	_____
Percent of orders involving a quality rejection	_____	_____	_____

Figure 3-5. Customer statistics—detailed information. (Coopers & Lybrand 1990)

In summary, the approach to collecting customer base line data requires the following:
• reviewing types of desired information
• identifying most likely sources
• conducting interviews and collecting data
• preparing data collection forms and graphic displays

CUSTOMER SURVEY

The purposes of the customer survey are to capture the voice of the customer and to answer the following questions.
• What criteria do our customers use to select suppliers and evaluate their performance?
• How well are we doing in meeting our customers' expectations?
• What changes should we make to improve customer satisfaction?

Customer survey questions are found by selecting target responses. Once the questionnaires are prepared and the surveys are conducted, the responses are analyzed, checked, and then compiled into a final output. This approach should be applied to each customer category. Figure 3-6 depicts the customer criteria for selecting a supplier. Figure 3-7 shows a similar form for customer criteria to evaluate the delivered product.

Customer Category : __Motors__ Date: _____

Customer perception of us vs. a representative competitor

	CRITERIA	IMPORTANCE	Worst 1	2	3	4	Best 5
1	The price quoted	5					
2	Speed of delivery of the proposal	5					
3	The range of after sales services offered	4.5					
4	Finance facilities offered	4.5					
5	The ease of contacting the supplier	3.5					
6	Willingness to allow penalty clauses	3					
7							
8							
9							
10							
11							
12							
13							
14							
15							

5 = Most important ● Our company
1 = Least important ☐ Representative competitor
0 = Not a criteria

Figure 3-6. Customer criteria for choosing supplier. (Coopers & Lybrand 1990)

Customer Category : __Motors__ Date: _____

Customer perception of us vs. a representative competitor

	CRITERIA	IMPORTANCE	Worst 1	2	3	4	Best 5
1	The fit of the product to your actual needs	5					
2	The product achieves specification	5					
3	The product's reliability	4.5					
4	The product's performance	4.5					
5	The length of service intervals	4					
6	The product is technically advanced	4					
8							
9							
10							
11							
12							
13							
14							
15							

5 = Most important ● Our company
1 = Least important ☐ Representative competitor
0 = Not a criteria

Figure 3-7. Customer criteria for evaluating delivered product. (Coopers & Lybrand 1990)

It is also important to understand what customers like most; what customers dislike most; and most importantly, what changes customers recommend. Figure 3-8 provides an example of displaying the detailed results by customer criterion. The questionnaire is an important part of understanding the customer. The population and sample size must be defined. The survey should be designed to obtain at least twenty-five to thirty responses. Having an independent organization conduct the survey

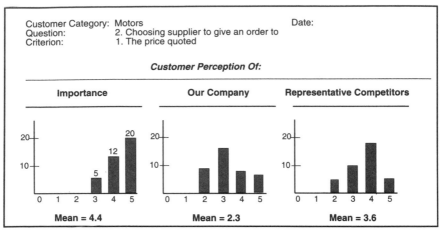

Figure 3-8. Detailed results by customer criterion. (Coopers & Lybrand 1990)

usually will improve the integrity of individual responses. The questionnaire and survey process is shown in Figures 3-9 and 3-10. Some useful example questions to be included in the questionnaire are listed below.

• When you are selecting suppliers to invite to bid:
(a) what importance do you attach to the following criteria?
(b) how do you rate our company and a representative competitor in the ability to satisfy these criteria?

• When you are choosing which supplier to give an order to (i.e., appraising a proposal or offer):
(a) what importance do you attach to the following criteria?
(b) how do you rate our company and a representative competitor in the ability to satisfy these criteria?

• When you are evaluating the quality and performance of the delivered product or service:
(a) what importance do you attach to the following criteria?
(b) how do you rate our company and a representative competitor in the ability to satisfy these criteria?

• When you are appraising the level of after-sale service that you received from a supplier:
(a) what importance do you attach to the following criteria?
(b) how do you rate our company and a representative competitor in the ability to satisfy these criteria?

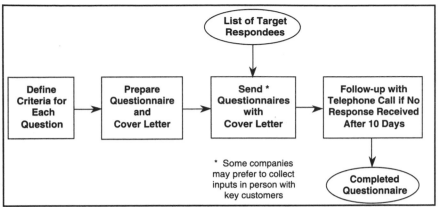

Figure 3-9. Prepare questionnaires and conduct survey.
(Coopers & Lybrand 1990)

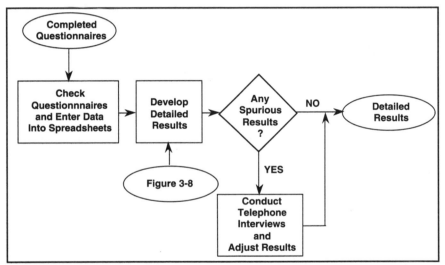

Figure 3-10. Analyze and check responses. (Coopers & Lybrand 1990)

- What do you most like about our company?

- What do you most dislike about our company?

- Do you have any suggestions on how we could improve?

QUALITY FUNCTION DEPLOYMENT

The word quality is derived from the Latin word *qualis,* which means how an object is constituted. Quality has also been defined as fitness for use, and the quality function as that area of responsibility in industrial companies through which we achieve quality (Juran 1980). The definition of quality deployment is "to convert customers' requirements into substitute characteristics, establish the design quality of a final product, and deploy the relationship systematically starting with the quality of each functional component, to the quality of each part and process" (Akao 1987).

Quality function deployment (QFD) has been defined as: "Taking the voice of the consumer all the way through product development to the factory floor and out into the market place. A system for translating consumer requirements into appropriate company requirements at each stage from research and product development to engineering and manufacturing to marketing/sales and distribution" (American Supplier Institute 1987).

Quality function deployment is an effective technique for defining requirements to introduce products into the market place. It provides a customer-driven product design. Compared with traditional new product development processes, QFD can reduce development time by fifty percent while decreasing overall costs.

An important concept of QFD is the use of cross-functional teams to manage product development. The teams consist of marketing, product engineering, manufacturing engineering, quality, suppliers, and customers. With everyone involved from the beginning, the organization can perform concurrent engineering for the design, manufacturing, and quality requirements. This will save time and reduce quality problems.

A basic aspect of QFD is a systematic collection and analysis of information that flows from the customer through the design process including production, testing, and process planning. At each step in the process, information is checked and rechecked as to its importance and impact on the customer, manufacturing, testing, and design.

The four basic phases of QFD are product planning, parts development, process planning, and production planning. In the product planning phase, the team defines the customer requirements and then translates them into design standards. Phase two is parts development, in which the design requirements are linked to assembly, subassembly, and part criteria. In the third phase, process planning is addressed. With the information from phase two, the process of manufacturing and testing the product can be determined. Finally in phase four, production planning, the production requirements can be defined (e.g., the size and layout of the manufacturing area).

THE HOUSE OF QUALITY MATRIX

In most cases the product planning phase is of most interest to the customer and is the first phase in the process. Figure 3-11 depicts the "house of quality" matrix, which is used to directly relate customer requirements to product features.

Customer requirements, the "what." An organization must first listen to the voice of the customer via interviews, questionnaires, and product and service records to determine what the customer really wants. Customer requirements are translated into quantitative criteria, e.g., color, size, and function. In most cases customer requirements are defined as primary, secondary, or tertiary (see left side of matrix in Figure 3-11).

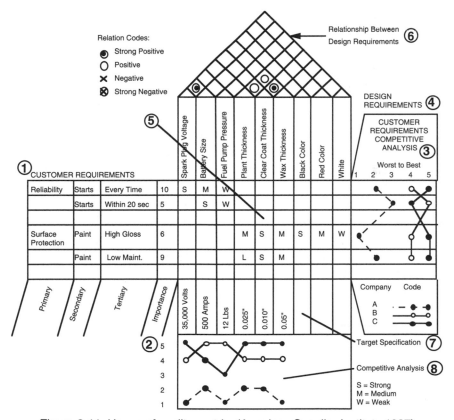

Figure 3-11. House of quality matrix. (American Supplier Institute 1987)

Importance to users. Each requirement must be rated as to its importance to the user. The ratings can range from a 1 to 10 with 10 being very important to the customer. For example, one would expect the reliability of a car to be more important than having a high-gloss paint surface. So, reliability would get a 10 and high-gloss paint might receive a 6 or 7.

Customer requirements competitive analysis. The relative position of each competitor's product to meet each customer requirement can be determined by testing or surveying. Rate each product on a scale of 1 through 5. Referring to Figure 3-11, the rating is placed on the right side of the matrix.

Design requirements, the "how." Next, the team determines "how" to meet the customer requirements by identifying design specifications based on the requirements. The specifications will be placed near the top of the matrix.

Relationships between customer and design requirements. Now describe the relationship between customer requirements and design specifications in the middle of the matrix. The relationship is either strong (S), medium (M), or weak (W). In the example, there is a strong relationship between reliability and spark plug voltage, so special attention must be given to spark plug voltage.

Relationship between design requirements. Some requirements will support each other while others will conflict. Mark these relationships on the top of the house. In the example, there is a strong positive relationship between spark plug voltage and battery size.

Target specifications, the "how much." The "how much" section is the target or nominal specification for each design requirement. Sometimes tolerances are identified in this section. The information is close to the bottom of the matrix. Use these data to set up assembly, subassembly, and part criteria.

Relationships between target specifications and competitive products. Determine the relative position of each competitor's product. As before, rate each item with a 1 through 5. Place the rating at the bottom of the matrix.

SUMMARY

There are several versions of the house of quality matrix. Some include more elaborate rating systems and ways of balancing design requirements to customer requirements.

After completing the product planning house of quality matrix, the next step is to start the parts house of quality matrix, which uses the same matrix format. The design specifications are used as input to the left side of the parts house. Next, the output from the parts matrix becomes the input into the process planning matrix. After completing the process planning house, it is time to start the production planning matrix. All of the matrices are linked through common information that starts with input from the customer.

In summary, the QFD product planning process, the house of quality, and cross-functional teams are powerful tools when used to understand the customer. These methods produce improved product designs, higher quality, lower costs, and increased customer satisfaction—a critical element of TBM.

REFERENCES

Akao, Y. 1987. *Quality Deployment: A Series of Articles.* MA: G.O.A.L., Inc.

American Supplier Institute, Inc. 1987. *Quality Function Deployment.* Dearborn, MI.

Coopers & Lybrand. 1990. *TBM/TQM Methodology: Customer Survey.* New York: Coopers & Lybrand.

Covey, S. R. 1989. *The Seven Habits of Highly Effective People.* New York: Simon & Schuster.

Juran, J. M. and F. M. Gryna. 1980. *Quality Planning and Analysis.* New York: McGraw-Hill.

Myer, R. 1989. Suppliers—manage your customers. *Harvard Business Review.* November-December: 160-68.

The Product Supply System   4
Requires a Product Portfolio

FOR any business, the appropriate product lines and product variety must be driven by customer demand supported by a well developed and understood product supply system (PSS). Today, diversity and individual personal choice have all but eliminated the homogeneous, easily predictable market place. This individualism is apparent throughout our society; it ranges from personalized auto license plates to the large choice of colors in many products. Individual choice is not necessarily linked to traditional status symbols or buying patterns. For example, Sam Walton, one of the world's wealthiest individuals, for years drove a pickup truck daily to and from his office.

THE NEW MARKETING OPPORTUNITY

Consumers demand and get more variety and options in all kinds of products, from cars to clothes. Auto buyers, for example, can choose from three hundred different types of cars and light trucks, domestic and imported, and get variations within each of those lines. Beer drinkers now have four hundred brands to sample. The number of products in supermarkets has soared from thirteen thousand in 1981 to twenty-one thousand in 1987. Marketing in the age of diversity includes the following (McKenna 1988):

- more choices for consumers, more options for producers
- less perceived differences among similar products
- increased competition and promotional efforts
- newly minted phrases as marketers try to "invent" product differentiation
- information overload as consumers try to cope with inputs from all forms of media and communication
- customization
- changing leverage criteria as economies of scale are replaced by the power of customer knowledge
- changing company structures as large corporations downsize to compete with smaller niche firms
- smaller wins and fewer chances for mass market success, but more opportunities for profits in smaller markets

These sudden market shifts have created terrific revenue and profit opportunities for manufacturers. Overnight, organizations have moved into markets and market niches previously closed to them. In some cases, companies have invented new markets through product variety. This consumer windfall has been the manufacturers' downfall in many cases, however, as the PSS was ill-equipped to provide the product proliferation initiated by the new marketing opportunities.

TRADITIONAL MANUFACTURING

In contrast to the fast-changing, opportunistic marketing systems driving today's leading manufacturers, the PSS typically was built at a time when consumers and marketing systems differed greatly. Many facilities were built more than twenty years ago when a more traditional manufacturing mindset existed. As a result, these manufacturing plants have the following types of characteristics:
- rigid production systems designed to produce only a few products
- high-speed, volume-driven equipment
- large material batch sizes
- long changeover times
- highly utilized capacity based on average sales volumes
- hidden production bottlenecks
- long supply cycle times
- many material vendors supplying a few parts

The explosion of product variety placed a demand on product supply systems that has thrown many out of control. These systems are being asked to meet requirements that were never imagined when they were originally designed.

PRODUCT VARIETY

Many symptoms are found in the firm with excessive product variety. Common among these are:
- decreasing margins
- inventory buildup—finished goods, in-process products, and raw materials
- poor service performance, including failure to deliver on time, and poor product availability
- reduced supply system capacity
- increased changeovers and changeover downtime
- low product yields
- increased overhead costs
- greater system complexity
- longer quoted lead times

Few individuals would disagree that product variety and new offerings are a must for most businesses. Figure 4-1 depicts our experience with a wide range of manufacturing companies. Five years from now existing products will account for only about forty percent of today's sales revenue. Therefore, sixty percent of current sales plus planned growth must be generated from new products. Consequently, in most organizations there is considerable ongoing pressure from customers, shareholders, and top management to develop, manufacture, and sell new products. Some supplier firms, working to "manage" their customers, are even suggesting new potential products.

Conversely, little pressure is put on companies to eliminate products. The need for a complete product line, or just the feeling that "we can't get rid of that one," prevails in many businesses. A substantial number of companies do not even have a definition for an obsolete product, let alone a systematic way for elimination.

An excellent conceptual analysis has been presented by Hal Mather that illustrates the problems associated with product variety (Figure 4-2). The graph contains three axes: vertically on the left is cumulative annual percent; vertically on the right is money, zero at the horizontal intersection,

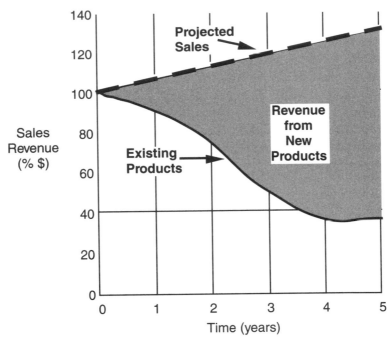

Figure 4-1. Projected sales revenue from existing and new products.

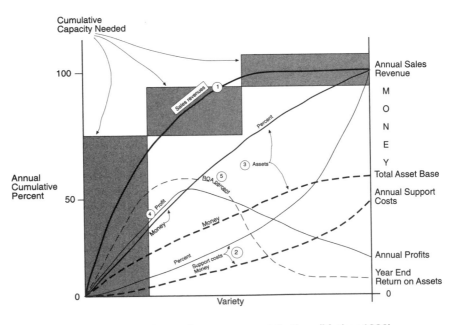

Figure 4-2. Product variety versus contribution. (Mather 1988)

plus above, minus below; the horizontal axis is variety, zero on the left, total variety on the right.

The graph begins with a simple Pareto analysis of sales revenues by product variety. Typically, a small number of products (i.e., 80/20 rule) generates most of the revenue.

The second curve looks at support costs, which are the total costs of doing business less direct materials and direct labor. The support costs relationship is typically the reverse of the sales revenue accumulation. Support costs are small when there is very low variety and high volume; they then grow as variety increases and unit volume per product decreases.

The third curve represents company assets: plant, equipment, inventory, and accounts receivable. Typically, asset requirements relate fairly directly to increased product variety, resulting in a curve drawn relatively down the middle, between the sales and support cost curves. The solid line uses the left axis, i.e., one hundred percent of the assets. The dotted line uses the right curve, i.e., the total assets in dollars.

The fourth curve is the profit contribution curve. It is derived by taking revenues minus direct materials and labor minus support costs, which equal profit contributions for each item. It uses the right axis, which is in dollars. It reaches a peak, then decreases to the amount of money equaling annual profits.

The last curve is used to derive return on assets. This formula is simply profits divided by assets. On a cumulative basis, the curve peaks then decreases quickly. The result is a percentage that uses the left axis. The end point on the right is the year-end value for return on assets.

What do the curves tell us? The curves show how some product profits subsidize others, a commonly felt but not well understood business problem. When further compared with capacity, the situation is magnified. When operating in a capacity-constrained situation, many companies increase capacity through overtime, new equipment, and additional shifts to make products that are losing money. This analysis helps companies understand that there are "winners and losers" in the product portfolio (Mather 1988).

Increasing product variety also drives a proportional increase in the parts required to support it. This proliferation of parts is very costly to the company. Its effects are far reaching, for several reasons. First, the more parts in the portfolio, the more parts that must be designed. This requires a larger engineering support staff. With the increase in parts comes an increase in staff required for materials planning and control. Additionally, as these two functions grow (with increased parts) so will their requirements for information systems. Therefore, the amount of information system support typically grows with increased parts. Obviously, an increasing number of parts directly affects the overhead needed to support the company.

Part proliferation involves other costs. The more parts that exist, the more forecasts that are needed for part usage. More forecasts mean more forecast errors. This means carrying more inventory to protect against these errors, so raw material inventory carrying costs rise. Additionally, more parts lead to more machine changeovers on the manufacturing floor. More machine changeovers mean either longer run sizes (resulting in increased inventory) or lost capacity, both having negative cost effects.

Time to market is a powerful competitive weapon in time-based manufacturing (TBM); however, the number of parts in a product has a significant impact on this time. The more parts in a product, the more parts to be designed and developed. Additionally, more parts mean more planning and control time in the design and manufacturing stages. If there are no attempts to minimize parts in the early product planning stage, a company needlessly increases the time to market for the product. Obviously, part proliferation affects a company's ability to compete on a cost and time basis. The product planning strategy should include a framework for reducing proliferation to improve design and reduce costs.

An interesting approach relating to variety has been suggested by Suzue and Kohdate. They have defined two types of cost: functional and variety. Functional costs are those generated to provide product functions. There are usually several different alternatives to provide function, e.g., different material, added process, or design alteration. Variety costs occur when the number of products increases. These costs come from additional new components, processes, and equipment. Functional costs tend to decrease as product variety increases, while variety costs go up as the number of products increases (Suzue and Kohdate 1990). Their variety reduction program (VRP) approach is to provide products that meet diversifying market needs while also reducing the number of required parts and production processes. Their approach is similar to the *typen und teile* (TUT) types and parts approach developed by the Siemens Company of Germany.

In most organizations, the product reduction strategy is likely a combination of activities best suited for the company's business, customers, and suppliers. In many organizations, a major difficulty in determining the true cost of producing a product is the lack of activity-based cost accounting. Product reduction in a business may be analogous to the federal government reducing the budget; it's not easy and you probably will never make the progress you should.

ACTIVITY-BASED COSTING

While the TBM emphasis is on time, quality and cost remain vital components of the PSS. The following points are universally applicable in the business world (Ames and Hlavacek 1990):

- Over the long term, it is absolutely essential to be a lower-cost supplier.

- To stay competitive, inflation-adjusted costs of producing and supplying any product or service must continuously have a downward trend.

- The true cost and profit picture for each product, for each product/ market segment, and for all key customers must always be known, and traditional accounting practices must not obscure them.

- A business must concentrate on cash flow and balance-sheet strengths as much as on profits.

Most costs can be managed. What is needed is the accounting and information system to support product-based cost management decisions within the TBM organization.

Activity-based costing (ABC) recognizes that support costs are a growing portion of total costs and that they are not uniform across every product. Using ABC, indirect costs are applied based on the actual activities performed or on the real causes for the costs.

Activity-based costing incorporates all the costs of major activities required to develop, support, and deliver products into the costs of the product. The focus on the cost drivers usually results in making management aware of significant improvement opportunities.

WHY ABC?

Many manufacturers have implemented or are considering TBM. The decision to change manufacturing methods is becoming more of a necessity than a choice to stay competitive. It is important to change cost accounting and management techniques to align with the concepts and operations of TBM. This is particularly critical when looking at product costs in light of today's increasing product variety and complexity. Activity-based costing looks beyond the traditional cost methods and provides a systematic way for measuring the total delivered cost, direct and indirect, of products. In this way, management can make informed decisions concerning pricing and variety reduction when product proliferation has become a supply-system issue.

IMPLEMENTING AN ABC SYSTEM

First, it is important to understand the following definitions:

- *Activities* are the tasks or processes performed within a company to develop, manufacture, and distribute its products and services. For example, all costs of requisitioning, purchasing, and receiving materials would go into a cost pool.

- *Activity cost profiles* refer to the resources, types, and amounts of expenses associated with activities on either a total or per unit cost driver basis. This could be the total budgeted costs associated with an activity.

- *Cost drivers* refer to the primary measures of the activities being performed. It is the best index to measure an activity. The cost driver for requisitioning, purchasing, and receiving materials could be either requisitions or purchase orders.

The steps to implement an ABC system are outlined below:

1. Identify activities. Include all activities performed to develop, manufacture, and sell the product or service such as marketing, sales, purchasing, production control, and distribution.

2. Identify the activity cost profile associated with support activities. Determine the costs associated with each activity and identify a mechanism to track and report these costs. To simplify reporting and tracking, group activities by the same cost driver.

3. Select the cost driver for each activity group. Identify how the costs are consumed by, or how they will be assigned to, the product.

4. Identify cost application basis. Identify the condition that makes one product cost more than another. For example, if the cost driver is procurement of materials, assign these costs to a product based on the number of requisitions or purchase orders required for that product. Subsequently, a highly customized product with many unique material requirements would be costed at more than a standard product that uses stock material.

A simple example of ABC follows. The XYZ company makes both standard products and custom products. Processing an order for a standard product involves a single-step order entry activity. Processing an order for a custom product requires an engineering design activity, a product structure creation activity, and a multi-step order entry activity. Traditionally, the engineering and order processing costs would be applied through an overhead rate, or would be expensed. Differences in activities and costs between the orders would not be recognized so that the orders would be priced differently.

ADDED BENEFITS OF ABC

Because ABC reveals the links between performing particular activities and the demands those activities make on the organization's resources, it can give managers a clear picture of how products, brands, customers, facilities, regions, or distribution channels both generate revenues and consume resources. The profitability picture that emerges from the ABC analysis helps managers focus their attention and energy on improving activities that will have the biggest impact on the bottom line (Cooper and Kaplan 1991).

The ABC system tracks and assigns costs where they actually occur. Once total life cycle costs are clearly identified, companies can begin to decide which markets and products are most profitable. For example, a company may decide to build a new product overseas because the direct labor expense per hour is significantly lower than in the United States. Although traditional accounting practices would support this decision, activity-based accounting practices often reveal that the hidden and support costs make this move unprofitable. Some of those hidden costs when subcontracting may be training people to communicate in a different language, extra inventory, travel cost for support personnel, rework of quality problems on large batches, additional production control personnel, shipping materials, inspection, mailing expenses, and turnaround time. Once the accounting department appropriately allocates these hidden costs back to the product, it is evident that an offshore manufacturing decision may be unprofitable (Huthwaite 1989).

MATCHING PRODUCTS, CUSTOMERS, AND THE PRODUCT SUPPLY SYSTEM

There is no single-dimensional right solution to the product proliferation problem, although a variety of choices exist, depending on the specific circumstances of the business. A series of short-term decisions ("band aid" solutions) may give way to an overall longer-term strategy of the TBM organization. Potential short-term actions include:

- reducing products offered
- retrofitting products to the supply system capability
- standardizing products and packaging
- extending lead time for selected products
- implementing focused cost reductions
- outsourcing low-volume products
- changing product prices to reflect true costs based on ABC analysis
- increasing PSS capacity

The long-term solution is simple. The TBM company must redesign the PSS for low-volume, high-variety capability. Doing so will provide the single most sustainable competitive advantage in the market place. Benefits include the following:

- capacity synchronized with customer demand
- reduced customer orders and complexity
- standardized modular products permitting the benefits of variety without the high costs normally associated with variety
- reduced number of suppliers
- simplified packaging and product designs

PSS INVOLVEMENT

The three levels of PSS involvement in the product design function in the TBM organization are marketing, design, and production (Figure 4-3). The later the PSS becomes involved in product design and development, the lesser the opportunity to make a product that can compete on the basis of time, cost, and quality.

The production level generally is the lowest, latest, and most frequent level of PSS involvement in product design. At this level, the product has already been designed and "thrown over the wall" to the PSS to produce and deliver. The best the PSS can do at this point to improve products is communicate problems and offer standardization possibilities. In this retrofitting stage, the PSS provides appropriate tooling design and uses quick changeover techniques where possible.

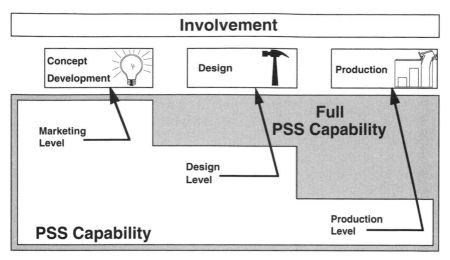

Figure 4-3. Three levels of product supply system involvement.

The next level of PSS involvement in product design is at the design level. Here the PSS provides knowledge about the supply system capabilities, the ramifications of design choices, and any tricks to using the PSS more effectively. At this level, the PSS attempts to assure that product design uses the supply capability most effectively (e.g., product flow and changeovers) and that product parts are rationalized and standardized (e.g., packaging, options, etc.).

The highest level of PSS involvement in product design is at the marketing level. Here the PSS offers creative ideas to bring the product concept in line with supply system opportunities. Also, the organization attempts to assure that the marketing system direction is consistent with the supply system strategy. Only when the PSS is involved at this level can the TBM organization hope to achieve the best overall result. This means increasing product variety at the lowest supply system cost with complete flexibility to respond to change.

REDUCING PART PROLIFERATION

Several proven approaches exist for reducing the number of parts within an organization (Suzue and Kohdate 1990). They are the *foundation technique,* the *building block technique,* and *part implosion.*

The foundation technique. This approach requires the design team to understand what product features are likely to change. With this understanding, the designers can then standardize parts across product families that support features that are not likely to change.

The designers, with input from others, classify parts as fixed or variable. Fixed parts are not likely to change and are designed as common components for use across product lines. Their purpose is to meet the functional requirements that are common to many products; they build the foundation of the product.

Variable parts are designed to meet changing product specifications. Their main purpose is to respond to changing market needs; as market needs change, so do the variable parts.

By standardizing the fixed parts and minimizing the variable parts, a company reduces the number of parts needed to support specific product lines. Figure 4-4 illustrates a simple example of this technique. In designing this clamp, the company expects the clamp length will be the changing feature. Therefore, the arm (part D) will be the variable part. With this in mind, the designer can standardize parts A, B, and C. When the specifications change on the arm length, the new arm can be designed accordingly. All fixed parts remain the same, so the rest of the design is complete.

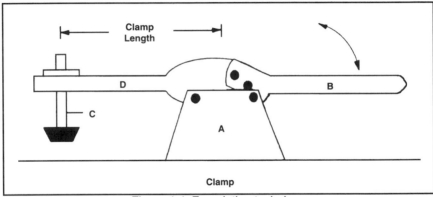

Figure 4-4. Foundation technique.

The building block technique. This approach uses a building block or modular approach to designing products. The modules are developed with standard parts for each product function. When a product with specific functions is required, the products are manufactured by selecting the appropriate modules. Additionally, the company meets product specification changes by introducing new modules. This eliminates the need to change the entire product structure. A good example of this approach is found in the automotive industry. The design of automobiles accommodates options in a modular fashion. If someone orders a radio and an air conditioner in a car, the standard modules for these functions are retrieved and inserted during final assembly. Because this approach uses standard units and parts, and does not affect the basic product structure, the company significantly reduces the number of parts.

The part implosion technique. This technique focuses on reducing parts within a particular product or product group. First, the designer reduces the number of parts that perform a particular function, for example carrying a load. Second, increases are made in the number of functions that a particular part can perform. Figure 4-5 gives a step-by-step progression of this technique.

At the start (Figure 4-5a), seven parts are performing three functions. First, the number of parts performing a particular function is reduced by standardizing these parts (Figure 4-5b). Now three parts perform these functions. Next, more functions are found that use these parts. This is often done by using new materials or process technologies. Now two parts perform three functions (Figure 4-5c).

In summary, the number of parts has reduced because of two factors. First, the number of parts performing the same function has decreased. Second, the number of designed parts performing multiple functions has increased.

	1	2	3	4	5	6	7
a) A	X	X	X				
B				X	X		
C						X	X

	2	5	7
b) A	X		
B		X	
C			X

	2	7
c) A	X	
B	X	
C		X

Figure 4-5. Part implosion.

PERFORMANCE MEASURES

In assessing the level of proliferation, an organization must measure the number of part types (e.g., screws, brackets, etc.) and count the amount of each part (e.g., the number of screws, etc.). Additionally, the company should assess these numbers at different product levels. These measures should be minimized at the product level, the product line level, and the total company level. By using these measures, companies can assess their level of part proliferation and determine where to focus their efforts. Note that these are relative measures, and they should be used to measure improvement trends.

CONCURRENT ENGINEERING AND DESIGN FOR MANUFACTURING

The PSS is highly dependent on the product design and the manufacturing processes. Concurrent engineering is a methodology that completes the product design and also promotes manufacturability. It ensures that the product design will be producible and accepted at the manufacturing shop floor. It is essential for TBM because of the shortened throughput requirements from marketing research to final product delivery (see Figure 4-6). The traditional practice of sequentially performing each function from marketing research to product delivery is no longer acceptable.

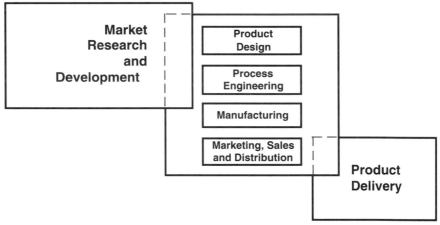

Figure 4-6. Concurrent engineering.

In addition to parallel activities, concurrent engineering efforts should provide products that can be supported by the PSS. The following guidelines are suggested (Mather 1988):

- Design for short stacked lead times. Provide the flexibility to respond quickly to the changing market place. Do not force reliance on long-range, supposedly accurate forecasts.

- Add variability at the last possible moment. Create products with standard materials and processes for the early stages of procurement and manufacture. Product varieties should be added in later steps.

- Select standard materials and components from a preferred list, especially those with long lead times. If unique items are needed for desired functionality or to differentiate your product from the competition, these unique items must have short lead times.

CONCLUSION

In these times of demanding customers and product diversification, it is possible to expand product lines and control costs. Doing so requires that the organization get a "marketing feel" for the product. By understanding what product specifications are likely to change, and using creativity, a company can design product lines that minimize the costs of proliferation. Reducing proliferation yields a competitive advantage that allows companies to meet customers' demands for expanding product variety while maintaining profitability.

REFERENCES

Ames, C. and J. D. Hlavacek. 1990. Vital truths about managing your costs. *Harvard Business Review*. January-February: 140-47.

Cooper, R. and R. S. Kaplan. 1991. Profit priorities from activity-based costing. *Harvard Business Review*. May-June: 130-35.

Huthwaite, B. 1989. The link between design and activity-based accounting. *Manufacturing Systems*. October: 44-47.

Mather, H. 1988. *Competitive Manufacturing*. Englewood Cliffs, NJ: Prentice-Hall.

McKenna, R. 1988. Marketing in an age of diversity. *Harvard Business Review*. September-October: 88-95.

Suzue, T. and A. Kohdate. 1990. *Variety Reduction Program* (English Translation). Cambridge, MA: Productivity Press.

Daily Demand Synchronizes
the Product Supply System   5

ALIGNING the product supply system (PSS) components to satisfy customer needs is one of the most important and least understood elements of time-based manufacturing (TBM). Understanding this principle simply means that each link in the PSS must be individually capable of producing and delivering what customers order each day. The entire PSS is only as capable as the weakest system link, and the overall throughput of the system depends on the slowest system component, i.e., the system bottleneck.

In contrast to achieving system alignment, most PSS are woefully unbalanced versus customer requirements. As a result, the overall supply system lead time is dramatically longer than the customer expected replenishment lead time (see Figure 5-1). To the extent this situation exists, the PSS directly carries excess costs in the way of inventory and factory overhead to support finished goods and work-in-process inventory. In addition, the supply system must either stock the customer's product to adequately respond to lead time requirements or extend the customer's replenishment expectations to meet the supply system capabilities. This second option is rapidly going away as more competitors shorten their supply lead times.

Long supply lead times also require increasing dependence on the sales forecast for insight into what the system should produce to meet customer demand. The shortcomings of forecasting are well understood by manufacturing managers. Accuracy is inversely proportional to the forecast period.

Traditional

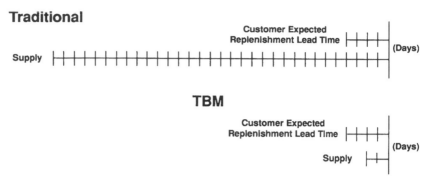

Figure 5-1. Replenishment lead time versus supply lead time in days.

The only good forecast is no forecast at all. The longer the supply lead time, the greater the need to forecast. The more forecasts are used to drive supply decisions, the worse the supply system performs; this is as true and predictable as anything can be in manufacturing. The true TBM competitor seeks to execute the customer's demand in less time than the customer-expected replenishment lead time. In this way, all customer demands can be supplied to order, resulting in a substantial supply chain waste reduction and cost savings.

Figure 5-2 illustrates a major movement from the traditional manufacturing world of long lead times and bottlenecks to the TBM world of synchronized supply to short-term demand. To achieve this synchronization, the TBM organization must address the total supply system including the customer demand profile, run cycles, batch sizes, system capacity, and customer order visibility.

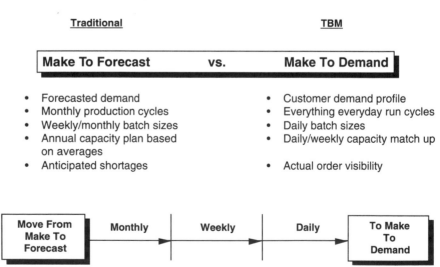

Figure 5-2. TBM supply system strategy.

SYNCHRONIZE SUPPLY TO DEMAND

Synchronizing the supply to customer demand requires that each major activity in the PSS (e.g., assembly, subassembly, and fabrication) be performed so that the activity output matches the customer demand profile (see Figure 5-3). Doing so allows the overall system output to be calibrated and linked to the customer order rate.

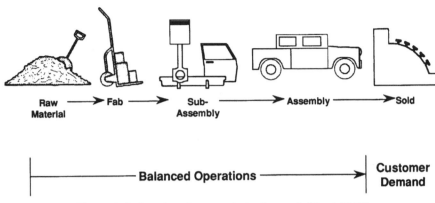

Figure 5-3. Synchronize supply to demand. (Ford 1926)

In the synchronized supply system, the production rate equals the sales rate—not the machine rate, nor the ability to produce (capacity)—and it is not constant from period to period. A simple example of a repetitive manufacturing cycle time calculation is shown in Figures 5-4 and 5-5.

Sales				Supply time/unit min.	Total minutes /cycle
Model	/week	/day	/hour		
A	8,000	1,600	200	0.150	30.0
B	6,000	1,200	150	0.100	15.0
C	4,000	800	100	0.075	7.5
D	2,000	400	50	0.150	7.5
			500		60.0

Figure 5-4. Repetitive manufacturing cycle time.

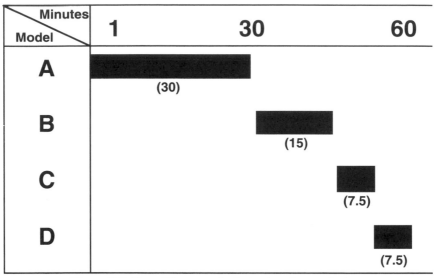

Figure 5-5. Repetitive manufacturing hourly run strategy.

The principles of synchronization are summarized as follows:

1. All activities within the PSS are synchronized to customer demand.

2. Manufacturing is done to support the end customer schedule. Nothing is produced for stores except C inventory items manufactured or purchased in larger quantities (lot sizes).

3. The daily customer order schedule is the only schedule and drives system priorities.

4. Products are only produced and supplied in the required quantities when needed. If manufacturing cannot economically produce daily or smaller lot sizes, then the smallest possible quantities are produced for eventual consumption at the point of next use.

5. The synchronized system is coupled to the negative feedback of the pull system, which keeps all facets of the manufacturing pipeline in balance. This effectively schedules and prioritizes all aspects of the supply chain.

CUSTOMER DEMAND PROFILE

The customer demand profile provides the language that drives the PSS synchronization. It marries products with customers to determine pre-

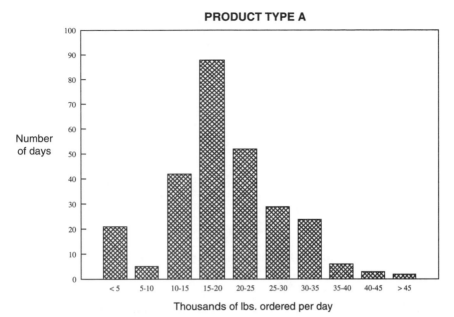

PRODUCT TYPE A

Thousands of lbs. ordered per day

Figure 5-6. Customer demand profile—histogram.

cisely what the PSS must provide daily. It is the critical input that allows management to configure the PSS for the TBM organization design.

Figure 5-6 is an example of the customer demand profile. The period represented by this histogram is approximately one year of daily shipments, or 277 days. The vertical axis on the graph represents the number of days out of 277 that customers ordered the number of pounds shown on the horizontal axis for product type A. For example, forty-two out of 277 days, customers ordered between ten thousand and fifteen thousand pounds of product type A. In addition, two days out of 277, customers ordered between forty thousand and forty-five thousand pounds. Because these histograms do not illustrate trends in customer orders, they should always be coupled with a run chart (see Figure 5-7). These two graphs show the demand load on the supply system as well as seasonability and trends in demand.

Characteristics of the customer demand profile are:

• The profile should cover at least one year. More history is acceptable and may be necessary.

• The profile's time bucket (manufacturing requirements) should be daily, unless customers expect to communicate in weekly buckets. This would happen for larger products with high value-added times (weeks). Only in rare cases should the customer demand profile bucket be monthly.

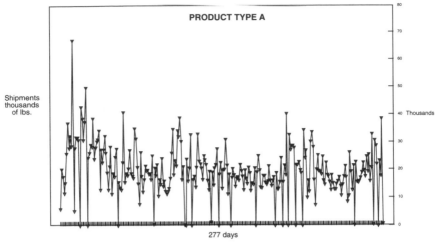
Figure 5-7.Customer demand profile—run chart.

- Along with collecting demand data, management should also under-stand the characteristics of the sales and marketing system and the types of events that drive demand. A reason always exists for very high and very low demand. Management should be looking to separate common cause variations in demand from special causes.

- Individual product profiles can be grouped together when flowing through the same PSS component. This grouping provides an overall system view for all products. Different configurations can then be studied by changing product mixes.

RUN CYCLES
A major synchronization step in TBM is calibrating the PSS to a supply bucket that matches the customer demand bucket. In other words, when the customer buys products daily, the PSS should produce and deliver products daily. As a TBM organization, the goal should be to supply a little bit of everything everyday (see Figure 5-8).

Aligning run cycles with customer demand cycles is a large departure from the traditional manufacturing strategy. In these companies, run cycles are determined on an individual machine basis, typically driven by long changeover times and large minimum order quantities. Often, run cycles are not looked upon from a total supply system perspective and their individual influences on overall PSS lead times are not examined. Dra-matic examples of long supply system lead times frequently occur from run cycle imbalances. For example, customers could purchase products each

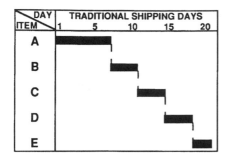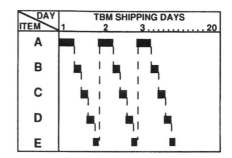

SELL DAILY!
SUPPLY DAILY!
Figure 5-8. Run cycles.

day from a company, while final assembly produces fifty each week, fabrication produces fifty every two weeks, and a supplier provides all raw materials once a month. In this example, it is easy to see how the supplier's monthly replenishment cycle is dramatically out of synchronization with the customer's buying cycle.

BATCH SIZES

In conjunction with matching the supply system run cycles with the customer's demand cycle, the PSS batch size must match the customer demand batch size. For example, looking at Figure 5-6, if the minimum batch size in the fabrication department was 35,000 units, then the PSS could never be synchronized daily with the customer demand profile for product type A. The average cycle would be as follows:

35,000 units ÷7,000 units (average daily demand) = 5 days run cycle

This one-week run cycle would add an additional week to the supply system lead time for product type A. This problem can easily be compounded when adding multiple components with large minimum batch sizes sequentially in the supply chain.

The goal in the TBM organization is to have all batch sizes equal the batch size required to meet the customer's daily demand profile. The barrier to smaller batch sizes is typically long changeover times, especially on capacity-constrained equipment. For example, if a changeover requires eight hours on a key machine, it is not possible to run three products across that machine in a twenty-four hour period. The entire twenty-four hours would be spent on changeover time, and no time would be available to run products. The only solution to overcoming this barrier is to adopt a formal changeover reduction program. Reducing changeover times will be addressed later in this chapter.

CAPACITY

Capacity is the highest sustainable rate of output that can be achieved with current production specifications, product mix, worker effort, plant capacities, and equipment. It is important to note that in most manufacturing plants, overall output is not equal to the input workload because of work-in-process, queue or wait time, and items in temporary storage (see Figure 5-9). The function of capacity planning determines the resources required to meet PSS supply (customer demand) objectives. Capacity control is necessary to monitor output, compare it with the customer profile, determine if variations exceed limits, and take corrective action.

To obtain the needed manufacturing capacity, capacity control must balance human resources, plant facilities, equipment, and finances. The importance of matching capacity and demand are illustrated in Figure 5-10.

It is critical when implementing TBM that the company understand thoroughly the relationship between market demand patterns (daily sales variability) and daily supply system capacity. This knowledge must exist for each product manufactured and delivered in the PSS. Understanding this relationship provides management with the basis to design inventory levels for finished goods as well as each work in process (WIP) location.

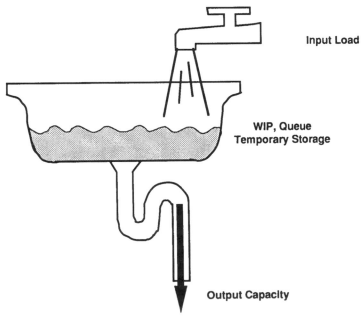

Input Load

WIP, Queue
Temporary Storage

Output Capacity

Figure 5-9. The capacity sink.

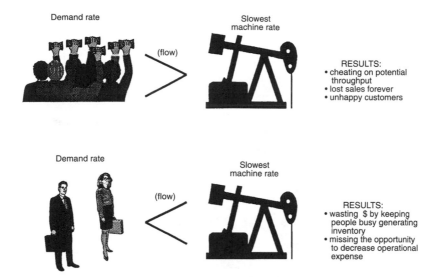

Figure 5-10. Capacity rates and results.

The more highly variable the demand pattern and the greater the number of days that sales exceeds supply system capacity, the higher the levels of inventory that the PSS will be forced to keep. The TBM organization needs to match PSS capacity with projected sales in order to satisfy its overall customer demands.

Figure 5-11 compares the customer demand profile for product type A against the plant capacities for company A and its major supplier. For ninety-six percent of the days, company A had the capacity to produce the amount ordered of product type A, while the major supplier could supply product type A for eighty-six percent of the days. The histogram shows that both company A and its major supplier are highly capable of supplying customer orders daily for this product type. In our experience, as capacity capabilities move below the sixty percent to seventy percent range, a company's ability to meet demand on a daily basis becomes highly questionable.

Interestingly, we have found that most outliers in the demand profile, i.e., the high-volume peaks and low-volume valleys, are usually due to sales and marketing decisions made by the organization itself. Most companies take a relatively smooth customer demand profile and introduce variability through customer incentives such as promotions, forward buys, and trade allowances. What on the surface appears to benefit the company through volume increases (temporarily) in actuality adds costs to the supply system. These costs come from the increased run time (i.e.,

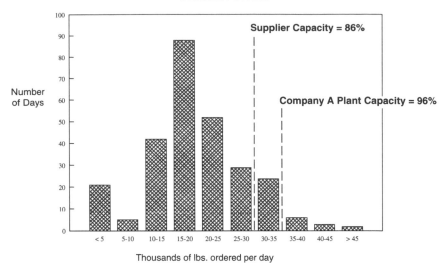

Figure 5-11. Output capacity versus customer demand profile.

overtime) or extra inventory required to cover the capacity shortfall initiated by the temporary volume spike.

CUSTOMER ORDER VISIBILITY

The final component of the synchronized PSS is order visibility. As PSS lead times decrease, the ability to supply to actual customer orders becomes a reality. This represents a major shift in thinking, as most organizations are resigned to producing to stock based upon long product lead times with forecasted demand.

Implementing visible scheduling extends into two areas. The first area is determining the total product quantity to manufacture each day. The second area is determining the variety of each product within that total quantity. As stated earlier, the goal of the PSS is to make a little bit of everything every day. This requires substantially reducing batch sizes and running these smaller batch sizes on more frequent cycles. Table 5-1 provides an example of run cycle times.

The product quantities and mix in Table 5-1 provide results in a visible scheduling sequence on the manufacturing shop floor during eight one-hour run cycles in a day (see Figure 5-12).

As the PSS moves toward a supply lead time approaching the customer-expected replenishment lead time, the need to see the customer order daily becomes important. The organization must know what is ordered, how much is ordered, and any special instructions. In this way, the

Table 5-1. Run cycle times.

Daily Customer Demand	Hourly Run Cycle Quantity to Meet Daily Demand (8-hr. shift)
Product A = 1,000 units	Product A = 1,000/8 = 125/hr.
Product B = 800 units	Product B = 800/8 = 100/hr.
Product C = 480 units	Product C = 480/8 = 60 hr.

PSS can begin each day with new customer orders and supply them out of daily PSS capacity using a daily run cycle and batch size in the precise quantities needed to meet that day's demand.

This mixed product supply requires strict first-in first-out control of product flow, by using pull scheduling. Using visible scheduling within the synchronized PSS results in drastically reduced pipeline inventory and very high customer service levels. The PSS now produces and delivers to the perfect schedule, which contains the actual products and quantities ordered by customers. There is no need to expedite or change from true customer demand.

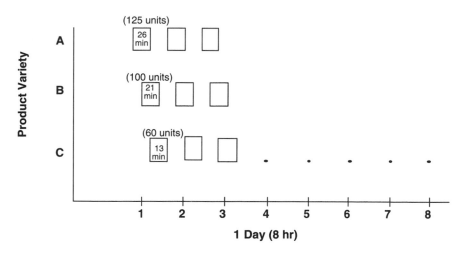

Figure 5-12. Daily visible schedule.

SUMMARY

Developing the synchronized PSS is more than just calculating capacity and developing production schedules (see Figure 5-13). It extends into customer demand profiles, run cycles, batch sizes, capacity, and order visibility.

Synchronization creates the basis for standardizing many activities in addition to direct production work; hence, the benefits can be very extensive. Smaller batch sizes running more frequently result in less inventory, which in turn results in less waste and lower inventory holding costs. Furthermore, smaller batch sizes and smaller inventories actually increase customer service levels (see Figure 5-14).

Synchronizing the PSS is difficult because nearly all the variables of production and most facets of running the business are affected. However, synchronizing the PSS and untangling the material flow is the key to realizing TBM.

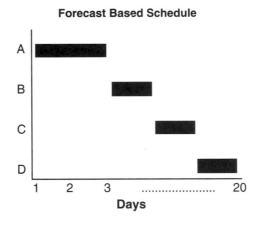

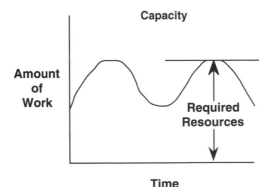

Figure 5-13. Traditional schedule and required capacity.

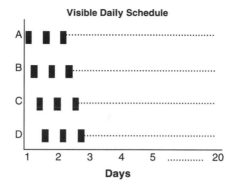

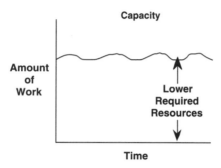

Figure 5-14. Synchronization around the daily customer schedule.

THE IMPORTANCE OF REDUCING CHANGEOVER TIMES

Reducing changeover times is vital to synchronizing the PSS. Unfortunately, many companies still have a traditional changeover paradigm that includes the following views:
• equipment design dictates long changeover times
• changeovers require a high level of knowledge and skill
• large lot productions offset these long changeover times
• better equipment efficiencies justify high inventory holding costs
• combining changeovers increases equipment efficiencies

This paradigm is underscored by the mindset illustrated by some common quotations heard in the plant.
• "We can't find the tools to do this changeover."
• "Now that it's finally running well, keep the equipment running. We'll sell the stuff eventually."

- "That is a tough changeover. Do we really need this product?"
- "We can't start that changeover today. The mechanic didn't show up."
- "We were late starting because all the changeover parts were mixed up."
- "Leave the changcover for the next shift."

Once the TBM organization reduces changeover times, these truisms are no longer valid. The economic order quantity relationship, Figures 5-15 and 5-16, illustrates how lot sizes can dramatically decrease as changeover costs decrease. Table 5-2 shows the impact on cycle as changeover time is reduced from sixteen hours to two hours.

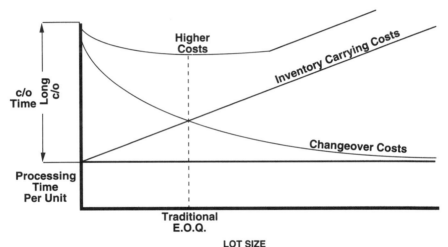

Figure 5-15. Economic order quantity (traditional).

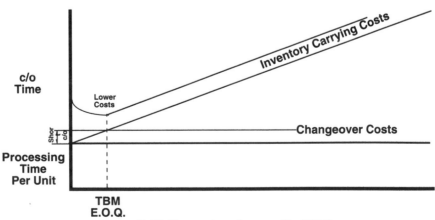

Figure 5-16. Economic order quantity (TBM).

Table 5-2. The impact of changeover time on cycle.

Example	Changeover Time (hours)	Lot Size (Standard Cases)	Process Time Per Standard Case (hours)	Cost (Avg. Process Time/Case)	Cycle Time (Hours)
1	16	80	1	(16/80 +1 hr.) = 1.20 hr.	96
2	8	40	1	(8/40 + 1 hr.) = 1.20 hr	48
3	4	20	1	(4/20 + 1 hr.) = 1.20 hr.	24
4	2	10	1	(2/10 + 1 hr.) = 1.20 hr.	12

BENEFITS OF REDUCED CHANGEOVER TIMES

Quick changeover times provide the flexibility to manufacture what is needed, when it is needed, in whatever batch size is required. Quick changeovers provide a stream of benefits, which flow as follows:
• more frequent changes ... allow
• shorter production cycles ... which
• lower inventories ... and offer
• more flexibility ... to deliver
• faster customer response ... along with
• fresher product ... which is
• better quality ... and provide
• higher return on assets.

Quick changeovers also deliver a favorable impact on quality. For example, minimizing trial processing reduces material waste: fewer adjustments mean less chance for variation; smaller batches provide a quicker feedback loop and deliver fewer defects in inventory should an undetected problem develop; and standardized changeovers improve process yields.

CHANGEOVER IMPLEMENTATION

A simple definition of changeover time is: The time between the last good item of one run and the first good item from the next run at target run rates. Table 5-3 outlines the changeover implementation methodology.

Table 5-3. Changeover implementation methodology.

Methodology
1. Create changeover team
2. Select changeover to study
3. Determine changeover reduction goal
4. Videotape changeover
5. Document activities
6. Identify internal vs. external elements
7. Housekeeping
8. Shift internal to external
9. Improve elemental operations
10. Implement and test new methods
11. Analyze new method videotape
12. Standardize new method
13. Goal attained

Brief descriptions follow of each of the thirteen steps in the changeover reduction methodology.

1. Create changeover team. The changeover team should consist of a cross-functional group of operators and support personnel such as:
• changeover technicians
• equipment operators
• technical support (engineers)
• equipment vendors
• raw material suppliers
• other support (accounting, marketing)

The changeover team's mission is to search for better overall results by improving the changeover process and job methods. The objectives of using a changeover team are:
• blend the team process with the systematic changeover methodology
• move decisions to the source of the work
• develop and use internal experts
• facilitate implementing difficult changes
• expand efforts quicker throughout the plant

The changeover team should plan to meet twice weekly for two hours for the first four to six weeks of study. After the initial data collection and study period, the team should meet once per week for one hour until the team objectives are achieved.

2. Select changeover to study. Before jumping into a changeover reduction effort, the changeover team should collect a variety of plant data to determine improvement priorities, current changeover operating procedures, and plant practices relative to changeover policies, staffing, timing, and performance measurement.

Initial data collection should include information such as the following:
• historical changeover times
• average run cycles and batch sizes
• number of changeovers per week, month, and year
• causes of changeovers
• changeover procedures
• staffing
• personnel types and skills required.

This data collection effort should initially lead the team to discuss the options available to avoid the need to changeover. Achieving flexibility with no changeover is a better option than performing a changeover with reduced times. Examining these options could result in eliminating an operation, dedicating equipment, or rationalizing parts. A company could eliminate an operation, for example, by substituting materials. This substitution could come by changing from a custom printed corrugated box (needing changeover with each new product) to moving to online printing of boxes requiring no product change, only a simple recoding with each new product.

Dedicating equipment is frequently possible when multiple machines run multiple products. Performing a Pareto analysis of product volumes relative to equipment capabilities often provides insight into realigning products to reduce changeover downtimes. Parts rationalization typically comes from reducing multiple varieties of the same item (e.g., cap size on a bottle) to a single variety. This type of change is usually one of the most obvious changeover wastes and is easily identified and corrected.

The last downtime improvement option to consider is reducing the changeover time itself. For large changeovers, we have found the Gantt chart technique to be particularly useful in understanding the current changeover method and procedures (see Figure 5.17). Several reasons for using the Gantt chart approach follow.

- It develops a common base of understanding.
- It expresses the changeover process in a pictorial form.
- It shows task dependencies.
- It develops a critical path.
- It documents the current procedures.

3. Determine changeover reduction goal. Once there is common understanding of the current changeover frequency, time, method, and staffing, the changeover team must select a goal for changeover time reduction. It is in this area that teams frequently flounder. Because they don't understand what is needed to support the synchronized PSS, they typically select a thirty-three, fifty, or seventy-five percent reduction as a good goal. This method is largely ineffective and will be explained in the next section.

4. Videotape changeover. Videotaping the changeover is an objective technique that permits detailed study of the changeover method without the confusion and disruption of the shop floor. Before performing the videotaping session, the changeover team should meet and discuss the process with changeover operators and make certain they are comfortable with the study technique.

The pre-video preparation should include checking the camera and making sure the logistics are correct. The logistics include adequate lighting, sufficient audio, camera mobility, adequate power, accessible camera location to the entire changeover process, and a nondisruptive

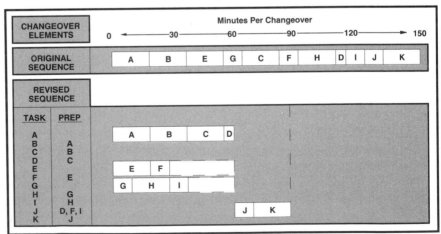

Figure 5-17. Changeover Gantt chart.

camera location. The videotape process should begin by taping the last good unit from the previous production run and end with the first good unit following changeover. The camera operator should narrate important facts during taping. This study should include the operator explaining the changeover as performed so that individual elements can be distinguished. Focus should be on the machine as much as possible and a zoom lens should be used for close-ups of hands. The videotaping should include the following:
• moving tools and materials
• removing old hardware
• installing new hardware
• trial processing
• inspecting first items
• searching for missing tools
• problem solving

A summary of a videotape analysis is shown in Figure 5-18. Typical changeover activities are shown in Table 5-4 (Shingo 1985).

Seq. no.	Element description	Time (min.)	Int	Ext	Threads	Adjustments	Mgmt. contr. problems	Useless work	Necessary	Purposes, additional facts, distance, comments
			✔	✔						
A	Raise old assm shaft	5	✓						✓	
	Detach shaft @ top	2	✓			✓			✓	
	Detach shaft @ bottom	3	✓			✓			✓	
	Test machine	5	✓					✓		
	Cut & attach wire	1.5	✓						✓	
	Detach assm. shaft	1	✓			✓			✓	
	Attach crane to shaft	5	✓						✓	
	Remove assm. shaft	5	✓						✓	
	Take away old assm. & get new one	3.5		✓				✓		Walked a good distance
	Remove plates	3	✓			✓			✓	Why so many plates?
	Take away old & get new plates	1		✓				✓		Walked a good distance
	Install new plates	4	✓			✓			✓	Why so many plates?
	Hook up machine	.5	✓					✓		
	Trial run	1.5	✓				✓	✓		
	Attach crane	.5	✓						✓	
	Attach new assm. shaft	1	✓				✓		✓	A lot of jockeying to install
	Remove crane	.5	✓						✓	

Figure 5-18. Changeover reduction videotape analysis.

Table 5-4. Changeover activities.

Typical Activities	Percent Occurrence
Preparation and function checks	30
Attachment and removal of parts	5
Centering, dimensioning, setting conditions	15
Trial processing and adjustments	50

5. Document activities. Upon completion of the videotaping, the changeover team should meet to review the changeover. This review should be done in a single meeting, if possible, and is done to facilitate the group's understanding of the entire changeover process. To support the team effort before the meeting, the team leader should analyze and document the tape for the following tasks:
• listing each changeover element and sequence
• timing each element
• documenting pertinent details
• laying out dependencies
• developing a Pareto chart of elemental times

6. Identify internal versus external elements. Reducing changeover time requires identifying all required activities and then shifting as many of those as possible from inside to outside machine operation. The initial step in this shift is to classify each activity as either internal or external. Internal tasks are those that must be done while the equipment is shut down. Common examples include:
• removing and installing operating hardware
• internal cleaning
• connecting and disconnecting

External tasks are those that can be done while the equipment is running on the previous product. Common examples include:
• obtaining instructions and specifications
• presetting gauges
• obtaining and returning hardware and materials
• organizing tools
• off-line cleaning and adjusting

7. *Housekeeping.* Housekeeping is the most basic of the changeover improvement elements. This approach alone, however, can yield a forty percent time reduction. It is based on four basic principles: simplify, organize, participate, and discipline.

- *Simplify* means to identify needed tools, parts, etc., and remove everything else from the work area. The operator should sort through, then sort out.

- *Organize* means to designate locations for everything and set quantity limits. Locations should be designated with the objective of minimizing material handling, distance traveled, and unnecessary work.

- *Participate* means to involve the local operator in determining what he/she needs to do a better job, and then meeting those needs.

- *Discipline* means developing standard operating procedures and sticking to them. This provides the basis for not only reducing changeover times but also performing changeovers to achieve consistent, stable results.

8. *Shift internal to external.* After setting the baseline, the team should determine what elements currently performed in-line (internal) can be shifted to off-line (external). This is often an inexpensive method for achieving significant gains. Several approaches can be used to achieve this shift. One method is to prepare checklists that identify and list the steps necessary for external operations. These steps should include parts, tools, measurements, and people. Using a checklist prevents forgetting the necessary items to perform a changeover. Another method is to inspect and prepare hardware, such as tools and dies, before equipment shutdown. This inspection prevents unexpected breakdowns in the middle of a changeover. A final method is to create parts storage at the machine. This storage provides the necessary supplies closest to the point of use.

9. *Improve elemental operations.* Elemental operations improvements come from a variety of tricks pioneered by Shigeo Shingo (Shingo 1985). These techniques include thread reduction, adjustment elimination, and methods improvements.

Thread reduction means eliminating the unnecessary use of threads to secure devices. Threads are a particularly inefficient way to attach items, and there are a variety of effective thread alternatives that save substantial attaching/detaching time.

Adjustments elimination means standardizing tools, molds, dies, etc., to reduce the need to perform large changeover activities. It also includes using gauge stops and calibrators to reduce searching for the optimal gauge setting.

Methods improvements represent a variety of techniques including:

- duality—keeping two of an item
- minimum interchange—combining tools, components, etc. into one removable fixture
- interface elimination—removing barriers to operator performing changeover
- fail-safing—designing changeover to prevent human error (e.g., leaded gas hose cannot go into unleaded gas tank)
- parallel operations—two operators performing changeover tasks simultaneously
- handles—putting handles on everything difficult to carry

10. Implement and test run methods. Implementation of new changeover procedures is diagrammed in Figure 5-19. The desired results should show reduced time for the changeover, reduced variability in the changeover process, improved quality, and improved start-up yield and efficiency.

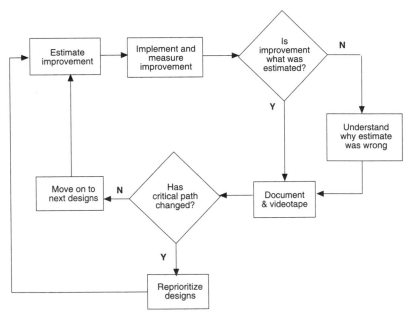

Figure 5-19. Changeover implementation flow chart.

11. Analyze new method videotape. Documentation of the improved changeover should include definitions, tasks with required tools, step by step procedural execution of tasks with illustrations, and any other pertinent reference information. The changeover documentation is used for training operators and technicians, and for detail reference (not during changeover). As with all documentation this material should be updated as improvements occur.

12. Standardize new method. Recommendations for standardizing the new changeover methods are as follows:

- Standardize the changeover reduction process across the plant, company, etc.
- Train operators on the new changeover process and the standard operating procedures.
- Develop standard operating procedures for monitoring changeover time.
- Measure and post results.
- Develop plans for communicating improvements early in the process. The main targets for this communication are the appropriate operators and team member managers.
- Communicate improvements using newsletters, storyboards, or presentations.

13. Goal attained. It is well documented that any changeover can be reduced by seventy-five percent or more. The real question is, "To what level must the changeover be reduced to support the business?" When viewed as an integrated part of the synchronization strategy, changeovers take on new-found importance as priorities and levels of improvement are pursued to optimize overall PSS throughput. The next section offers an effective approach to answering this often misunderstood question.

SETTING THE CHANGEOVER REDUCTION GOAL

To produce products in a synchronized TBM environment, companies must place significant emphasis on reducing changeover times. Because changeover reduction success stories of seventy-five to ninety percent improvement abound these days, companies often embark on a changeover program without a focus or a specific goal. All they know is that they need to reduce changeovers to make cost reductions or support lead time reduction efforts. They assemble teams and they usually experience quick success. Invariably, however, someone asks, "When are we done?" In some cases a manager may have said, "Reduce changeovers by seventy-five percent." Even if this is the case, why seventy-five percent?

The method to determine the changeover time reduction needed to support TBM is a data-driven, straightforward approach that is based on product demand. This method shows that not all manufacturers have to reduce changeovers from twenty hours to two hours, or ninety minutes to five minutes. In many cases, a level of changeover reduction supporting a synchronized PSS may not be ninety percent.

THE CHANGEOVER REDUCTION CALCULATION

For explanation purposes, changeover time is the amount of time required to make the change per run cycle. A run cycle refers to the time it takes a company to cycle through its entire product line. This run cycle may be three months, a month, a week, or a day. The simple equation for changeover time (CO) is:

$$CO = AT- RT$$

where
AT = available time (shift hours)
RT = run time (production hours)

To obtain the required changeover time, an estimate of customer demand is necessary. Sources to help determine this future demand include customer order history and marketing forecasts. Future demand analysis provides the framework for what customers will expect during the cycle. For example, assume cycles are monthly and products X and Y are made on the same machine. The production time, changeover time, and demand data for X and Y follow:

Product	Production Time (hours/unit)	Changeover Time (hours)	Demand Per Cycle (units)
X	1.00	8 (from Y)	88
Y	0.25	12 (from X)	176

In the example, 132 hours of production time per month are needed to satisfy demand (88 units × 1.00 hours/unit + 176 units × 0.25 hours/unit = 132 hours). After understanding the production time required, the hours available for changeovers can be calculated. Assume this facility runs one eight-hour shift for twenty-two days per month, which equates to 176 available hours per month. The equation for determining the time available for changeover (CO) follows:

$$CO = 176 - 132 = 44 \text{ hours}$$

Because changeover time is twenty hours (8 hours + 12 hours) per cycle, the demand can be produced on a weekly run cycle. The remaining available time (24 hours) can be used for additional capacity or maintenance activities.

Historic Perspective

Before the push toward TBM, producers commonly lived with long changeover times. There was no business need to reduce them. Typically, large batch sizes were scheduled to avoid wasting capacity. With large batch sizes, there are longer run cycles and fewer changeovers. These long cycles can create problems elsewhere in the organization. For instance, with a one-month run cycle the company must keep a month's worth of finished goods in inventory. Additionally, because monthly forecasts are not accurate, constantly changing production schedules must be maintained to meet customer needs. The final result is that capacity is wasted by either producing the wrong product or performing unplanned changeovers.

Shorter Run Cycles

As companies adopt TBM, they must also adopt shorter run cycles. However, shorter run cycles result in more changeovers which—unless they require less time—mean lost capacity. As mentioned, many companies have assembled changeover teams with great success. The downfall of these teams often is that they do not know where to target changeover reduction efforts. Some teams reduce changeovers beyond what is necessary to support business objectives, resulting in the needless spending of costs, time, and resources. These efforts could be better spent on reducing changeovers on other machines that support PSS throughput. Where teams do not adequately reduce changeover times, there is lost capacity to the machine. The company needs to develop target changeover times at each resource in the PSS so that resources are used most effectively. But what is the allowable level of changeover time?

DETERMINING CHANGEOVER TIME FOR SHORTER RUN CYCLES

In reducing run cycle lengths, management must make sure that capacity is available to accommodate the customer demand. For example, if a company moves from a monthly cycle to a weekly cycle, it must determine the new cycle demand on the supply system. Assuming a five-day week, following are the weekly demand data:

Product	Demand per month (units)	Demand per week (units)
A	88	20
B	176	40

Therefore, thirty hours (20 units • 1 hour/unit + 40 units • 0.25 hours/ unit = 30 hours) of production time is needed a week to satisfy demand. There is one, eight-hour shift for five days a week which leaves forty hours available. Hence, the time available for changeover (CO) is:

$$CO = 40 - 30 = 10 \text{ hours}$$

However, in this example, changeover time per weekly cycle has not changed; it is still twenty hours. To accommodate the new run cycle, changeover time must be reduced from twenty hours to ten hours, i.e., a fifty percent reduction.

This analysis can be easily completed when demand within a cycle is constant throughout the year. However, the real world has seasonality and promotions creating variations in demand. If the PSS is designed according to average yearly demand, it will not be capable of responding to demand peaks. As an example, assume the numbers used earlier are average numbers. If changeover time is determined according to these numbers, then it is clear that changeovers must be reduced by fifty percent. However, most manufacturers have variable demand patterns. In this example, assume that demand surges require up to 37.5 production hours per week. With changeover times determined by average data, the company is incapable of responding within forty available hours. It needs 47.5 hours (37.5 production hours + 10 changeover hours). Therefore, it is necessary to determine how many production hours should be set aside for demand variability.

The following example will illustrate this concept. Start by collecting anticipated demand data by week for the coming year; the past year's shipments are an excellent source for this data. Input from marketing would also be valuable. This demand forecast should be converted to production hours for the fifty-two weeks in the coming year (see Table 5-5).

Table 5-5. Weekly production hours.

Production hours required per week	No. weeks in this range	Cumulative weeks (%)
22.5 - 25.0	5	10
25.0 - 27.5	10	29
27.5 - 30.0	11	50
30.0 - 32.5	13	75
32.5 - 35.0	8	90
35.0 - 37.5	5	100
	52 total	

Management's role at this point is to determine the number of weeks per year that the PSS should be capable of producing to demand, or cover demand. The more weeks covered, the less inventory carried. However, the more weeks covered, the more production hours are needed to cover demand and the greater the reduction in changeover time needed. Therefore, this decision is the result of a cost/benefit analysis between carrying inventory and reducing changeover times. For example, management determines it needs the capability to accommodate ninety percent of the weeks in the year. From Table 5-5, thirty-five hours of production are needed to accommodate ninety percent of the weeks.

The calculation for required changeover (CO) hours is shown below:

$$CO = 40 - 35 = 5 \text{ hours}$$

Therefore, in moving from a monthly cycle to a weekly cycle changeover time must be reduced by seventy-five percent (from 20 to 5 hours per cycle).

SUMMARY

To use resources effectively, the objectives for changeover time reduction must be known. The method described earlier provides a simple, straightforward approach for determining changeover time reductions. For a given cycle, product demand data (which considers demand variability) drives the entire process. Furthermore, it requires a cost/benefit analysis between inventory carrying cost and changeover reduction investment. Applying this method will help make productive use of the resources needed to implement TBM.

CONTINUOUS PROCESS FLOW

A continuous process flow is essential to TBM. The benefits of a continuous flow include the following items:
• problems are uncovered
• the overall supply system operation is streamlined
• a focused factory within the TBM organization is created
• everyone involved is brought together
• applies to the entire enterprise

All activities in an organization are completed through the steps in a process. The maximum benefits of a continuous process flow design are obtained when all processes are considered at the same time, from order entry and product concept to delivering customer requirements.

The traditional manufacturing layout commonplace in job-shop production requires that machines and equipment with common functions be located in proximity (Figure 5-20). This layout requires that products flow in large lots using separate schedules by functional department with the associated problems of increased inventory, excessive move distances, delays, overhead costs, and other inherent inefficiencies.

Typically, paperwork processing and order entry processing are also organized in the traditional functional layout (see Figures 5-21 and 5-22). The results of analyzing a traditional order entry process in a manufacturing firm are summarized in Table 5-6. In this example, six different tasks were performed a total of forty-nine times over a five-day period to complete the process. Redesigning the order entry process reduced the task occurrences to nine and the cycle time to one day (see Figure 5-23).

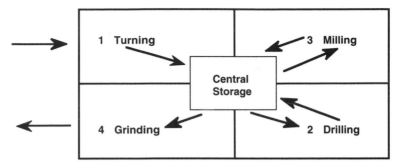

Figure 5-20. Traditional manufacturing layout. (Coopers & Lybrand 1987)

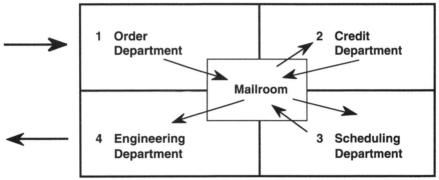

Figure 5-21. Traditional paperwork processing. (Coopers & Lybrand 1987)

6 DAYS CYCLE TIME

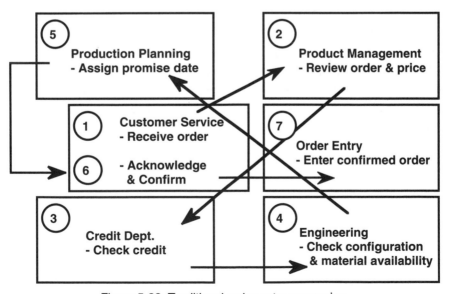

Figure 5-22. Traditional order entry processing.

1 DAY CYCLE TIME

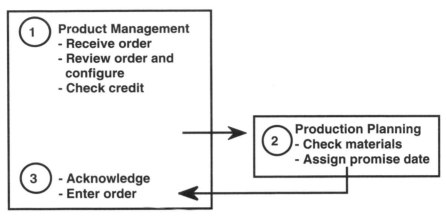

Figure 5-23. TBM order entry processing.

Table 5-6. Order entry analysis.

Action	Move To	Sort, Split, Decide Where to Move	Review Check Change Correct	Copy Re-Copy	File Pull File	Do	Total
Occurrences	16	9	9	2	6	7	49

CELLULAR PROCESSING

Cellular processing maximizes product flow efficiency by incorporating all required processes into a single integrated system (see Figure 5-24). The same cellular concept can be applied to paperwork processing (see Figure 5-25). The prerequisites for cellular processing include:
• fast changeover times
• ability to balance processes and operations
• part and product families
• sufficient volume
• cross-trained workforce

The characteristics of cellular processing include:
• people-dependent versus machine-dependent processes
• frequent rebalancing because of demand changes
• flexible equipment

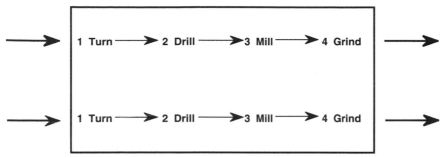

Figure 5-24. Cellular processing for component manufacturing. (Coopers & Lybrand 1987)

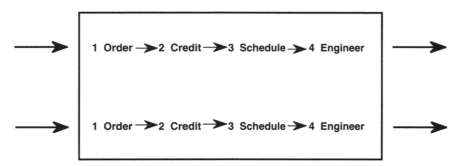

Figure 5-25. Cellular processing for paperwork. (Coopers & Lybrand 1987)

- small batches (lot sizes) moved short distances to realize faster through-put
- space-saving compact physical layout
- immediate quality feedback and "feedforward" information
- minimum material handling
- enhanced worker satisfaction

CELL DESIGN

The objective of a cell design is to categorize product routings for smooth work flow. It is important to understand the flow patterns of materials, components, subassemblies, and the final assembly of the product.

Similar routing flows among components and products are grouped to define a possible cell. The process of cell design is highly interactive. Figure 5-26 defines the flowchart sequence for a furniture item. All resources needed to support the cell design must either be available within the firm or acquirable at a reasonable cost.

EVENT	SYMBOL	DIST (ft.)	MH*	LABOR	DESCRIPTION
1					Receive lumber
2					Receiving clerk inspects rejects to hold area
		25	F	1	
3					Raw stores
		125	F	1	
4					Rip saw floor stock
		25	F	1	
5					Rip saw - to width
		25	C		
6					Cut-off saw queue - FIFO
		25	J		
7					Cut-off saw to length
		175	F	1	
8					Tenoner queue - FIFO
		25	J		
9					Operator inspects
10					Tenon parts ends rounded; center split
		75	F	1	
11					Planer queue - FIFO
		25	F	1	
12					Plane parts
		100	F		
13					Sander queue - priority - wide to narrow cycle
		25	J		
14					Sand parts
		250	F	1	
15					WIP storage
		900			

* MATERIAL HANDLING KEY: F =Fork truck J = Hand jack C = Conveyor

Figure 5-26. Process cell design flowchart. (Coopers & Lybrand 1987)

CELL STAFFING

The objective of cell staffing is to determine the minimum number of personnel required to support the production level. The steps to determine cell staffing follow:

1. Determine operation work content.
2. Determine work content per part.
3. Set the production rate equal to the demand rate and convert to seconds or minutes/unit (cell load).
4. Divide work content by cell load to get theoretical minimum staffing.

5. Group operations together by cell load total (could be many groupings).
6. Determine the most effective grouping.

An example of cell staffing is given in Table 5-7:

Table 5-7. Cell staffing.

Operations No.	Description	Cycle Time (sec.)
10	Make component	10
20	Make component	20
30	Sub assemble	5
40	Final assemble	10
50	Inspect and pack	15
Work content/unit = 10 + 20 + 5 + 10 + 15 = 60 sec.		
Demand Rate = 1,200 units/day = 24 sec/unit		
Staffing = 60/24 = 2.5 = 3 people		
Capacity = 3 units/min = 1,440/8 hour (480 min.) shift		

In this example, operators could be assigned tasks in the following manner to balance the flow. Operator 1 is assigned operations 10 and 40; work time = 20 seconds. Operator 2 is assigned operation 20; work time = 20 seconds. Operator 3 is assigned operations 30 and 50; work time = 20 seconds. A possible layout for this three-person cell is depicted in Figure 5-27.

CELL DESIGN GUIDELINES
The following guidelines relate to assigned workers:

1. Make it easy (ergonomically correct) and safe for the operator to perform all assigned tasks.
2. Do not isolate the operator.
3. Use all human resources.
4. Concentrate idle time and eliminate unnecessary activities.

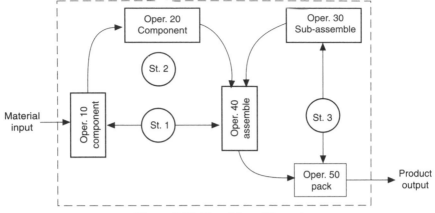

Figure 5-27. Possible cell layout.

Guidelines for the physical cell layout are:

1. Keep operators inside the cell and in view of others.
2. Have high reliability in all machines and equipment.
3. Minimize space available for inventory.
4. Minimize operator and part (item) travel distance.
5. Make any cell waste visible.
6. Provide for easy maintenance and housekeeping.
7. Place cell function above appearance.

The following cell operation guidelines are useful:

1. Stop the line when imbalances occur and correct.
2. If a cell fails, solve the problem; do not keep people busy making inventory.
3. After eliminating nonvalue-added activities, work to improve value-adding activities on an ongoing basis.

LAYOUT CONFIGURATIONS

The U-shaped layout has several advantages in cell manufacturing, including the following:
- more flexibility and reach for workers
- more alert workers when rotating tasks
- more variety, resulting in higher worker satisfaction
- simpler equipment handling
- better communication and visibility
- better balancing capability

Figures 5-28, 5-29, and 5-30 illustrate the U-shaped layout for a single operator, multiple operators, and straight-line cells that achieve the U-effect.

Time-based manufacturing requires flexibility of output. An important element of flexibility includes layouts that can accommodate variable demand and respond to operational changes. Figures 5-31, 5-32, and 5-33 give examples of layout configurations that are well suited for flexible production.

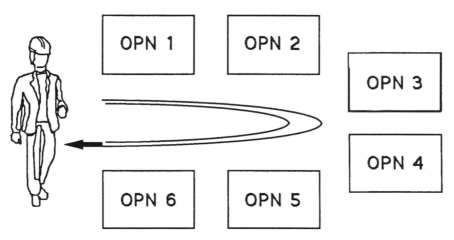

Figure 5-28. U-shaped layout configuration for a single operator.

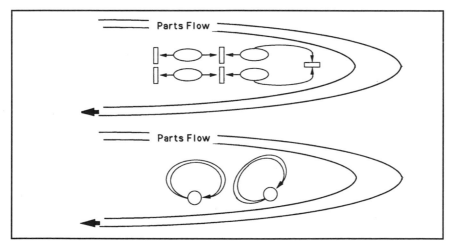

Figure 5-29. U-shaped layout configuration for multiple operators.

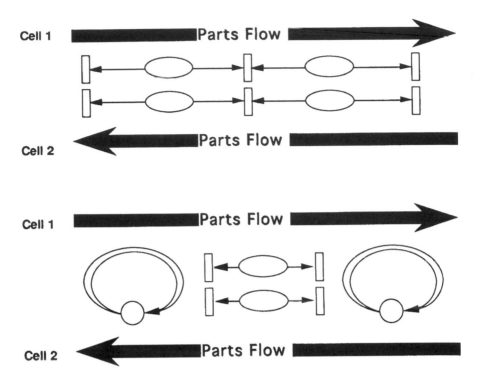

Figure 5-30. Straight-line layout configuration that achieves the U-effect.

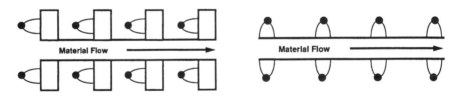

Not Good: Operators are isolated. No ability to trade elements of work.

Improved: Operators can trade elements of work. Can add and subtract operators. Trained ones can self-balance at different output rates.

Figure 5-31. Flexible layout configuration.

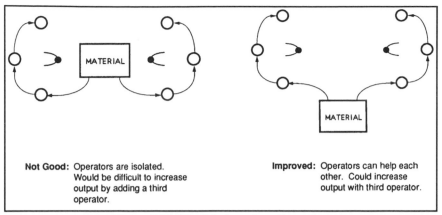

Figure 5-32. Flexible layout configuration.

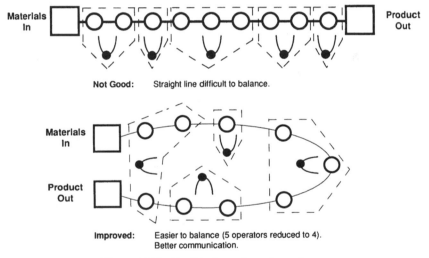

Figure 5-33. Flexible layout configuration.

BALANCING AND SYNCHRONIZING WORK ACTIVITIES

As previously discussed, TBM comprises various activities occurring from customer demand to product delivery. Some activities are performed in sequence and some in parallel. For any given process flow, it is essential that each activity have balanced human and physical resources, i.e., the capacity of each activity in the sequential process flow should be the same rate. In a sequential flow, the rate of throughput is dependent on the activity with the longest cycle time.

The percent efficiency (E) of a balanced sequential flow path can be computed as a ratio of the total individual activity times to the maximum activity time within the flow path as shown below:

$$E = \frac{\sum_{i=1}^{n} ST_i (100)}{ST_{max}}$$

where

ST_i = Standard time for individual work activities
ST_{max} = Standard time for the longest work activity

Standard times may be established for each work activity required in the flow path. The methodology suggested for standard time determination will be discussed in Chapter 10.

For example, assume that a customer order rate has been established at one hundred units per day (500 per week) for a period of six months. Nine distinct work activities are required to produce the units as outlined in Table 5-8.

Table 5-8. Standard time for work activities.

Work Activity	Standard Hours/Order	Standard Hours/Unit
1. Customer interface	20.0	0.00
2. Order entry and data base	8.0	0.00
3. Design/specification review	24.0	0.05
4. Tooling/test equipment check	12.0	0.05
5. Release to production	4.0	0.00
6. Material procurement	20.0	0.10
7. Produce units	40.0	5.00
8. Test units	10.0	1.00
9. Package and ship	2.0	0.50

All nine of the work activities require time for the initial order processing (standard hours/order). In addition, work activities 3, 4, 6, 8, and 9 require some time for ongoing support during production (work activity 7). The staffing and capacity of each work area must include human and physical resources for the initial order processing and the hours per unit. The flow path efficiency (E) is ideal when each work area is staffed to accommodate the standard time summation for the work activities of all orders, and when the total summed time of each work area is identical (i.e., a perfect flow balance).

Ideal synchronization requires the assignment of resources without any delay so that work activities can be performed as soon as an order enters. This equates to a balanced process flow.

THE PULL SYSTEM

The control of synchronization in TBM is accomplished with a pull system, which signals for production based on the present demand for a product. Items are produced only as demanded for use or to replace those taken for use. This method is in contrast to the more traditional push system (see Figure 5-34), where items are produced through production schedules based on forecasted demand. The pull concept, which was initiated at Toyota Motor Company, requires that the product supply schedule be

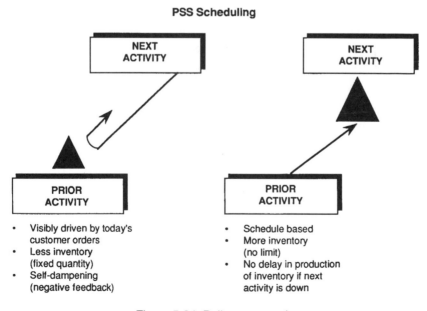

Figure 5-34. Pull versus push.

established from customer demand. The PSS schedule is set to produce and ship the quantity of each product every day matching customer requirements. Pull scheduling also requires that the PSS be balanced and synchronized before initiation. As production occurs according to the customer schedule, final assembly consumes standard containers of materials from its inbound stock.

The pull system is a very visible method of shop floor control. When a work center needs material, a signal is sent to the preceding activity to replenish according to the pull signal (a standard container's worth). The types of replenishment signals include:

• Containers—totes, pull signal squares
• Physical—cards, tags
• Electronic—telephone, bar code, fax, computer linkage

The pull system is a self-dampening method based on negative feedback. There are two major elements: a fixed upper volume limit and a pull signal for replenishment. Negative feedback means if no call is made for production, then production is not authorized. In this way, work centers cannot get out of balance with the customer schedule.

The fixed upper-volume limit is set between activities in the PSS to assure that excess inventory is not generated between any components of the PSS. If the fixed upper limits are met, then the PSS shuts off until products are withdrawn to cover demand.

The pull signal for replenishment is the method used to execute specific products and quantities through the PSS. Pull signals should always be executed based upon a first-in first-out priority sequence. Pull signals should be in standard batch sizes throughout the materials continuum; doing so facilitates a much smoother flow of production. It is important not to deviate from pre-established quantities in the pull signal transfer.

The pull system is an effective scheduling method only within a synchronized PSS; this method does not accommodate large fluctuations in demand (greater than twenty percent). Capacity planning is still a key element of the synchronization requirement for TBM.

There are five basic pull system rules (Monden 1983).

Rule 1. An activity should withdraw products from the preceding activity in the right quantities at the right time. No signal means no withdrawal: only standard quantities should be used.

Rule 2. The preceding activity should only produce products in the quantities withdrawn by the subsequent activity. Use pull signals for first-in first-out priority.

Rule 3. Defective products should never be delivered to the subsequent activity. The pull system will shut down the PSS unless this rule is followed. Product supply system stoppage is very obvious and visible to everyone.

Rule 4. The number of pull signals should be minimized; start simple and reduce lot sizes. Pull signals should decrease as confidence increases.

Rule 5. The pull system should be used to adapt to small fluctuations in demand. "Fine tune" supply through pull signals. Capacity management is still necessary.

PULL SIGNAL CALCULATIONS

An example of a simple pull signal (PS) calculation follows:

$$PS = \frac{T_r \cdot D_r \cdot F_m}{U_k}$$

where
T_r = replenishment time (for feeder) = 50 minutes
D_r = demand rate = 62.5 pieces/hour
U_k = pieces per signal = 36 pieces/skid
F_m = management factor = 1.3

$$PS = \frac{0.833 \text{ hrs.} \times 62.5 \text{ pieces / hr.}}{36 \text{ pieces / skid}} \times 1.3$$

$$= 1.88 = 2 \text{ signals}$$

Pull scheduling and its linkage with MRP will be discussed in Chapter 9.

REFERENCES

Coopers & Lybrand. 1987. *Just In Time Improvement Program Diagnostic and Conceptual Design Methodology.* New York: Coopers & Lybrand.

Ford, H. 1926. *Today and Tomorrow.* Garden City, NY: Doubleday, Page & Co.

Monden, Y. 1983. *Toyota Production System.* Norcross, GA: Industrial Engineering and Management Press.

Shingo, S. 1985. *A Revolution in Manufacturing: The SMED System.* Cambridge, MA: Productivity Press.

The Product Supply System Must Be Reliable and Capable 6

THE time-based manufacturing (TBM) organization must understand the critical importance of synchronization; it must also match the product supply system (PSS) capacity to the customer demand profile. This match provides the foundation for successful TBM. To the extent that it can supply daily customer demand with adequate capacity, the PSS will achieve a time-based competitive advantage. In many companies, however, actual capacity is not adequate on a daily basis to respond to customer orders. This capacity shortfall causes extended supply system lead times, a strategy based on forecasted demand, and weekly, monthly, or even quarterly run cycles.

The ability of a PSS to produce to its full potential is affected by a variety of factors (see Figure 6-1). While each factor may reduce only a fraction of the potential capacity, in total these degradation factors often represent a substantial portion of the overall potential PSS capacity.

As the supply system capacity is lowered, the chance to improve capacity degradation increases in importance. Often the rate of output can be increased by improving factors contributing to reduced capacity. For example, in Figure 6-2 the increase in the level of demand coverage from fifty-six percent to seventy-five percent was achieved in this way.

Improving supply system capacity involves several important elements. These elements can be grouped under reliability, which is a measure of the effectiveness of PSS resources, and capability, which is a measure of the PSS' ability to produce products meeting the customer's quality specifications.

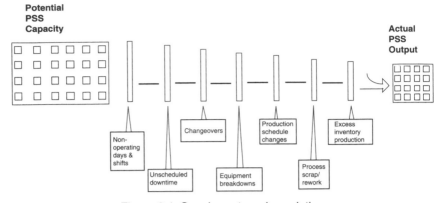

Figure 6-1. Supply system degradation.

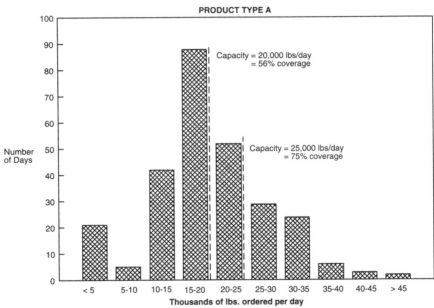

Figure 6-2. Capacity shortfall versus the customer demand profile.

PSS RELIABILITY

Reliability measures the effectiveness of a PSS resource to supply a product relative to its maximum potential capacity. Through reliability management, a company monitors its effective use of assets to satisfy customers and return profits. Increasing reliability requires constantly searching for ways to improve resource performance by reducing waste.

Measuring, managing, and improving reliability can be achieved through extensive use of the following methodology and formula.

$$\text{Reliability} = \text{Uptime} \times \text{Dependability} \times \text{Yield}$$

UPTIME

Uptime is the ratio of a resources scheduled operation time versus the available operation time. Maximum available operation time is defined as 7 days, 24 hours each, for a total of 168 hours a week.

Uptime = Scheduled Operation Time / Available Time (168 hours/week)

Uptime measures a resource's use. The uptime goal is to schedule a resource to work only as required to supply to the customer demand profile. By doing so, a company uses the appropriate level of capacity to supply customer demand. The goal of the uptime measure is definitely not one hundred percent, as full use of a resource would likely result in a PSS bottleneck. This is a sure way to extend supply lead times and lower overall PSS performance. As a general rule, a PSS resource should provide eighty-five percent or more capacity coverage versus the customer demand profile.

Factors contributing to a difference between available time and scheduled work time include:

- company downtime including holidays, meetings, building closures, etc.
- scheduled downtime, including unscheduled operating hours such as off shifts, weekends, etc., that occurs because a resource is not needed to meet customer demand
- planned maintenance, including preventive upkeep measures, over-hauls, and rebuilds
- changeovers

The methodology to evaluate uptime is as follows:

1. Select a representative period of time to develop a baseline.

2. Use historical data or collect new data to identify:
   - available operation time (AT)
   - company downtime (CD)
   - scheduled downtime (SD)
   - planned maintenance (PM)
   - changeover (CH)

3. Calculate uptime (UP):

$$UP = \frac{AT - (CD + SC + PM + CH)}{AT}$$

4. Analyze the results and develop the ratio, expressed as a percentage.

Example results of equipment uptime calculations are shown in Table 6-1.

Table 6-1. Uptime calculations.

Process Number	Equipment Number	Available Time	Company Downtime	Scheduled Downtime	Planned Maint.	Changeover Time	Equipment Uptime %
10	1010	168	24	--	8	8	76
	1020	168	24	24	--	16	62
	1030	168	24	48	--	--	57
	1040	168	24	48	--	--	57
	1050	168	24	48	8	24	38
20	2010	168	24	72	--	4	40
	2020	168	24	--	16	--	76
	2030	168	24	48	--	12	50

*Note: All time in hours.

DEPENDABILITY

Dependability is the ratio of a resource's actual output rate versus the potential output rate, as follows:

$$Dependability = \frac{Actual\ Output\ Rate\ (units\,/\,hr)}{Potential\ Output\ Rate\ (units\,/\,hr)}$$

Dependability measures the efficiency of a resource. When scheduled to work, a resource should perform to its maximum efficiency relative to its potential. The dependability goal should be one hundred percent. In this way, no activities are wasted and a resource achieves its maximum output potential relative to its design rating.

Factors contributing to a loss in dependability include the following:
- unplanned equipment downtime including breakdowns, minor stoppages, and failures
- support-related downtime including production schedule changes, lack of materials, inspection waiting, and communications
- actual equipment running speed less than design speed

The methodology to evaluate dependability follows:

1. Identify the maximum or designed output rate (units/hour).
2. Use historical data or collect data to measure the actual run rate (units/hour).
3. Calculate dependability (D).

$$D = \frac{\text{Actual units output / Actual hours worked}}{\text{Potential rate / hour}}$$

4. Compile and analyze the results.

Example results of dependability calculations are shown in Table 6-2.

Table 6-2. Dependability calculations.

Process Number	Equipment Number	Actual Units Processed	Actual Hours Worked	Potential Rate (units/hr)	Dependa-bility %
10	1010	2500	128	20	98
	1020	2450	104	45	52
	1030	1764	96	25	74
	1040	1500	96	22	71
	1050	1350	64	25	84
20	2010	12,000	68	200	88
	2020	11,880	128	125	74
	2030	12,000	84	300	39

YIELD

Yield is the ratio of good products produced by a resource versus the materials input to the resource, as follows:

$$\text{Yield} = \text{Good Products Output} - \text{Total Products Input}$$

Yield measures a resources ability to produce acceptable results the first time without generating fallout. The yield goal should be one hundred percent. This represents the most effective processing of materials to eliminate waste and achieve the lowest possible costs.

Factors contributing to fallout (yield loss) include:
• scrap
• rework
• repair
• process loss
• additional nonstandard operations

The methodology to evaluate yield loss follows:
1. identify what constitutes fallout on a resource
2. establish input quantity of materials
3. count output quantity of good products
4. calculate yield

Example results of yield calculations are shown in Table 6-3.

Table 6-3. Yield calculations.

Process Number	Equipment Number	Total Units Input	Good Units Output	Yield %
10	1010	2500	2450	98
	1020	2450	1764	72
	1030	1764	1500	85
	1040	1500	1350	90
	1050	1350	1242	92
20	2010	12,000	11,880	99
	2020	11,880	9860	83
	2030	9860	8973	91

OVERALL RELIABILITY AND PSS THROUGHPUT

The overall resource reliability is the product of uptime, dependability, and yield (see Table 6-4). This reliability performance can then be compared with equipment rates to determine overall process throughput capacity for the two examples shown in Table 6-5 as well as bottlenecks for each. As can be seen, process number 10 has an overall throughput capacity of 1,218 units per week. Equipment number 1050 is the process bottleneck. For process number 20, the overall throughput capacity is 9,072, and equipment number 2030 is the bottleneck.

Table 6-4. Reliability calculations.

Process Number	Equipment Number	Uptime %	Dependability %	Yield%	Reliability %
10	1010	76	98	98	73
	1020	62	52	72	23
	1030	57	74	85	36
	1040	57	71	90	36
	1050	38	84	92	29
20	2010	40	88	99	35
	2020	76	74	83	47
	2030	50	39	91	18

Once the throughput bottleneck is identified, further data collection and analysis should be used to improve capacity. For example, looking at the reliability formula for process 10, equipment 1050, suggests that increased uptime from thirty-eight percent would yield the greatest impact to improve process 10 throughput. This would likely be achieved through a changeover reduction effort on equipment 1050. Looking at process 20, equipment 2030, improved throughput would come from increasing dependability from the thirty-nine percent baseline. This would likely be achieved by collecting and analyzing downtime data and implementing maintenance improvements.

Table 6-5. Throughput capacity calculation.

Process Number	Equipment Number	Potential Rate (units/hour)	Available Hours	Reliability %	Actual Output per Week
10	1010	20	168	73	2453
	1020	45	168	23	1739
	1030	25	168	36	1512
	1040	22	168	36	1330
	1050	25	168	29	1218
20	2010	200	168	35	11,760
	2020	125	168	47	9870
	2030	300	168	18	9072

FIRST RUN YIELD

First run yield (FRY) is the extrapolation of the resource yield measure to the overall PSS. It measures the units started at the beginning of the PSS versus the good quality units delivered by the PSS. First run yield represents a powerful view of the level of effort required by a system to supply the product. It measures losses due to scrap, rework, repairs, and process failures. Figure 6-3 shows the power of yield loss and its impact on the PSS cost per carton. Because product yield is taken at each step in the PSS, the product of mediocre yield combinations can result in very low overall supply system yields. In Figure 6-3, 1,000 cartons are started into the system, while only 543 good cartons emerge. This yield factor of fifty-four percent results in a base material cost of $1.00/carton and a good unit cost of $1.84/carton. This is a dramatic cost increase on a per unit basis.

The second major impact of a poor FRY is lost system capacity. The fifty-four percent yield in Figure 6-3 results in a forty-six percent loss in system capacity on this one dimension alone. When evaluated as a total PSS, this factor is frequently substantial and represents an enormous opportunity to improve PSS capacity versus the customer demand profile.

The methodology for measuring and evaluating FRY follows:

1. Develop a plan to collect FRY information.
2. Define the common PSS unit of measure and the definition of fallout.
3. Identify all areas where fallout occurs.
4. Develop data collection methods to capture fallout quantities and reasons.

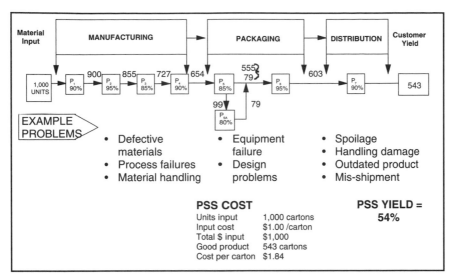

Figure 6-3. PSS first run yield.

Table 6-6 looks at the reliability example and extends the two process flows into their FRY calculations. First run yield calculations are as shown:

Process number 10
  FRY = (98%)(72%)(85%)(90%)(92%) = 50%

Process number 20
  FRY = (99%)(83%)(91%) = 75%

Table 6-6. First run yield.

Process Number	Equipment Number	Uptime %	Dependa-bility %	First Run Yield % Yield%	Reliability %
10	1010	76	98	98	73
	1020	62	52	72	23
	1030	57	74	85	36
	1040	57	71	90	36
	1050	38	84	92	29
			FRY	50%	
20	2010	40	88	99	35
	2020	76	74	83	47
	2030	50	39	91	18
			FRY	75%	

First run yield may also be evaluated for a PSS made up of sequential and parallel processes. The recommended procedure (see Figure 6-4) is:

1. Determine the FRY of all processes in the system.

2. Graphically layout the system to determine which processes are performed sequentially and which occur in parallel.

3. First run yield for a system of sequential processes is the product of the individual FRY of the processes that comprise the system. For systems with parallel processes, use the branch with the lowest FRY when calculating the system FRY.

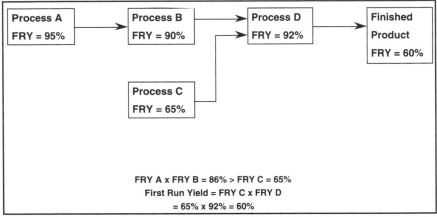

Figure 6-4. FRY evaluation for sequential and parallel processes.

THE MAINTENANCE CONNECTION

Maintenance effectiveness can contribute significantly to the total PSS cost. In many firms today, maintenance costs are increasing two to three times faster than overall production costs. This is due to more machines and equipment with new technology replacing direct labor, higher labor wage rates for skilled maintenance technicians, higher costs for more complex and intricate spare parts, and suppliers' needs for profits from after market sales.

Interestingly, management does not always recognize and accept the premise that every dollar invested in capital equipment is also a commitment to spend proportional dollars on preventive and corrective maintenance. In fact, it is common to include projected maintenance and repair cost savings in the capital justification for new equipment. With some equipment, however, these costs may represent an increase, not a savings!

The costs for poor maintenance should not be measured by general ledger machine repair expense entries. A machine down, particularly in a TBM environment, propagates stoppages or disruptions up and down the manufacturing line; this results in costs that cannot be recovered. The more closely coupled the operation, the more critical maintenance becomes. Also, the greater the need for increased capacity and the lower the reliability, the greater the opportunity for a positive maintenance impact. Customer delivery and quality satisfaction can be directly attributable to the ability of the equipment to perform dependably and to specification. Employee safety and health can also be jeopardized by poorly maintained equipment.

Properly maintained machines are reliable machines. To improve dependability and yield, effective maintenance addresses the following major loss types:
- equipment failure (lost capacity due to unexpected breakdowns)
- changeover downtime and start-up losses to target run rates
- unplanned downtime, including minor stops, gaps, jams, or blockages in flow
- reduced speed versus design speed
- process defects resulting in time wasted doing rework and scrapped products

TOTAL PRODUCTIVE MAINTENANCE

Since the early 1970s, several maintenance philosophies have been developed to meet the evolving challenges of modern manufacturing. Total Productive Maintenance (TPM) is best suited to a TBM environment. Total productive maintenance applies integrated quality principles to maintenance and focuses resources to support the equipment user. It is simple, straightforward, and relies heavily upon the equipment operator; the approach integrates well into the TBM philosophy.

Total productive maintenance is concerned with keeping a physical resource functionally available so that it will perform reliably. This means equipment will work when needed, produce a quality product the first time, and perform dependably without breakdowns. Total productive maintenance is heavily based on total quality concepts. Table 6-7 presents the quality profile and elements that are the foundation for TPM methods.

Table 6-7. TQM/TPM relationships.

	TQM	TPM
Problem	Product Defects	Equipment losses
Traditional Solution	End of line inspection Sorting and rework	Breakdown maintenance Plant overhauls
Improved Solution	In-process inspection Error proofing Taguchi experiments Design for quality	Condition-based maintenance Operator preventive care Failure analysis Design for reliability
Information	Quality data collection & analysis Statistical process control	Reliability data collection & analysis Work order planning & control
Basic Approach	Continuous improvement teams Education Process ownership Cost of quality	Continuous improvement teams Education Process ownership Cost of reliability

TPM OBJECTIVES

Total productive maintenance has three major aims:

1. Maximize overall equipment reliability.

2. Create operator ownership of the equipment through his or her involvement with maintenance activities.

3. Foster continuous efforts to improve equipment operation through continuous improvement teams.

Maximizing equipment reliability involves a systematic effort to eliminate the causes of waste. Equipment is analyzed for opportunities to improve its maintainability (mean time to repair), reduce changeover times, and eliminate nonvalue-adding functions. Total productive maintenance also focuses on implementing enablers, which are aids to help identify services and parts required to perform maintenance tasks. Examples of enablers include:

- color coding service lines
- making quick connections for lubrication and maintenance points
- clearly identifying components as discards or repairables
- providing wheels or air lifts for overhaul maintenance

Creating operator ownership means that the operators assume primary responsibility for the condition of their equipment. Operators collect and analyze reliability data on their equipment, constantly seeking to understand root causes of poor performance. In addition, operators monitor performance and detect obvious problems, replenish most consumables, and perform first-level preventive maintenance (PM) tasks themselves. Complex PM—tasks, diagnostics, corrective maintenance, and major repairs—are still carried out by the maintenance specialists. In many situations, the operator will assist the formal maintenance team.

Finally, TPM aims to eliminate the sometimes adversarial division between operations and maintenance. Led by managers or supervisors, the owner operators and skilled maintenance personnel, including engineers, are teamed in continuous improvement efforts to increase operational reliability. Such efforts often involve experimental analysis to determine the root cause of malfunctions. This will usually lead to changes such as substitutions or redesigning of equipment components, or to beneficial improvements to the process itself.

TPM BENEFITS

Complete implementation of TPM in time-based manufacturing may take twenty-four months or more to become fully effective. Once equipment is restored to its design specifications and a rigorously applied PM inspection schedule is in place, the first visible result will be a dramatic reduction in unplanned downtime. As time passes, operators and maintenance specialists will become more confident and competent in their new roles. Their continuous attack on equipment related waste will gradually reduce operating wastes of all kinds. Improvements that may be expected include:

- overall supply system rates will increase, creating greater available PSS capacity
- spoilage, rework, and scrap resulting from equipment malfunction will be reduced
- need for standby equipment and just-in-case spare parts inventory will be reduced or eliminated
- product costs will be lowered as costs for indirect labor, spoilage, and warranty costs are reduced

SUMMARY

Maintenance is becoming a larger factor on the overall cost effectiveness of the PSS. The cost of poor maintenance should include the costs of lost PSS throughput and failure to deliver product, as well as the direct repair expenses. The aims of TPM are to maximize equipment reliability, create operator ownership of equipment, and foster continuous efforts to improve equipment operation. Total productive maintenance benefits include increased reliability, improved quality, elimination of redundant equipment and spare parts, lower product costs, and enhanced customer satisfaction.

QUALITY THROUGH PSS CAPABILITY

Achieving high quality in products and processes is not optional, it is essential. In years past, American industry has thought of quality as one of many relative factors used as a basis for gaining a competitive advantage. In today's climate of increasing consumer expectations and global competition, quality is an essential ingredient for success.

Many companies now realize they must make fundamental changes in the management of their businesses to achieve quality levels that would have been considered impossible just a few years ago. The following approach to quality improvement is compatible with the most successful of these companies and is integrated tightly into the TBM philosophy and principles woven throughout this book. Quality and lead time compression are highly interdependent concepts, and true time-based manufacturers have discovered the power of quality improvement in the lead time compression paradigm.

The four basic principles outlined below are essential for achieving high quality (Coopers & Lybrand 1988).

1. Understand and meet the customer's requirements. Quality is meeting the customer's requirements, a simple concept yet powerful enough to be the driving force of the entire process. The customer is the end consumer. Meeting the consumer's needs, however, involves everyone with whom an employee deals—not only the person who buys a product or service but also a co-worker, supervisor, subordinate, or supplier. Vital to meeting the requirements of the end consumer is mutually understanding what the requirements are, documenting the requirements, and reviewing them regularly to plan for necessary changes.

Understanding customer requirements provides the basis for defining the design quality for a product. The design quality is the product grade and characteristics chosen by the manufacturer to best satisfy customer requirements. This product definition is based on a company's policies, its marketing strategy (i.e., the understanding and interpretation of customer requirements), and research and development. A design's quality level can be better understood by measuring and comparing customer requirements with the chosen product design and its characteristics. A product grade more closely meeting customer requirements contains a better design quality (see Figure 6-5).

For A Customer--Desired Product Characteristic

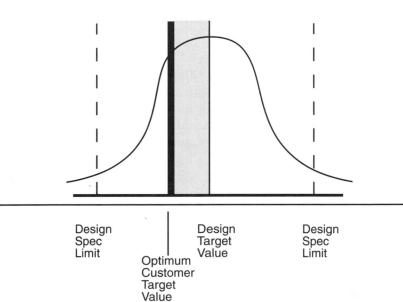

Figure 6-5. Design quality versus customer target.

2. Perform error-free work. The standard for meeting customer requirements is error-free work: doing the right activities right, the first time, every time. This drives the concept of process quality, which is the product uniformity of a manufactured item around the target value (i.e., design quality), shown in Figure 6.6. This does not mean that errors will not happen or that waste will not occur. It does mean there is an attitude that errors and waste are not acceptable. There is no more acceptable quality level with its allowable percentage of defects. A company having the new attitude continually asks "why" when an error occurs, tracks down the root cause, and then takes action to keep that error from happening again.

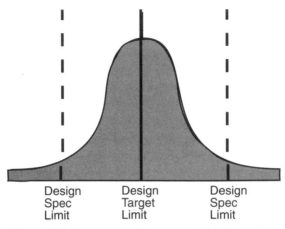

Figure 6-6. Process quality versus design target value.

3. *Manage by prevention*. Managing by prevention means that quality must be built into the process; it cannot be inspected in at the end. This requires studying problems and making permanent changes to prevent errors. The more emphasis that is placed on preventing errors, the more often a customer's requirements will be met by doing the right activities right the first time, every time (see Figure 6-7).

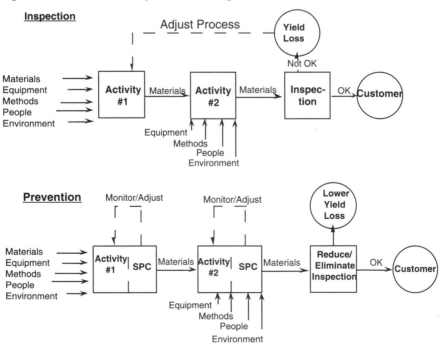

Figure 6-7. Inspection versus prevention.

4. Stabilize variations, then reduce them. Quality management in the TBM company emphasizes understanding, stabilizing, and continuously reducing variation. Process variation is normal. This variation must be controlled, however, and ultimately reduced to allow the PSS to operate a stable, reliable system that consistently delivers products meeting design quality targets. The variation reduction strategy shown in Figure 6-8 builds a very high confidence level into the PSS so that the system consistently meets customers' expectations.

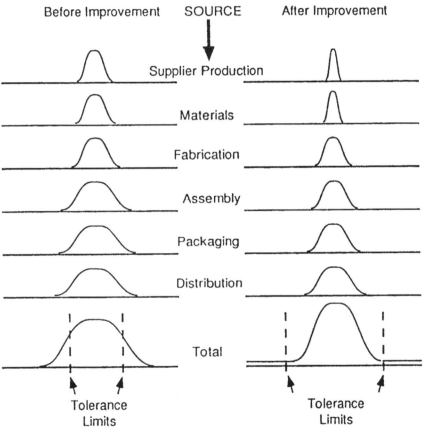

Figure 6-8. Supply system capability: sources of variance.

UNDERSTANDING VARIATION

Variation is the tendency of a process to produce different results under the same given set of conditions. Variation is a natural law of life. No two items of anything are exactly alike. Brian Joiner offers the following points as the most common range of views on variation (1991).

Pessimist's View of Variation:
"I hate variation. If only things would be done the same way every time, many of my problems would go away. It is difficult to understand why it is so pervasive."

Optimist's View of Variation:
"I respect variation. The only way that we can learn about the cause and effect mechanisms operating in a process is by studying variations in outputs and inputs. Once we understand cause and effect mechanisms, then we can reduce variation and do a better job of meeting customer needs."

Majority View of Variation:
"Huh???" This majority view has led many managers to make incorrect decisions and take the wrong actions to solve problems. Understanding the true nature of variation will have a profoundly positive impact on management decision making.

The level of variation contained in a process will directly affect the output quality of the process. The supply system goal then is to produce to the product's design target value all the time (Sullivan 1984). This is a substantial shift in thinking from the traditional conformance to requirements mindset. This traditional view allowed that all products within acceptable specification limits were good and shipped to the customers. Products could, in fact, vary greatly from the target and still get shipped as good products. A better approach is to measure and improve uniformity around the product design target value and invest improvement resources and efforts into continually reducing this variation. Any deviation from the target value is clearly considered a loss. The approach shown in Figure 6-9 will yield greatly improved consistency of output and improved customer satisfaction.

Reducing variation begins with an understanding of the two types of variations: common cause and special cause (Gitlow and Oppenheim 1989). Common causes of variation are inherent in a process. They make up the natural variation of a process given the present set of environmental and operating conditions. Characteristics of common causes are highlighted in the following list (Joiner 1991):

- Process inputs and conditions regularly contribute to the variability of process outputs.
- Common causes contribute to output variability because they themselves vary.
- Each common cause typically contributes a small portion to the total variation in process outputs.

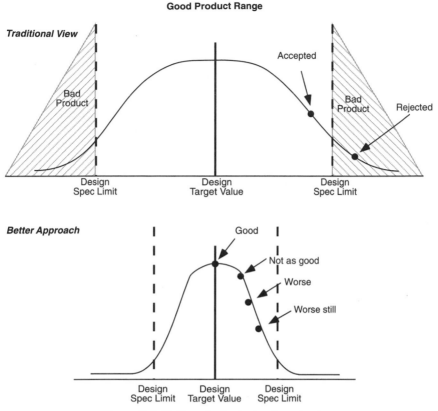

Figure 6-9. Uniformity to design target value.

- The aggregate variability due to common causes has a nonsystematic, random-looking appearance.
- Because common causes are regular contributors, the process variability is defined in their terms.

Special causes of variation are those of specific, assignable causes that lie outside of the process. Characteristics of special causes are highlighted in the following list (Joiner 1991):

- Special causes have process inputs and conditions that sporadically contribute to the variability of the process outputs.
- Special causes contribute to output variability because they themselves vary.
- Each special cause may contribute a small or large amount to the total variation in process outputs.
- The variability due to one or more special causes can be identified by the use of control charts.

* Because they are sporadic contributions, due to specific circumstances, the process variability is defined without them.

A process with only common cause variation is statistically stable and in control. A process containing special cause variation is statistically unstable and out of control. About eighty-five percent of process variation is typically due to common causes and responsibility for this variation rests with management (Juran and Gryna 1980). The remaining fifteen percent of process variation is due to special causes and can be addressed directly by operators (see Figure 6-10).

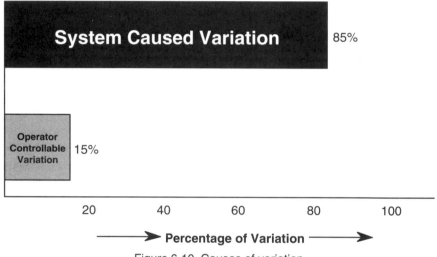

Figure 6-10. Causes of variation.

It is important to understand the difference between common cause and special cause variation because the improvement strategies appropriate for each type are different. The use of statistical control charts helps in understanding and separating the causes of variation. Using a special cause improvement strategy to solve a common cause problem is called tampering, and will result in worse results than if no action had been taken at all. Using a common cause improvement strategy on a special cause problem will only yield frustration, as the assignable special cause will not have been addressed. Special cause variation requires fast, specific action to eliminate the source of the cause. Common cause variation requires fundamental changes in the process to further reduce.

Several consequences of inappropriate managerial reaction to variation are given in the following list (Joiner 1991):

- wasted time and energy
- diverted attention
- more variation in the process
- loss of productivity
- loss of morale
- loss of confidence in manager
- jobs put in jeopardy
- careers put in jeopardy
- problem goes on

In the search for higher PSS reliability and FRY, all processes must first become stable (i.e., eliminate special cause variation), and then become capable (i.e., reduce common cause variation) around the product design target value. This progress can be tracked through the following variation reduction continuum (Chambers and Wheeler 1992):

- When a process is in the state of *chaos,* it is producing product statistically out of control and outside of the customer's specification. The process is unpredictable relative to acceptable product output.

- When a process is on the *brink of chaos,* it produces product within the customer's specification, but the process is statistically unstable. There is no certainty the product will continue to be acceptable.

- When a process is in the *threshold state,* it is statistically stable, but producing some product outside of the customer's specifications. This process can only be improved through a common cause variation reduction strategy.

- When a process is in the *ideal state,* it is a stable process producing all products within customers' specifications.

The PSS objective is to move all processes along the path from their widely varying beginning state (chaos, brink of chaos, etc.) into the ideal state, where all processes are measured as being in control and capable around the product target value, and where natural variation is less than customer specifications.

GAINING STATISTICAL CONTROL OF THE PROCESS*

Statistical process control (SPC) is a key element in TBM and quality improvement. Through SPC, it is possible to manage consistency in the manufacturing environment and to gain competitive advantage through improved reliability and capability. The purpose of this section is to provide guidelines for implementing positive change through the ongoing use of SPC.

Statistical process control is the application of statistical methods to ensure the integration of quality into each element of the TBM supply system. The major goals of SPC are to:
• differentiate between common cause and special cause variation
• develop techniques that allow early detection of defective products
• give an objective means of assessing product characteristics
• apply statistics to control process quality for the benefit of making more consistent product

Statistical process control determines what the process is capable of doing, regardless of what the customer requires from the process. Benefits of SPC include:
• reduced yield loss
• more consistent product quality
• improved market position and customer satisfaction
• better understanding of supply system processes
• better communications along the PSS

The main purpose of statistical control charts is to identify and distinguish special cause variation from common cause variation. Statistical control charts are best used as a preventive tool rather than a detection tool for defective product after it is manufactured. Statistical control charts are also best used as an action-oriented tool rather than an after-the-fact reporting tool.

Statistical process control has been a powerful weapon in the quality improvement arsenal; however, a word of caution is needed. Experience has shown that it is much easier to acquire the basic statistical skills than it is to translate those skills into actions having a positive impact on product

---

*This section is adapted from Coopers & Lybrand's SPC Methodology. (Coopers & Lybrand 1988)

quality. The major reasons for failure of SPC programs include the following:
• lack of management support
• not understanding customer requirements
• failure to get worker input and involvement
• failure to provide adequate employee training
• overdependence on engineers
• not understanding process drivers of quality
• not providing money to implement positive changes

Successful implementation of SPC requires an ongoing, disciplined, company-wide effort. The methodology to develop and implement statistical process control is diagrammed in Figure 6-11.

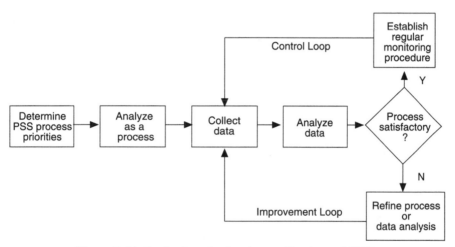

Figure 6-11. Basic steps to develop and implement SPC.

DETERMINE PSS PROCESS PRIORITIES

The development of SPC begins with deciding what changes need to made to improve the process. The one change that would provide the greatest improvement for overall PSS performance should be given priority. In every PSS, there are key leverage processes where improvement delivers a disproportionately higher gain in the overall PSS performance level. While the TBM manufacturer eventually will want all processes under control and operational, the company should begin with the key leverage processes that are more critical to overall success.

Processes that should be selected as priorities for SPC application include:

- processes where yield loss is highest, especially if overall FRY is low and the system is experiencing substantial wasted dollars
- processes where reliability is low, especially if overall system capacity versus the demand profile is constrained, causing a bottleneck, or if uptime already high
- processes where customer data suggest a problem exists
- certain high cost processes caused by operation defects
- processes suspected to be out of control and causing downstream difficulties
- processes where key design characteristics are manufactured and must be tightly controlled to the design target values

The use of SPC in the PSS should not be limited to manufacturing processes only. The factors listed earlier could well apply to a non-manufacturing process. For example, the daily shipping of finished goods could be the process bottleneck in the overall PSS output. Applying SPC to this process would provide insights into the average shipping rate—whether the process is stable or not—and potential sources of opportunity to improve shipping process performance.

ANALYZE AS A PROCESS

A process is the conversion of inputs (materials, equipment, methods, people, and environment) into outputs (products or services). A principle process may include a single machine, a single person, or a single method of measurement. A more complex process could include a multiple station assembly line; processing a customer order; or any combination of people, equipment, methods, materials, and environment that operates in series or parallel to produce an output (see Figures 6-12 and 6-13).

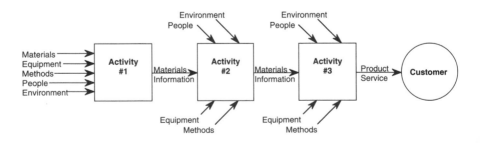

Figure 6-12. Processes operating in series.

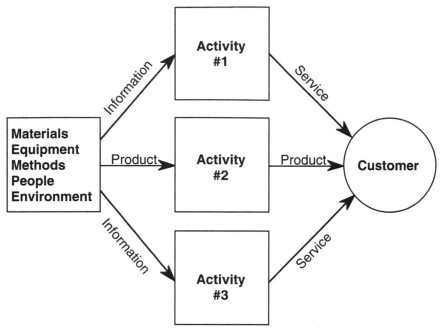

Figure 6-13. Processes operating in parallel.

As discussed in Chapter 2, it is useful to initially create a flowchart of the process to visually help determine which activities in the process are interdependent. Flowcharting also helps identify logical places for data collection or process control activities and stratification points where several different sources of variation exist.

Once the flowchart has been created, cause and effect diagrams are also useful for sorting and segregating the possible causes of a problem into logical order (see Figure 6-14). They also identify areas for data gathering. Development of the diagram is educational, serves to guide discussions, and helps to keep meetings on target. Cause and effect diagrams can be developed into a complete project management tool that displays actions taken and results achieved. The Seven Basic Quality Tools (see Figure 6-15) are valuable in SPC process control and improvement. Applying the tools helps to identify the key process characteristics of the product that must be controlled and improved. In doing so, the company sorts through the trivial many improvement possibilities to get to the vital few process characteristics where improvement efforts will yield the maximum benefit.

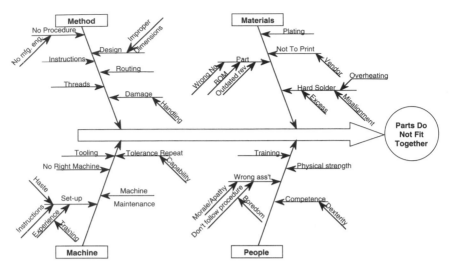

Figure 6-14. Cause and effect diagram.

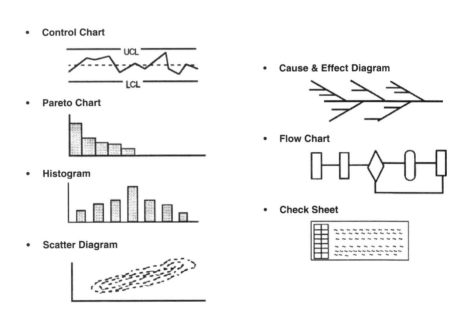

Figure 6-15. Seven basic quality tools.

COLLECT DATA

Statistical process control is completely dependent on collection of accurate and timely process data. It is important to remember that in SPC data are nothing more than numbers that represent a particular characteristic. There are two major types of data. Variable (continuous) data are measured and represented by numerical values, which are created by measuring the values of a particular characteristic. Attribute (categorical) data are obtained by counting observations that occur in particular categories. Before collecting data, there must be a well defined purpose. Management must understand the intent of the data collection exercise, and whether or not it will answer the question at hand. Before collecting data, management must do the following:

- Determine the frequency, method, and unit of measure to be used.
- Determine whether manual or automatic data collection is best for the situation.
- Ensure that appropriate and calibrated instruments are used.

Four kinds of statistical data are useful in SPC: prioritization statistics, descriptive statistics, process control statistics and relationship statistics (Figures 6-16, 6-17, 6-18, and 6-19 respectively).

The simple check sheet is useful for the initial data collection. For variable data, a measurement scale is provided and a mark is placed in an appropriate interval. Actual measurements are recorded in compliance with a specific plan. For attribute data, a mark is recorded at each occurrence of a characteristic. Examples of check sheets are illustrated in Figures 6-20, 6-21, 6-22, and 6-23.

ANALYZE DATA

Control charts are statistical tools used to analyze and understand process variables, to determine a process' capability to perform with respect to those variables, and to monitor the effect of those variables on the difference between customer needs and process performance (Gitlow and Oppenheim 1989). Control charts accomplish these functions by allowing a manager to understand the sources of variation in a process and to manipulate and control those sources to decrease the difference between customer needs and process performance. This decrease can be managed only if the process under study is stable and capable of improvement.

The control chart is the ongoing test of the process. Initial analysis using the control chart should allow users to answer the following questions (Ehley 1991):

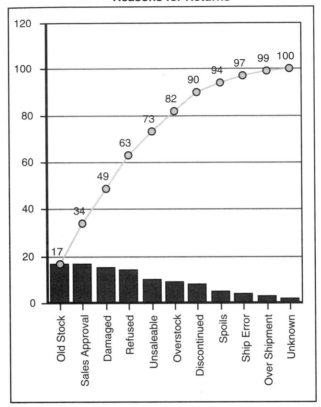

Figure 6-16. Prioritization statistics—Pareto chart.

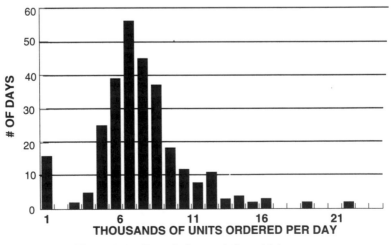

Figure 6-17. Descriptive statistics—histogram.

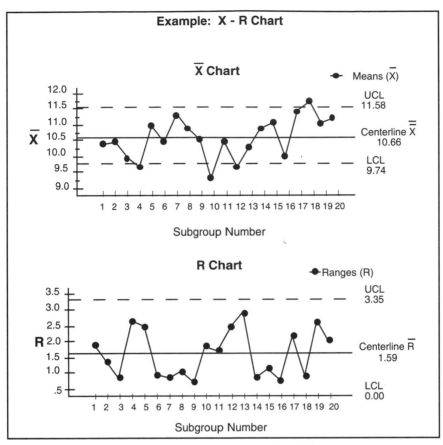

Figure 6-18. Process control statistics.

Example: SCATTERPLOT

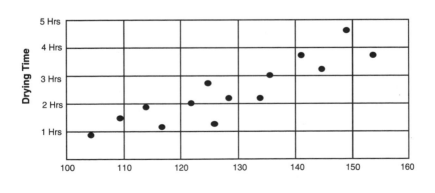

Moisture Index
(Baseline = 100)

Figure 6-19. Relationship statistics. (Coopers & Lybrand 1988)

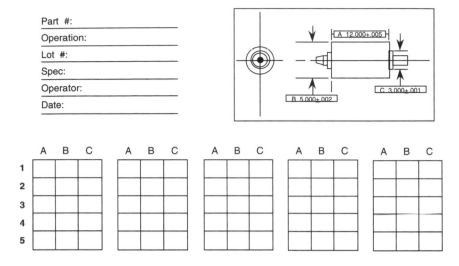

Figure 6-20. Variable measurements check sheet. (Coopers & Lybrand 1988)

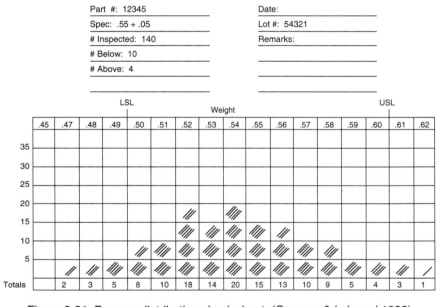

Figure 6-21. Process distribution check sheet. (Coopers & Lybrand 1988)

Defect-By-Type Check Sheet

Part #: _____ Date: _____

Oper. #: _____ Operator: _____

Remarks: _____ _____

_____ _____

Defect	Numbers	Totals
Oversize	⫲⫲ ⫲⫲ ⫲⫲ ⫽⫽⫽	18
Undersize	⫲⫲ ⫲⫲ ⫲⫲ ⫲⫲ ⫲⫲ ⫲⫲ ⫽	31
Cracked	⫲⫲ ⫲⫲ ⫲⫲ ⫲⫲	20
Scratched	⫲⫲ ⫲⫲ ⫲⫲ ⫲⫲ ⫲⫲ ⫲⫲ ⫲⫲ ⫽⫽	37

Figure 6-22. One factor attribute check sheet. (Coopers & Lybrand 1988)

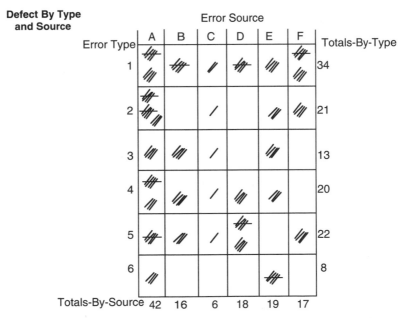

Figure 6-23. Two factor attribute check sheet. (Coopers & Lybrand 1988)

- Is the population distribution represented by a normal curve?
- Is there random variation around the center line?
- Is the frequency of distribution values consistent with the probability of making those values according to a normal curve?

Answering these questions helps the user understand if the process is in control (i.e., experiencing only common cause variation) or if the process is out of control (i.e., experiencing special cause variation). A process communicates through collected data; control charts provide the means to understand what the data are telling the user. Effective SPC requires using control charts as a preventive measure, not for inspection. Successful use of control charts depends on the speed with which a change in the process is detected and corrective action is taken. For example, the best time to address a special cause variation is when it happens, not the next shift or the next day.

INDIVIDUALS CHART

The individuals chart plots single data points collected within a time sequence. This chart can be used for most any type of data collected over time. When using the individuals chart, the user should consider the following elements:

- characteristics to measure and plot
- number of data points to plot (at least 25)
- time interval between data points (i.e., hourly or some time interval sample)

The individuals chart includes two measures: one is charting process average for single measurements and the other is charting process variability. The process average is calculated as follows:

$$\overline{X} = \frac{X_1 + X_2 + X_3 + \ldots + X_n}{n}$$

Example:

	Daily Sales	Range
	1252	
	927	325
	1007	80
	836	171
	1082	246
	1012	70
	778	234
	999	221
	1311	312
	1222	89
Total	10426	1748

$$\overline{X} = \frac{1252 + 927 + 1007 + ... + 1222}{10} = 1042.6$$

centerline $\overline{X}$ = 1042.6

The process variability is charted as the range (R) which is calculated as follows:

$$R_P = |X_n - X_{n-1}|$$

Example:

Data 1252, 927, 1007, 836, 1082,
      1012, 778, 999, 1311, 1222

$R_1 = |927 - 1252| = 325$
$R_2 = |1007 - 927| = 80$
$R_3 = |836 - 1007| = 171$
  etc.
$R_9 = |1222 - 1311| = 89$

$$\overline{R}_P = \frac{325 + 80 + 171 + ... + 89}{9} = \frac{1748}{9} = 194.2$$

Upper control limit (UCL) = $\overline{X}$ + 2.66 $\overline{R}$

Lower control limit (LCL) = $\overline{X}$ + 2.66 $\overline{R}$

UCL ($\overline{X}$) = 1042.6 + (2.66 × 194.2) = 1559.17

LCL ($\overline{X}$) = 1042.6 − (2.66 × 194.2) = 526.03

The resulting individuals chart is illustrated in Figure 6-24.

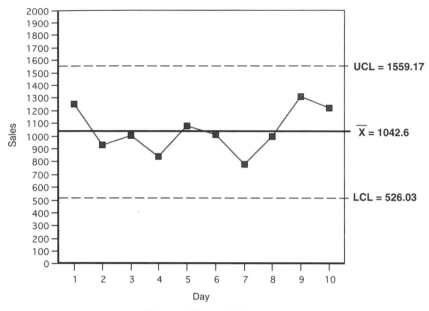

Figure 6-24. Individuals chart.

Three additional types of control charts are commonly used in statistical process control. The X bar-R chart is used for variable data with subgroup sized n between 2 and 10. The P chart is used for defective data. The C chart is used for defective data, count data, or both.

X BAR-R CHART

The X bar-R chart plots subgroup averages and subgroup ranges of variable data collected over a time sequence. The X bar-R chart uses the subgroup mean $\overline{X}$ to chart the process location and the subgroup range R to chart the process variability (Gitlow and Oppenheim 1989). Considerations of the subgroup before data collection should include defining the following elements:

- characteristics to measure and evaluate
- general definition of subgroup
- number of subgroups (should be greater than twenty)
- time interval between subgroups
- number of samples in each subgroup
- time interval of samples within subgroups

The central tendency is expressed as the mean or average ($\overline{X}$), which is the sum of all the samples being examined divided by the number of samples (n). The equation is shown below:

$$\overline{X} = \frac{X_1 + X_2 + X_3 + ... + X_n}{n}$$

An example is presented in Table 6-8. For Subgroup 1:

$$\overline{X} = \frac{11.5 + 10.2 + 9.4 + 10.4 + 11.0}{5}$$

$$\overline{X} = \frac{52.5}{5} = 10.5$$

Table 6-8. Number of subgroups.

Group		1	2	3	4	5	6	7	8	9	10	11	12	13	14	15	16	17	18	19	20
	1	11.5	11.4	9.9	10.0	9.5	10.2	11.6	10.3	10.1	10.1	10.0	11.0	12.1	10.7	10.6	10.5	10.9	12.0	12.9	11.7
Sample	2	10.2	10.5	10.1	9.0	11.7	11.0	11.1	11.0	10.9	9.2	11.4	8.6	9.1	10.6	10.9	9.8	12.6	12.0	11.1	10.6
Size	3	9.4	10.1	9.9	11.0	11.2	10.2	11.3	11.1	10.8	8.3	9.7	10.9	10.1	11.5	11.2	10.0	11.5	11.9	10.4	10.5
	4	10.4	10.5	10.6	10.7	12.0	11.1	11.0	10.9	10.7	9.7	11.3	8.6	10.9	11.2	11.2	9.9	10.5	11.2	10.7	10.7
	5	11.0	10.5	10.0	8.3	12.1	10.5	12.0	11.2	10.5	9.7	10.6	8.4	9.3	11.0	11.6	10.3	11.5	11.4	10.4	12.5
Sum		52.5	53.0	50.5	49.0	56.6	53.0	57.0	54.5	53.0	47.0	53.0	47.5	51.5	55.0	55.5	50.5	57.0	58.5	55.5	56.0
Average (X)		10.5	10.6	10.1	9.8	11.3	10.6	11.4	10.9	10.6	9.4	10.6	9.5	10.3	11.0	11.1	10.1	11.4	11.7	11.1	11.2
Range (R)		2.1	1.3	0.7	2.7	2.6	0.9	0.8	0.9	0.8	1.8	1.7	2.6	3.0	0.8	1.0	0.7	2.1	0.8	2.5	2.0

The range (R) is the difference between the smallest (X_{min}) and largest (X_{max}) observation in a data set, and may be expressed as:

$$R = X_{max} - X_{min}$$

Example data for Subgroup 1:
$$X = 11.5, 10.2, 9.4, 10.4, 11.0$$
$$R = 11.5 - 9.4 = 2.1$$

The mean for the X portion of the chart may be calculated as follows:

$$\overline{\overline{X}} = \frac{\overline{X}_1 + \overline{X}_2 + \overline{X}_3 + \dots \overline{X}_n}{n}$$

$$\overline{\overline{X}} = \frac{10.5 + 10.6 + 10.1 + \dots 11.2}{20} = \frac{213.2}{20} = 10.66$$

The range mean ($\overline{R}$) for the R portion of the chart maybe calculated as follows:

$$\overline{R} = \frac{R_1 + R_2 + R_3 + \dots R_n}{n}$$

$$\overline{R} = \frac{2.1 + 1.3 + .7 + \dots 2.0}{n20}$$

$$\overline{R} = \frac{31.8}{20} = 1.59$$

The upper and lower control limits for the X portion of the chart may be calculated as follows:

$$\text{Upper control limit} = UCL(\overline{X})$$
$$\text{Lower control limit} = LCL(\overline{X})$$

$$UCL(\overline{X}) = \overline{\overline{X}} + A_2\overline{R}$$
$$LCL(\overline{X}) = \overline{\overline{X}} - A_2\overline{R}$$

where

A_2 equals:

Number of observations in a subgroup (n)	A2
2	1.88
3	1.02
4	0.73
5	0.58
6	0.48
7	0.42
8	0.37
9	0.34
10	0.31

For example:

$$\overline{\overline{X}} = 10.66$$
$$\overline{R} = 1.59$$
$$n = 5$$
$$A_2 = 0.58$$

Upper control limit for the $\overline{X}$ portion of the chart:

$$UCL(\overline{X}) = \overline{\overline{X}} + A_2\overline{R}$$
$$UCL(\overline{X}) = 10.66 + (.58 \times 1.59)$$
$$UCL(\overline{X}) = 10.66 + 0.92$$
$$UCL(\overline{X}) = 11.58$$

Lower control limit for the $\overline{X}$ portion of the chart:

$$LCL(\overline{X}) = \overline{\overline{X}} + A_2\overline{R}$$
$$LCL(\overline{X}) = 10.66 - (.58 \times 1.59)$$
$$LCL(\overline{X}) = 10.66 - 0.92$$
$$LCL(\overline{X}) = 9.74$$

The upper and lower control limits for the R portion of the chart may be calculated as follows:

$$\text{Upper control limit} = UCL(R)$$
$$\text{Lower control limit} = LCL(R)$$

$$UCL(R) = D_4 \overline{R}$$
$$LCL(R) = D_3 \overline{R}$$

where
D_3 and D_4 equal:

Number of observations in a subgroup (n)	D_3	D_4
2	.00	3.27
3	.00	2.57
4	.00	2.28
5	.00	2.11
6	.00	2.00
7	.08	1.92
8	.14	1.86
9	.18	1.82
10	.22	1.78

For the example:

$$\overline{R} = 1.59$$
$$n = 5$$

$$D_4 = 2.11$$
$$D_3 = 0.00$$

Upper control limit for the R portion of the chart:

$$UCL(R) = D_4 R$$
$$UCL(R) = (2.11 \times 1.59)$$
$$UCL(R) = 3.35$$

Lower control limit for the R portion of the chart:

$$LCL(R) = D_3 \overline{R}$$
$$LCL(R) = (0.00 \times 1.59)$$
$$LCL(R) = 0.00$$

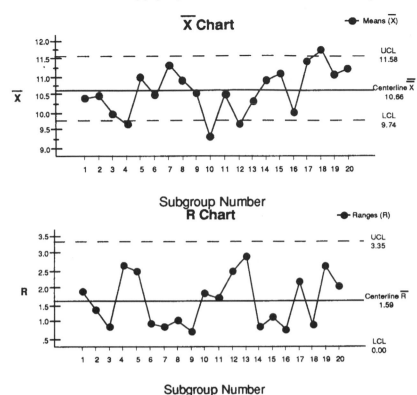

Figure 6-25. X bar and R charts.

The resulting X bar and R charts are illustrated in Figure 6-25. For practical interpretation, the X bar chart monitors process average, such as machine setting adjustment, raw material changes, and operator or technician changes. The R chart monitors process consistency such as machine repair, maintenance, and cleaning.

P Chart

The P chart is used to plot percent defectives, which are samples with one or more defects for a particular attribute. Each sample must be determined to possess or not possess some attribute. This attribute is usually nonconformance to specification. The samples must consist of distinct items to be evaluated, and the occurrence of the sample for an attribute is independent of the previous sample. The percent defective (P) is calculated by dividing the number of defectives found in a subgroup by the number of units sampled in a subgroup, or:

$$P = \frac{\text{Total number of defectives for all the subgroups}}{\text{Total number of units sampled for all the subgroups}}(100)$$

For this example:

$$P = \frac{6+7+4+...+7+5}{50+52+50+...+52+55}(100)$$

$$P = \frac{95}{1028} = .092\ (100)$$

$$P = 9.2\%$$

Calculation of the upper and lower control limits:

Upper control limit = UCL(P)
Lower control limit = LCL(P)

$$UCL(P) = P + 3\sqrt{\frac{\overline{P}(1-\overline{P})}{n}}$$

$$UCL(P) = P + 3\sqrt{\frac{\overline{P}(1-\overline{P})}{n}}$$

where
n = Average number of units sampled per subgroup

$$n = \frac{\text{Total number of units sampled for all the subgroups}}{\text{Number of subgroups}}$$

For this example:

$$P = .092$$

$$n = \frac{50+52+50+...+52+55}{20} = \frac{1028}{20} = 51.4$$

Upper control limit

$$UCL(P) = P + 3\sqrt{\frac{P(1-P)}{n}}$$

$$UCL(P) = .092 + 3\sqrt{\frac{.092(1-.092)}{51.4}}$$

$$UCL(P) = .092 + 3(.0403)$$

$$UCL(P) = .213$$

Lower control limit

$$LCL(P) = P - 3\sqrt{\frac{P(1-P)}{n}}$$

$$LCL(P) = .092 - 3\sqrt{\frac{.092(1-.092)}{51.4}}$$

$$LCL(P) = .092 - 3(.0403)$$

$$LCL(P) = .000$$

The centerline and control limits for the P chart are shown in Figure 6-26.

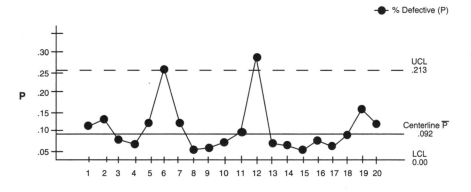

Figure 6-26. P chart.

C CHART

The C chart is used to count the total number of defects from a given number of samples when discrete defects occur within some constant subgroup size. This subgroup is the area of opportunity for the count of defects. The defects are independent and should be rare compared to the potential defects. The centerline (C) of the C chart may be calculated as:

For this example:

$$C = \frac{\text{Total number of defects}}{\text{Number of subgroups}}$$

$$C = \frac{8 + 9 + 5 + \ldots + 10 + 5}{25}$$

$$C = \frac{200}{25} = 8.00$$

Upper and lower control limits may be calculated as follows:

$$\text{Upper control limit} = \text{UCL(C)}$$
$$\text{Lower control limit} = \text{LCL(C)}$$

$$\text{UCL(C)} = C + 3\sqrt{C}$$
$$\text{LCL(C)} = C - 3\sqrt{C}$$

For this example:

$$C = 8.00$$
$$\text{UCL(C)} = C + 3\sqrt{C}$$
$$\text{UCL(C)} = 8.00 + 3\sqrt{8.00}$$
$$\text{UCL(C)} = 16.48$$

Lower control limit

$$\text{LCL(C)} = C - 3\sqrt{C}$$
$$\text{LCL(C)} = 8.00 - 3\sqrt{8.00}$$
$$\text{LCL(C)} = 0.00$$

The centerline and control limits for the C chart are shown in Figure 6-27. Table 6-9 indicates the types of control charts and the situations in which they should be used.

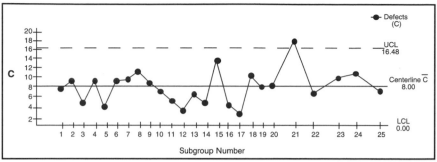

Figure 6-27. C chart.

Table 6-9. Types of control charts.

Type of Chart	Type of Use
Individuals chart	Single data points occurring over time
X-bar and R charts	Samples of measurements
P chart	Percent defective units
C chart	Number of defects per unit

IS THE PROCESS SATISFACTORY?

As a general guideline, control charts of variable data will provide a higher grade of information than will control charts of attribute data. This is because data based on measurements are more insightful than data that only indicates conformance or nonconformance. Where attribute charting is used, finding meaningful variables data should be the goal.

In seeking to answer the question, "Is the process satisfactory?" the user must first attempt to separate common cause variation from special cause variation; that is, the user needs to know if the process is in control. Rules for interpreting common cause versus special cause variation are shown in Figure 6-28.

Special cause variation is accepted to exist under the following conditions:

• one point lies outside of Zone A
• seven consecutive points lie above or below the center line
• two out of three successive points fall in Zone A or beyond
• four out of five successive points fall in Zone B or beyond

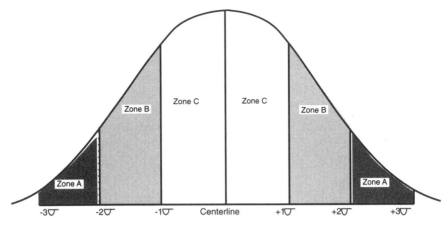

Figure 6-28. Identifying special cause variation.

• six points in a row steadily increase or decrease
• fourteen consecutive points alternate up and down
• seven successive points all have the same value

MAKING THE PROCESS CAPABLE

Process capability is the ability of a process to produce units whose variation is within the customer specifications and centered on the design target value. Capability involves only the variation among the measurements, not the actual size of the measurements.

The objective of a process capability study is to compare the existing customer specifications with the natural variation of the process. Doing this allows the user to further answer the question, "Is the process satisfactory?" An analysis of the natural variation of a process should be undertaken only after special cause variation is eliminated. The following assumptions are made when conducting a process capability study using variables data:

• The data come from a process that is operating in a state of statistical control.
• The data being used for the study come from a normally distributed process.
• The study should use at least fifty subgroups of data obtained from a control chart.

Cp Index

The Cp Index measures the actual spread of process variability (natural width) against the allowable spread of the customer specification. It is the specification width divided by the natural process width:

$$Cp = \frac{\text{Customer specification width}}{\text{Natural width}}$$

Customer Specification Width (SW) is the upper specification limit and the lower specification limit as defined to meet customer needs. *Natural Width (NW)* is statistically defined as the range of six standard deviations of individual data points. It can only be estimated for a process with constant variation, e.g., R-chart in control. The process spread is capable if NW <= SW.

The following interpretations of Cp are useful:
- if Cp>1.33, then the process spread is functioning more than adequately
- if 1.00<Cp<1.33, then the process spread is adequate but will require close attention, especially as the Cp approaches 1.00
- if Cp<1.00, then the process spread is not functioning adequately

Cpk Index

The Cpk index is the measure of the ability of a process to produce a product within customer specifications. It measures the degree of centering of the natural process spread versus the customer specification limits. The Cpk index is the range between the estimated process mean ($\overline{\overline{X}}$) and the closest specification limit divided by three process standard deviations:

$$Cpk = \frac{\left|\overline{\overline{X}} - \text{closest customer specification limit}\right|}{3\sigma}$$

The following interpretations of Cpk are useful:
- if Cpk>1.33, then the process spread and centering are more than adequate
- if 1.00<Cpk<1.33, then the process, including the spread, is centered adequately, but will require closer attention as the Cpk approaches 1.00
- if Cpk<1.00, then the process spread is not centered correctly or the spread is not adequate

Example calculations of the Cp and Cpk indexes are shown below:

Customer Width	Process
USL = 10.5	$\overline{\overline{X}}$ = 9.8
LSL = 7.5	1σ = .28
Target = 9.0	

1. $Cp = \dfrac{10.5 - 7.5}{6(.28)} = \dfrac{3.0}{1.68} = 1.79$

The spread of this process can more than adequately function within specification.

2. $Cpk = \dfrac{|9.8 - 10.5|}{3(.28)} = \dfrac{0.7}{.84} = 0.81$

This process is not centered correctly.

P chart data also provide useful process capability evaluations. It is assumed that the process must be operating "in statistical control" as evidenced by a control chart of percent defective data. In addition, at least fifty subgroups must be plotted on the control chart to perform the capability study. The process capability may be analyzed as the percentage conforming, that is, $(1-\overline{P})$. The average capability, not the changing individual values, must be compared against management's expectations for a particular characteristic. C chart data may be used in a similar fashion to evaluate process capability. Figure 6-29 indicates process capability variations. Figure 6-30 shows possible decisions resulting from a process capability study.

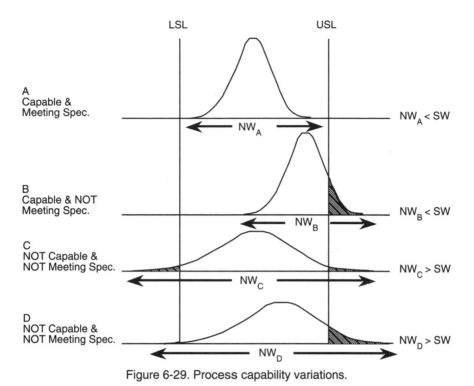

Figure 6-29. Process capability variations.

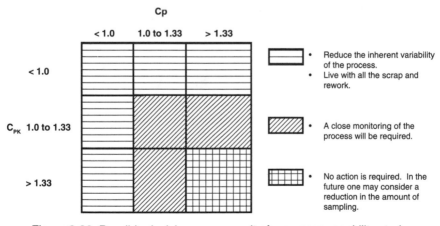

Figure 6-30. Possible decisions as a result of a process capability study.

LINKING PROCESS CAPABILITY TO FRY

Increased process capability directly correlates to FRY improvement in a PSS. As shown in Figure 6-31, the linkage is derived by:

1. developing the FRY baseline of performance and resulting dollars lost due to waste
2. defining the process drivers and their cause and effect relationship to yield loss
3. clearly understanding the customer specification widths, thereby setting process tolerances
4. applying SPC to process drivers to separate common causes from special causes
5. implementing quality tools to eliminate special causes
6. developing a new FRY performance level
7. measuring Cp and Cpk indexes
8. implementing common cause variation reduction strategy for Cpk indexes less than 1.33 (requires fundamentally changing the process)
9. monitoring process improvement activities, closely tracking capability improvement with measures showing increased yields and reduced dollars lost

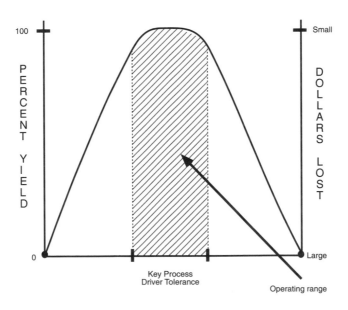

Figure 6-31. Relationship between process capability and FRY.

REFERENCES

Chambers, D. and D. Wheeler. 1992. *Understanding Statistical Process Control.* Second ed. Knoxville, TN: Statistical Process Controls Inc.

Coopers & Lybrand. 1988. *Integrated Quality: Statistical Process Control.* New York: Coopers & Lybrand.

Ehley, K. 1991. *Control Chart Interpretation, Parts I & II.* (Video). Wauwatosa, WI: Creative Solutions, Inc.

Gitlow, H., S. Gitlow, A. Oppenheim, and R. Rosa. 1989. *Tools and Methods for the Improvement of Quality.* Homewood, IL: Richard D. Irwin, Inc.

Joiner, B. L. 1991. *New Thinking for Managers: Variation and its Implication for Managerial Action.* A seminar for the Philadelphia Area Council for Excellence, Dec. 4-5.

Juran, J. M. and F. M. Gryna. 1980. *Quality Planning and Analysis.* New York: McGraw-Hill.

Sullivan, L. P. 1984. Reducing variability: a new approach to quality. *Quality Progress.* July: 15-21.

The Role of Suppliers 7

TRADITIONALLY, the relationship between buyer and supplier has been competitive and adversarial; the negotiation process focused on a win-lose outcome. However, to support time-based manufacturing (TBM), the buyer-supplier relationship must be quite different (see Figure 7-1).

In TBM, the purchasing function assumes the role of general manager for the external factory, making sure that the supplier's product supply system (PSS) is in sync with the customer's PSS. The purchasing department not only places orders, but investigates the supplier's technical, process, and human resource capabilities.

Long-term contracts are useful in developing these successful supplier relationships. In fact, there is an ongoing trend to move away from rebidding the requirements annually (or more frequently). It has been estimated that by 1995 three out of every four dollars spent by purchasing will go to key suppliers under long-term contracts (Raia 1989).

For many years, large vertically-integrated companies have reaped the benefits of their size, growing stronger with many competitors being eliminated. Today, however, it is possible for a group of smaller independent companies working closely together to manage the flow of goods and services along the entire value-added chain. By working in a partnership, small companies can realize the advantages and benefits of the large vertically integrated organization (Johnston and Lawrence 1988).

This chapter is adapted from Wheeler 1987.

Independent vs. TBM Partnerships	
Independent Suppliers	**TBM Supplier Partners**
• Arms-length negotiation	• Negotiations based on mutual linkage and problem solving
• Pressure by threat	• Pressure by establishing an obligation on both parties to perform
• Many suppliers with no time for each	• Few suppliers with significant time on important relationships
• Buyer as only contact	• Buyer as facilitator of many teams
• Allocation among suppliers based on bidding	• One supplier per product group to improve processes
• Formal specifications	• Deep understanding of technologies, capabilities, and customer requirements
• Prices established by firm quotations	• Cross organizational improvement teams to raise total PSS performance

Figure 7-1. TBM partnerships.

To fulfill its role in TBM, the purchasing function is responsible for forming partnerships with key suppliers and managing those suppliers in a successful relationship. The trend is toward fewer, smarter suppliers. The key is to link the company's needs for designing, marketing, and delivering a product with supplying companies. Getting this partnership going and keeping it competitive is no easy feat. It may be the single most important task of the people who run manufacturing organizations (Burt 1989).

THE TBM PARTNERSHIP

All manufacturers with businesses for customers are suppliers, and all suppliers are potential candidates for PSS synchronization and integration. In fact, a number of manufacturers have already been introduced to customers' TBM purchasing efforts. Although most programs have the proper intentions, not all are well planned or well executed. A proper TBM purchasing program does not make suppliers stock inventory to deliver just-in-time. If that is the customer's message, the supplier knows the customer does not understand TBM.

A TBM partnership consists of two (or more) companies that are working together side by side in the PSS to improve the flow of products and services. The PSS includes all activities and services necessary to transform basic raw material into the final, consumed product. The key objective is to enhance the value of the relationship, not just the physical materials, between the supplier and customer. The TBM relationship need not only be initiated by the customer, but may be pursued as a strategic initiative by the supplier.

CO-OP CONTRACTING

The heart of the TBM partnership is the co-op contracting philosophy that works toward eliminating waste across the entire materials continuum, i.e., the PSS. It is an integral part of the total TBM strategy. At first, co-op contracting may appear to be the easiest element of TBM to implement because the purchasing department only has to persuade the supplier (sometimes forcefully) to ship just-in-time for production. Properly executed, however, co-op contracting is the most difficult piece of the TBM program to implement. In order for a supplier to truly deliver "just-in-time" to the customer's need, the supplier and customer both must be on the same TBM strategy. This ensures that each organization is synchronized with the overall PSS requirement.

Successful co-op contracting depends on the ability of the customer organization to develop a highly interdependent leverage with key suppliers. There is much written about vendor partnerships, win-win agreements, and so forth. They all imply that the customer and supplier enter into these contracts on an equal footing. While that is the intent of the agreements, experience has indicated that few suppliers embrace the real benefit of continuous unit price reduction for the customer. Conversely, few customers are willing to concede that many supplier problems are caused by the customer's lack of definition and communication. Also, customers frequently want all the cost savings from the partnership, thereby driving down supplier margins until the partnership is ultimately unprofitable. Because of this, the enthusiasm for a TBM agreement often is viewed with skepticism at best, and more often, polarization at worst. To avoid this situation, the principal objective of co-op contracting is creating leverage with the chosen suppliers.

The co-op contracting strategy requires that the customer accomplish two initial major tasks:

1. Consolidate raw materials and parts into common product groups. By consolidating similar products that share the same manufacturing resources, raw materials, or both, the customer can offer more business opportunities to the supplier. This benefits both the customer and the supplier. The successful supplier enjoys more business with the customer than before through the same resources. In addition, more of the supplier's capacity is consumed by the customer who provides better visibility and more stable demand. The customer benefits from the higher confidence caused when supplier shipments are synchronized to support TBM efforts.

2. Consolidate the supplier base. Because of the magnitude of improvement activities needed within the materials continuum, the supplier base should be limited. The opportunity to reduce the supplier base as much as thirty percent exists when eliminating nonvalue-added activities from the PSS. With stakes this high, the effort required to realize that opportunity becomes a significant obstacle. By maintaining a large supplier base, the magnitude of effort required by the customer may actually increase exponentially. The customer resources required to support TBM partnerships would exceed the available personnel and increase potentially avoidable staff levels. Experience has shown that improvements made at one supplier usually do not transfer to another supplier because processes and equipment vary widely, even within the same product group or, more curiously, within different plants of the same company. With significantly fewer suppliers, it is easier to fine tune the few good suppliers than it is to fine tune many mediocre ones. By concentrating on fewer suppliers, the customer can treat each in a manner similar to its own employees, i.e., communicate a detailed understanding of objectives, provide training and certification, and assign responsibility for improvement that is consistent with the company's own objectives. Thus, by assigning the responsibility for improvement to a few co-op suppliers, the customer enhances its own company's capabilities.

After consolidating like parts to common product groups, the customer chooses one supplier as the primary source. That supplier benefits from increased revenues and becomes the servicer for the chosen product group. Since the two companies have entered into a highly interdependent relationship, the supplier is highly motivated to participate in continuous improvement, Each organization has substantially increased its accountability to the other.

Co-op Contracting Objectives

The objectives of co-op contracting are to assure continuous improvement of the PSS, synchronization between the companies, leveraged quality improvement, lower inventories, and technology sharing.

Continuous improvement of the PSS. By sharing common problems and seeking opportunities to eliminate waste, the customer and supplier can reduce overall lead times and improve quality. The two parties work together in improving products and processes that take advantage of the supplier's expertise. This cooperative effort ensures that the customer's products fit and function as planned and that they meet quality requirements.

To achieve continuous improvement, the supplier and customer share knowledge and expertise in TBM techniques, such as changeover reduction, statistical process control, total productive maintenance, and synchronization. With a single supplier for materials within a product group, the customer can focus valuable attention on joint improvement activities. In this way, resources are not diffused across many suppliers, which would substantially hinder improvement progress.

Both the supplier and the customer benefit from cost reductions. Costs are not just based on purchase price; they also include rework, testing, inspection, and transportation, for both the customer and the supplier. These can be reduced or eliminated to improve the PSS. Also, the supplier is able to offer design changes or technology improvements that the customer can take advantage of to reduce the number of components in the product or to reduce waste. The emphasis is on identifying and eliminating waste—initially in the linkage between the companies, and ultimately further up and down the supply system.

Synchronization between companies. When the supplier and customer act in each other's best interests, the PSS becomes a powerful strategic alliance to improve both companies' market and financial positions. Information is shared confidentially between organizations. Once both companies understand and agree upon the level of capacity required to service the customer, the puller manages the supplier's capacity by determining the production requirements and staying consistent to the plan. The supplier then dedicates a level of daily capacity that is consistent with the customer's production needs.

Daily customer order visibility is provided by the customer organization through the use of the pull system. In effect, the supplier and customer "go to the bank" with the daily schedule. By providing visible daily demand to the supplier, leverage is not only maintained but strengthened because the supplier's capability grows up around the managed pull system. Often information will be passed electronically, using electronic data interchange (EDI) technology. When one side is having a problem, the other is informed and both quickly take appropriate action to help ensure that the relationship remains strong. Joint strategic directions are set, particularly when they involve mutually beneficial investments.

Leveraged quality improvement. Quality problems usually represent the single greatest barrier to lead time reduction. The customer must often commit resources (technical experts) when working with the supplier to reduce process variation and improve product uniformity. As much as two-thirds of the supplier's defects may actually be traced to the customer. This usually comes from unclear or misunderstood expectations and quality specifications. When the root cause of a defect is identified and corrected, the solution can be applied to other products as well to improve yields. As nonvalue-adding costs such as inspection are eliminated, the supplier and customer become more dependent on each other for continued success, thus increasing leverage.

Lower inventories. Typically, lower inventories should not be considered a primary objective. If the continuous improvement efforts between the partners are working properly, inventory levels will drop as a normal progression. However, some customers are so conditioned to having large amounts of just-in-case inventories that it is sometimes necessary to state this as a primary objective to break out of existing mindsets.

In reality, low inventory and rapid throughput serve to uncover opportunities for improvement, and, therefore, cost reduction. The advantages are:

1. Low inventory requires that material be delivered in an extremely timely manner. Anything that prevents timely delivery becomes immediately apparent and is a candidate for concentrated improvement.

2. Low inventory requires that only correct products are delivered. This, in turn, requires that the customer reduce internal lead time to the point of making only what is needed of the potential product mix on a daily basis.

3. In order to achieve reliable delivery, the customer must require that suppliers ship just-in-time. This, then, requires an analysis of the entire PSS. The objective of the PSS analysis is to significantly reduce the entire throughput time. Similar to the internal organization, the major contributors to long lead times by different suppliers are widely varied. By identifying and eliminating these activities, the opportunity to lower inventory becomes available.

4. Low inventory requires that the items be supplied defect-free. Any rejection of the supplier's material quickly stops the production process and therefore forces focused quality action by both the supplier and customer.

Technology sharing. As the partnership matures, a more synergistic relationship develops between the supplier and customer. Each becomes more dependent upon the other because their fortunes are linked to the partnership's ability to improve. A basic assumption is made in co-op contracting that one reason a customer outsources is that the supplier is technologically more advanced than the customer in the manufacture of the supplier's product. Co-op contracting provides faster product launch because the supplier has already been identified and has participated significantly in the product design. What starts out as a somewhat unilateral arrangement evolves into mutually leveraged product/process development for the benefit of both parties.

CREATING THE TBM PARTNERSHIP

ROLES OF THE TBM PARTNERS

The rules that have traditionally governed the relationships between customers and their suppliers change with the implementation of the TBM partnership. For example, purchasing no longer focuses on identification of multiple vendors for sourcing each opportunity and negotiating the lowest purchase price and terms. Instead, purchasing focuses on identifying potential supplier partners who can contribute to the improvement of the PSS. In a TBM partnership purchasing personnel must become highly knowledgeable of the manufacturing process. They must understand how building customer/supplier relationships support the TBM principles of shorter lead times, reduced variation, smaller lot sizes, and manufacturability within the PSS.

The supplier should understand what the customer wants and be prepared to meet those expectations. In a recent survey (Raia 1989), customers looking for cooperative relationships with suppliers ranked their evaluation criteria in the following order:

1. reduced lead times and reliability of on-time delivery
2. quality performance
3. financial stability of the company
4. top management's commitment to the supplier-customer relationship
5. leadership in technology and innovation
6. proximity to their plant

Conversely, the customer should understand and appreciate what the supplier wants. In a different survey (Tonkin 1989), suppliers indicated they wanted the following in a TBM partnership with their customers:

1. information about the customer's future products and technical requirements
2. an understanding of how their performance will be measured and
feedback on results
3. an accurate demand on which to build, so that the supplier is not wasting
the customer's time and resources by building products that are not
needed or by expediting orders
4. the use of advanced information communication techniques such as
electronic data interchange to reduce or eliminate nonvalue-adding
paperwork, time, and energy

Each organization should enter into the partnership preparing to meet
at least these needs and eventually many others as the partnership defines
them.

What Makes It Work

Trust is the action word. Time-based manufacturing partnerships can only
work if the parties trust each other and are open to confronting negative, as
well as positive, aspects of each other's organizations and operations. The
relationship must truly promote the interests of both parties.

Previously, negative customer actions have created suppliers' skepticism and hesitancy toward entering into partnerships. How often has a
major corporation informed its suppliers that it wants them to enter into
some JIT program or quality program or else be eliminated as a source?
This is especially troublesome to the supplier when the demanding company has not implemented the same improvements in its own operations.
Also, how often has the customer tried to leverage the increased volume
into price concessions without offering to assist the supplier with education
or training to reduce waste and lower costs, which would ensure the long
term viability of the PSS? Yet, the realities of today's competitive world
are that more companies are pursuing the TBM strategy, and those
suppliers that do not choose to participate in these efforts will lose out.

The next key to making the relationship work is viewing the partnership as one competitive entity. Each side must be interested in both partners
making a profit. Cost reductions on the supplier side should not automati-
cally be viewed as price reductions to the customer. For example, the
supplier may need the increased profits to replace obsolete equipment or
to finance research and development to support new products or technologies for the customer. Remember, in the PSS, what's ultimately important
is the value of the product as it reaches the ultimate consumer.

WHO INITIATES THE RELATIONSHIP?

Typically, the customer implementing a TBM strategy initiates the TBM partnership. If this customer is a practitioner of TBM principles, then it provides its suppliers with education and assistance. There is no rule, however, that says the supplier cannot introduce TBM techniques to its customers. If the supplier believes in the concept of TBM partnerships and in helping the customer compete, then the supplier should carefully consider initiating the relationship. This approach has merit for the following reasons:

- The supplier who takes the initiative is better positioned to gain more leverage as the relationship develops.

- The supplier who understands the full scope of TBM will pass this understanding on to the customer to ensure that the customer does not just ask that the supplier stock extra inventory.

- The supplier may be able to open the door to sharing more information with the customer. This will usually identify opportunities to provide additional value-adding services to meet customer needs.

IMPLEMENTING CO-OP CONTRACTING

Implementing co-op contracting is not easy. It requires considerable effort from purchasing personnel, technical support staff, and management; management-to-management discussions will often occur at the highest executive levels. The goal of the co-op contract is to develop a mutually beneficial long-term participative partnership. The relationship should produce a better product that exhibits uniformity to mutually agreed upon requirements the first time, every time. The relationship should also consider quality, cost, lead time, and service. The benefits include elimination of incoming product inspection, reduced inventory, fewer false starts, and improved costs and quality.

The following is a comprehensive approach to implementing co-op contracting.

Step 1—Organize the effort. Implementing co-op contracting requires a multidisciplinary team of company professionals. This activity should not be looked upon as a purchasing responsibility. While purchasing certainly has a major role in co-op contracting, the responsibility for success lies with the entire organization. The customer co-op team should include representation from production control, quality, manufacturing, engineering, accounting, and production. This multidisciplinary group can provide a broader perspective on selecting supplier partners.

While recognizing that only management can set policy, the co-op team should begin by recommending company policy in three primary areas. First, the team should understand the Uniform Commercial Code (UCC) and be able to make recommendations on any potential legal issues (this should include company legal counsel) relative to planned agreements. Second, the team should establish an ethical framework for fair practice when dealing with suppliers. Finally, the team should establish guidelines for the level of mutual sharing with supplier partners. For example, the parties should reach an agreement on the method of sharing cost reductions. Improvement in co-op contracting is not a one-way street. Thinking through likely partnership issues will result in much better preparation for the co-op effort.

Step 2—Develop goals and priorities. The co-op team should determine what must be accomplished before beginning the work effort. As with other elements of TBM, there is a defined role for supplier partnerships to support the overall PSS improvement requirements. Understanding the key design drivers for supplier partnerships will guide the co-op team to leverage improvements to their best advantage for the company. Key design drivers will likely come from one or more of the following elements:
• synchronization
• quality
• lead time reduction
• first run yield
• reliability
• product rationalization

Step 3—Establish product groups. Defining product groups sharing the same manufacturing resources and technology in their production is one of the most difficult steps in the co-op contracting process. Careful consideration should be given to this step as it will dramatically affect the supplier consolidation process.

The co-op team must begin by collecting and analyzing product group data including inventory, quality rejects and rework, number of products in the group, lead times, delivery reliability, inventory levels, a basic process flow of the product group, and any issues specific to a product group. This allows the team to provide the most meaningful information to potential supplier candidates when going through the selection process.

After defining product groups, the customer must initially select the product group most important to the overall PSS improvement. This selection process can be based on several criteria including inventory, quality, cost, and degree of difficulty (see Table 7-1).

Table 7-1. Raw material product supply group.

Product Group	Annual $	Type*	No. of Items	Lead Time (weeks)	No. of Suppliers	Buyer
A	9,202,575	C	36	6	47	plant
B	4,189,234	F	16	1	6	corporate
C	2,271,761	C	209	6	3	corporate
D	2,185,923	B	9	4	8	plant
E	1,670,546	B	1	4	1	corporate
F	1,309,762	B	50	1	5	plant
G	1,014,257	C	139	9	6	corporate
H	854,446	F	93	4	13	plant
I	461,922	F	15	2	3	plant
J	275,000	C	3	5	2	plant

* F = forecasted
C = Contract (commitment for price and qty.)
B = blanket (commitment for price and estimated but no guaranteed qty.)

Step 4—Evaluate suppliers by product group. It is important to identify those suppliers where there is an opportunity to create a partnership. The ultimate objective is reduction of the active supplier base to lower resource requirements, travel costs, and administrative complexity to aid process simplification. In this step, the team should rate the current suppliers of a

product group based on their past performance level. When evaluating suppliers, a company should consider the following criteria:
- current quality, cost, lead time, and service
- responsiveness in creating process-to-process linkage including quality, inventory levels, and materials transfer
- technical competence to improve products and processes in the supply system
- stability of the management team for long-term improvement
- future business direction

The team should also be aware of other potential suppliers not currently doing business with the company. Often new opportunities for improvement emerge from looking at new suppliers. Initially, the company should visit those suppliers deemed most important and those with the top preliminary ratings.

Step 5—Conduct supplier orientation. During this step, top management from both companies and other key managers from quality, manufacturing, engineering, and purchasing meet to discuss the TBM partnership process.

A key element is establishing performance criteria for the partnership. While it would not seem obvious, a common problem in many companies is poorly defined customer procurement specifications. Considerable difficulty and delay will exist if either party is unclear about what the supplier will deliver and what the customer will accept. The requirement of consistency of production and shipment should be discussed. Price reduction objectives should be mutually established and periodically reviewed. The same can be said for lead time reduction, quality improvement, and reliability.

Step 6—Supplier visit. Following the orientation, the co-op team should conduct a site visit at the supplier's facilities. The objective is not to evaluate the supplier, but to better understand supplier processes and capabilities and to define potential for improvement. If possible, the visiting team should include materials procurement, technical support, and manufacturing management personnel. The visit should focus on identifying ways to reduce delays, lower major costs, attack raw material difficulties, improve quality, and reduce personnel problems.

In this step, the customer should determine if the supplier has the procedures, systems, organization structure, and technology to manufacture product uniformly. It is critical that the supplier's system provides for defect prevention as opposed to defect detection through inspection.

The results of the visit should be documented. As necessary, the company should discuss remedial corrective action and set a time schedule for implementation. Also, the supplier should be given the opportunity to discuss customer changes that would enhance the business relationship. For example, the supplier may need better customer specifications to process orders.

Step 7—Develop TBM partnership strategy. The purpose of this step is to develop the conceptual design for the TBM partnership process within a product group. The conceptual design presents "how the process will work here" by defining how the customer will improve its own business through the increased usage of supplier capabilities. In addition, it includes a discussion of supplier opportunities and the most pressing improvement needs, as well as major barriers. The TBM partnership strategy should address the following elements by product group:
- single versus multiple suppliers
- supply by distributor versus manufacturer
- selection by bid or appointed
- new candidates versus current suppliers
- timetable
- industry practice conflicts
- tooling
- specific selection criteria

Step 8 —Evaluate supplier partners. In this step the co-op team evaluates its group of potential suppliers against the criteria outlined in the TBM partnership strategy. A general rule for major product groups is that the co-op team should have five supplier candidates or fewer.

The evaluation step often includes developing a bid package for supplier candidates. Developing this bid package can be time consuming and should be as complete as possible because an incomplete package is often a signal of incomplete intent by the customer. The bid package should include the following sections:
- statement of intent and co-op philosophy
- product volumes and specifications
- customer's requirements
- supplier capabilities
- supplier improvement programs
- selection criteria
- due date
- query responsibility

Appendix 1 contains an example vendor bid package. The bid package typically includes a one-half to full-day group bid meeting where all potential suppliers for a product group convene with the customer to discuss the bid package. On the date due, each bidder should be given the opportunity to present a two- to three-hour overview of its bid. This provides for the co-op team and the potential supplier to discuss the bid and resolve questions. All co-op team members must be present for each presentation. Immediately following each presentation, the co-op team should evaluate its current supplier or suppliers against the competition.

Step 9 —Partnering negotiations and supplier selection. A key element of the selection process involves the partnering negotiations. Negotiations frequently are held with only one supplier, especially when it is clearly better than others. If there is not a clear leader, negotiations may be held simultaneously with two or more suppliers. Negotiations begin with the sales volumes and requirements and end with an understanding of what has to be done to ensure attainment of objectives. Questions that need to be answered include:

- What level of support will the supplier require?
- What are the schedules for cost and quality improvements?
- What are the lead time and service capabilities and commitments?
- What is the correct pricing and cost saving formula?

Several concessions can be offered and may appeal to the supplier. These include the following:

- The customer delays sharing cost improvement gains, e.g., the supplier retains all cost savings for a time.
- The customer provides short-term capital and technical support staff to assist in developing improvements.
- The customer trains the supplier's personnel in TBM. The training subjects that are most useful for management and other employees include:
  - supplier partnership goals
  - benefits of a TBM partnership
  - plans for continuous improvement
  - lead time reduction
  - waste elimination
  - TBM improvement techniques such as changeover reduction
  - performance measurement and rewards

The co-op team should insist that key decision makers be present at negotiations. If a supplier is unwilling to have key executives present, then it is sending a negative signal about its commitment to the partnership.

The supplier award should be made based on the established criteria and should be made as quickly as possible after the last negotiating session. Suppliers not chosen should be informed immediately.

The final element of the negotiation process for the selected supplier is to publish the joint agreement between the two companies. Each company should clearly and completely communicate the agreement to all concerned employees in their respective organizations.

Step 10 —Supplier/customer team. After completing negotiations, the supplier and customer should form a continuous improvement team consisting of sales, manufacturing, quality, engineering, and purchasing personnel. This team should develop an overall mission statement and goals along with action steps to address the areas outlined below.

Improved quality:
• clear product and process specifications, where the supplier under-stands customer needs and the customer understands supplier capability
• established customer service relationships
• consistent quality and reliability measures
• elimination of incoming inspection and count verification
• reduction of safety stocks that buffer quality problems
• preventive methods to ensure uniformity and reduced variation

Reduced lead times:
• synchronized supplier capacity
• quick changeovers and supplier flexibility
• order and volume visibility
• reduced inventories
• firm schedules with compressed lead times

The overall focus of the supplier/customer team should be to improve activity-to-activity linkages through mutual problem solving.

Step 11 —Product, process, and equipment qualification. In this step, the supplier focuses on controlling variations in the product due to raw materials, machines, gauges, fixtures, and processes. The supplier should use statistical methods to measure the level of variation to qualify the product, process, and equipment. The variation reduction tools used should include statistical process control and process capability studies, including the quality tools discussed in Chapter 6.

In addition, the supplier/customer team should map the supplier's manufacturing processes and design and implement an action plan to link the supplier's output with the customer's daily need for the product group. Depending on the geography and characteristics of the product group under study, the supplier linkage should be designed to use one of the three following methods.

1. Direct linkage. The supplier is completely linked into the customer's product scheduling system as though it were a customer department or work center. This is the closest of the three methods and treats the supplier as though it were a member of the customer's organization. Typically only two or three supplier situations require a linkage of this depth.

2. Pull system linkage. Here the supplier is linked through pull systems ranging from hourly replenishment to weekly replenishment. The majority (fifty to seventy-five percent) of a TBM company's suppliers are managed through pull systems.

3. MRP linkage. Through the MRP linkage method, the supplier is managed through the traditional forecasting of customer requirements. This relationship exists where volumes are too small to warrant greater attention. In TBM companies, this type of relationship covers twenty to twenty-five percent of the suppliers.

Step 12—Corrective actions. During the validation process, it may be necessary to make changes to get better uniformity or to improve the process. The supplier/customer team has the responsibility to determine the root cause of any problem and implement corrective actions. A temporary quick fix may be necessary while developing a permanent solution. It is time to move to the monitoring phase when:
- variation in product, process, and equipment is stable.
- the supplier and customer agree that products will uniformly meet requirements on a continuing basis.
- the supplier linkage to customer production is operational.

Step 13—Team monitoring. Depending on the history and location of the supplier, the customer should follow one of three methods to end incoming inspection.

For local suppliers:
This method is effective when the supplier is a short distance from the customer. When the supplier is manufacturing the product, for a series of five to twenty lots or shipments, the customer should conduct source inspection at the supplier's facility. This includes a review of the SPC charts and any inspection and process data that document process performance.

For out-of-town suppliers:
The customer should use this method to reduce travel costs. The customer inspects the first five to ten lots received. If they pass the inspection, the customer inspects every other lot received for the next ten to twenty lots. If each lot meets the requirement, the customer ends incoming inspection. If any lot fails to pass an inspection, the root cause of the failure should be determined and corrective action taken. When a lot fails, the decision of where to restart the qualification process should be based on knowledge of the process and the perceived effectiveness of the correction.

For suppliers who have a very good documented history:
The customer should use historical inspection results to end incoming inspection.

Step 14—Continued communications. To be sure all agreed-to procedures are operating effectively, the customer/supplier partnership progress should be reviewed monthly. These reviews should determine if any steps are necessary to prevent future problems. At this stage, the opportunities for improved product designs are substantial and can begin to be addressed. Questions should be asked about the need for equipment overhaul, tool replacement, and process and quality improvements.

TBM PARTNERSHIP GUIDELINES

The following are offered as guidelines for the successful TBM partnership:

1. All activities within the entire materials continuum (i.e., the PSS) should be synchronized to the end consumer demand rate. Negative feedback should assure synchronization throughout the materials continuum. The pull system is critical to negative feedback. Simplicity is best.

2. Time-based manufacturing is rarely implemented over a short period of time. Therefore, careful planning is a prerequisite for the effective migration to TBM. Every organization has both hindering and facilitating factors that must be addressed. The former must be minimized; the latter must be optimized before significant improvement can be seen. The partnership should concentrate on the most important items. Do not be deterred by the many trivial items that initially will confound progress. Education is expensive and time consuming, but it is the only way to assure long-term improvement.

3. Concentrating only on shop floor lead time will have little overall impact. Rather, the total materials continuum must be analyzed and attacked if true improvement is to be achieved. Furthermore, most breakthroughs in significant lead time reduction occur many steps up or downstream from the point of initial concentration.

4. The greater the variation in customer demand upon resources, the more difficult it is to manage responsiveness.

5. Of all the disciplines required of TBM, by far the most important is the perpetual search for and elimination of variation. Any quality defect adds to the lead time and therefore is unacceptable.

6. In the long run, inventory adds no value to the continuum. Therefore, at the outset its obsolescence must be planned so as to minimize the potential disruption of customer service.

7. The customer must avoid the mistake of starting TBM first with the supplier, for it often ends up in a confrontive relationship.

While the emphasis upon each guideline may vary from application to application, none of the above can exist by itself. All are interdependent and must be adhered to if the partnership is to realize the benefits of TBM.

REFERENCES

Burt, D. N. 1989. Managing suppliers up to speed. *Harvard Business Review*. July-August: 127-35.

Johnston, R. and P. R. Lawrence. 1988. Beyond vertical integration: the rise of the value-adding partnership. *Harvard Business Review*. July-August: 94-101.

Raia, E. R. 1989. JIT in purchasing: a progress report. *Purchasing.* September 14: 58-77.

Tonkin, L. 1989. Changing the rules in the supplier-buyer game. *Manufacturing Systems.* October: 28-32.

Wheeler, W. A. 1987. *Co-op Contracting. Just-in-Time Implementation Methodologies.* New York: Coopers & Lybrand.

Teams Drive the Time-Based Manufacturing Organization 8

THE focus and involvement of the entire organization is necessary for successful time-based manufacturing (TBM). While significant employee involvement is critical, it must be structured and leveraged from management's vision, involvement, and commitment.

MANAGING CHANGE WITHIN TBM

Time-based manufacturing is revolutionary. As with every revolution, companies often embark on the TBM journey with fervor and rhetoric but have no real knowledge of the consequences of large-scale change. Each employee interprets the leader's message in his or her own way according to their paradigm. For TBM to succeed within a company, common goals and understanding must unite the people. The TBM design creates a vision for the company and provides a road map for guiding the entire organization, from top management to front-line employees, toward TBM success.

TBM Change Must Be Cross Organizational

Just as the trumpet section does not make an orchestra, one function alone cannot implement TBM. For TBM to succeed, every function affecting the product supply system (PSS) must contribute. Most TBM improvement opportunities are found in the organization seams between functions. For example, by reducing manufacturing lead time, warehouse and distribution centers potentially can be made smaller or eliminated. The sales function must understand that producing a large volume order may cost more than producing a small one (a concept not easily accepted by more experienced sales people). Most cost accounting systems penalize the TBM implementation.

Time-based manufacturing must have a champion, but that champion is only the facilitator of broad-scale change affecting many. Responsibility and accountability for implementing change must reside at the top of the organization. Only in this way can TBM achieve the strategic status it requires.

TBM CHANGE REQUIRES THE "FAITH FACTOR"

The faith factor represents a classic paradigm example. In his paradigm studies, Barker (1992) learned that early paradigm pioneers must implement the paradigm change based on faith, because data and results are not yet available to support accepting the paradigm shift. Time and again this phenomenon has proven true when implementing TBM.

There are two levels of the faith factor in TBM. In the beginning of an implementation, many people either believe that the TBM design is unachievable or, in extreme cases, is too "far out" to be worthy of consideration. A first TBM implementation experience usually dispels these concerns. Subsequent activities lead to the next level of faith. Following the initial success, an enthusiasm arises that becomes infectious. The implementers take bolder and bolder steps in planning their next actions or fine tuning the existing ones. Linkages are planned even tighter, in process inspectors are planned out before one hundred percent quality is achieved, housekeeping takes on a new meaning, and technical support staff seek out front-line operators' advice and experience. Peer pressure often encourages the isolation and potential departure of anyone who is not converted. Change in the TBM company must be proactively managed to sustain the second faith level.

THE TBM ORGANIZATION SHOULD MIRROR THE PSS FLOW

Time-based manufacturing requires rapid response to problems. Matrix organizations, where technical support personnel do not report directly to operations, are ineffective in a TBM environment. At a minimum, support activities such as cost accounting, manufacturing and quality engineering, order entry and scheduling, and maintenance should report directly to PSS management. Support functions should be physically moved to the front lines where they are immediately accessible and can contribute to solutions for continuous improvement. This structure has additional benefits. It tends to flatten the organization for faster communication; it directly assigns support personnel to products, which is consistent with activity-based costing (ABC) accounting principles; it assures direct accountability for continuous improvement; and it makes certain that technical support is always available throughout the entire PSS flow.

TBM SIGNIFICANTLY CHANGES MANAGEMENT'S ROLE

As companies embark upon the TBM journey, they rapidly discover problems or impediments that they never knew they had. It is management's responsibility to prioritize the problems and assign specific teams to determine the root cause and implement corrective action. They must encourage creativity rather than inhibit it by not insisting that they themselves always play a direct role. These managers must now gain satisfaction by assuring that problems are solved by other people and not by themselves (sometimes this is difficult to accept for the individual trained as an engineer). Managers now have more time to do the tasks that they should be doing, i.e., managing and planning for the future direction and improvement.

Middle management should no longer spend hours filling out reports and assigning jobs. They should roam the front lines supporting their direct, value-added activities. Some managers are initially uncomfortable in this role. They must learn that they cannot manage via paper because paper must all but disappear in the high-visibility, quick-response environment of TBM.

TBM REQUIRES STRONGER ORGANIZATION SKILLS

Effective organizations require quality people, ongoing management development, and a work environment that is conducive to high output performance. Well-trained employees are a critical requirement. Today, many companies are not able to hire workers with sufficient education in basic math, reading, and communication skills. Motorola Corporation has taken a proactive approach to solving this problem by creating Motorola U. "We learned that line workers had to actually understand their work and their equipment, that senior management had to exemplify and reinforce new methods and skills if they were going to stick, that change had to be continuous and participative, and that education—not just instruction—was the only way to make all this occur" (Wiggenhorn 1990).

The worker requirements for TBM are drastically different from those needed in traditional production. Workers must change from specialists to generalists, from being reactive to proactive, from competitive to cooperative, and from passive to self-initiative. To accomplish these changes worker training is an absolute must (Chu 1990).

The following five separate but interrelated steps have been identified and are useful for human resources development in TBM organizations (Pearson 1987):

1. Set high performance standards for everyone and keep raising the standards.

2. Develop managers through fresh assignments and job rotation.

3. Adjust every facet of the work environment to facilitate and reward managers' development.

4. Infuse each level of the company with new talent.

5. Use the personnel department as an active agent for change.

SUMMARY

Successful TBM implementers have taken the time up front to plan the entire activity. They let the TBM design drive the implementation activities and the organization dynamics. They have a very different people-oriented value system (see Figure 8-1). They invest in extensive training with the belief that everyone is a real contributor to change and improvement. They believe that professionals can be more productive by allowing a synergy of multidisciplinary group problem solving. Successful TBM implementers realize that once the organization is focused and trained, the best leaders lead by following.

TRADITIONAL VALUES	TBM VALUES
• People are told what to do	• People tell management what they need to succeed
• Work efforts are closely controlled	• People are given clear direction and autonomy
• Management makes decisions, workers carry them out	• Teams make and implement their own decisions
• Stability is the goal	• Improvement is a must
• Departmental specialization is a sign of strength	• Cross-organization teams create breakthrough
• "Great" reactive problem solving	• Proactive process management
• Information is given out on a need to know basis	• Information is widely shared
• Management action is based on single data point results	• Management action is based on trended, data based decisions

Figure 8-1. Traditional versus TBM people values.

MANAGING THROUGH CONTINUOUS IMPROVEMENT TEAMS

The large amount of change brought on by implementing TBM is of two types. First, people's job duties, procedures, and methods of operation change with the TBM paradigm. Second, the volume of work effort required to address the many problems surfaced by TBM practices is more than managers can address. This challenge leads us to seek answers to the question, "How can a company most effectively manage change?" The answer to this question is simple, straightforward, and definitely not easy. It is this: Companies get better, quicker, and more permanent improvements through the use of teams than any other method, (see Figure 8-2). Why is this true? Understanding the answer to this question dates to World War II.

During World War II, psychologist Kurt Lewin and anthropologist Margaret Mead teamed up to find a method to reduce civilian consumption of rationed foods (Weisbord 1987). To obtain this knowledge, they conducted experiments with Iowa housewives by helping them decide, given facts about nutrition and scarcity, what to feed their families. They set up two groups in the experiment. For the first group, a nutritionist was brought in to lecture the housewives on what they should do—a traditional, reasoned exhortation to change. For the second group, the women were given the facts and invited to decide together what to do. From this experiment, Lewin and Mead learned two important facts that directly apply to organization change.

1. When attempting to make a change, we should always look for those people who directly control the situation.

2. We are likely to modify our own behavior when we participate in problem analysis and solutions and we are likely to carry out decisions we have helped make.

Teams provide better, faster, further, and more sustainable improvements than traditional approaches

Figure 8-2. Why use teams?

The decision to manage through teams requires much greater effort on the part of the total organization. Teams are harder to orchestrate, require much more attention to people, and create an entirely different set of challenges for the organization than more traditional methods. Managing through teams requires higher-level human relations skills, such as positive confrontation, communication, facilitation, presentation, and group leadership. These are skills that are generally nonexistent among all but a few members of the traditional organization.

Team management requires managing a diversity of people. Because giving orders without expecting a response is no longer acceptable, understanding cultural, racial, social, and educational differences is critical for the successful attainment of group objectives. In many companies, these issues were largely swept under the rug in times past.

Managing through teams does not mean all of the organization's problems go away; quite the opposite is true. It means that the organization trades a traditional set of problems such as lack of motivation, communication barriers, and lack of skills and knowledge, for a higher-level set of problems when they tackle areas such as resolving differences, individual self-esteem and leadership, and understanding each other.

Four Principles of What Makes Teams Work

Four simple principles have been developed that have differentiated successful team efforts from the many that have failed (Figure 8-3).

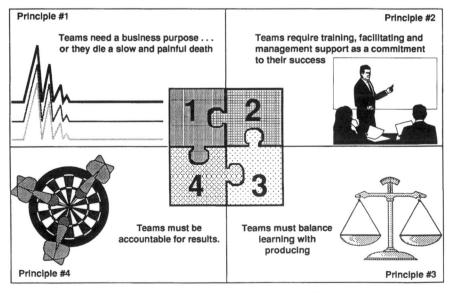

Figure 8-3. Successful team principles.

Principle No. 1. Teams need a business purpose, or they die a slow, painful death. Employee involvement for the purpose of good human relations management in an organization is essentially worthless as the many quality circle failures of the last decade have shown. Without a business purpose, teams sit around, not knowing what to do. They pick irrelevant problems to work on and do not care when they finish. All of this leads to a lack of focus, frustration, cynicism, and ultimately, failure. An organization should only use team management when it is tightly integrated into the business purpose, in this case the TBM vision and design. Why work on problems that, when they are solved, do not matter to the business?

The TBM challenge is to solve more problems, more quickly. The TBM organization needs every last resource working toward solutions that contribute to overall PSS lead time reduction and quality improvement.

Principle No. 2. Teams require training, facilitation, and management support to succeed. When first participating on teams, most team members will not have adequate skills and knowledge to succeed on their own. As team members, they will be asked to lead the group, use basic quality tools to solve problems, create project plans, collect and analyze data, and give presentations. Management must recognize the need to increase employee skills early on so that teams are organized to succeed and not fail.

In addition, early team facilitation is critical to ongoing success. In the past, problem solving for engineers, quality technicians, etc., meant collecting and analyzing data by themselves, getting management approval of their recommendations, and implementing the change by spending little time (thirty minutes or less) with people on the front lines. These technical support personnel must now grow into group members, leaders, and facilitators, where their people skills take on more importance than their technical skills.

Principle No. 3. Teams must balance learning with producing. The team paradigm suggests that time spent on improving organizational learning and skills development is as productive as time spent making and delivering products. This introduces the need to balance each requirement and the need to have adequate resources to commit to both. No longer will it be acceptable to avoid training because of never having time. The TBM organization should think about committing up to twenty percent of all employees' time to increased learning and skills development. While this seems quite high, in a relatively short time the overall organization resource needs are less than those using more traditional methods. This happens because employees are more highly skilled and have more flexibility to move among duties and to assume more individual responsibility.

Principle No. 4. Teams must be accountable for results. People often talk about the use of teams in the context of focusing on the process. A process focus is important, but it alone is not enough. Team management is not the abdication of accountability. Many teams have failed because management did not push them for results. The perception that expecting strong results would hurt team morale at a sensitive time developed somehow. This perception cannot be accepted. Management must get results from the team efforts because that is the way the organization runs its business. Teams that have a business purpose, a clear linkage to overall PSS improvement, and a focused line of accountability are powerful tools for the TBM paradigm.

TBM IMPLEMENTATION THROUGH TEAMS

The synergy of effective team efforts is the force that makes the whole greater than the sum of its individual parts. For example, a sports team composed of the top players in the nation may still be beaten by individuals who are less talented but function as a team. All of the players might even be superstars, but if they are not supporting and assisting one another, they are not performing up to their full potential as a team.

And so it is in work group teams. Effective teams do not just happen. An effective continuous improvement team, like a well-coached basketball team, is achieved through awareness, leadership, and effort. The synergistic results of team effectiveness will provide the following results (Coopers & Lybrand 1988).

- *Greater knowledge of quality and lead time problems and improved information resources*—Even when a person knows more about a process than anyone else, the limited and unique information from others can fill important gaps. There is simply more information, experience, and competencies in a team than in any one of its members.

- *Greater variety of problem-solving approaches*—Each person brings a different background of work experience and perspective to the problem. These differences can open avenues of opportunities beyond the awareness of any single individual. In addition, individuals can get into thinking ruts or patterned ways of defining problems and approaching issues. Using all team members expands the number of ways a particular problem can be approached and solved.

- *Increased acceptance*—When a solution is reached, two additional problems still remain: persuading others to accept the solution and carrying it out. When more individuals have an active part in the decision-making process, they have increased ownership of the outcome and enhanced responsibility for making the solution successful.

People management and the use of teams to improve performance can best be summarized by this statement by John J. Cotter (1991).

People need to be clear about the goals of the business and how they can contribute to achieving these goals. They need to know what to do, how to do it, and to understand their role and the roles of others. They need proper tools, skills and information. They need to be held accountable for their actions, get prompt, supportive feedback on their performance, and have a stake in the outcomes the business achieves. They need to trust those they work with, and be trusted in return. They need to feel safe and secure, and have a role in influencing decisions that affect them. They need to be challenged, empowered, and encouraged to make a difference.

Check how the organization stacks up against this list. Ask your employees how they view their world. Find the gaps, and act together to close them. It's simple, it's basic, it isn't necessarily easy, but it works.

TBM ORGANIZATION FOR CONTINUOUS IMPROVEMENT

Time-based manufacturing execution has no line reporting relationships. Rather, it is a hierarchical structure for problem definition and solution. This structure is intended to drive the TBM implementation, solve TBM generated problems, address TBM surfaced issues, fix accountability for results, and ensure company-wide involvement. Three distinct levels within the TBM organization are summarized in the following sections:

EXECUTIVE COMMITTEE

This group of top-level managers is usually composed of the CEO, function heads, and the TBM coordinator. Its overall role is to provide direction and leadership to the continuous implementation of TBM. More specifically, it defines policy, allocates resources, reviews and amends (if appropriate) TBM priorities, appoints and supervises the TBM coordinator, and approves expenditures that are consistent with the TBM design. Finally, the executive committee prioritizes and assigns specific problems requiring solution to task groups.

TASK GROUPS

The majority of all breakthrough improvements come from the efforts of task groups. Every element of TBM (changeover reduction, quality improvement, reliability, etc.) has a specific methodology for developing breakthroughs. These methodologies are learned and applied by task groups. The task group is charged by the executive committee with a specific goal, for example, to reduce the changeover time on a machine from one hour to fifteen minutes. The group then works toward the solution until the goal is consistently achieved. Once this happens, the group either disbands or is given another task by the executive committee.

A task group is a multidisciplined team usually composed of several front-line managers and employees familiar with the problem area, technical support professionals, and a facilitator who instructs in the methodology and facilitates meetings. A task group usually meets once or twice a week for up to two hours.

CONTINUOUS IMPROVEMENT TEAMS*

Improvements in lead time reduction and quality are made by focusing the efforts of continuous improvement teams (CIT) on single, identifiable problems. This concentrated effort continues until a problem is resolved. This focused approach to problem solving provides lasting solutions rather than temporary repairs. Specifically, the functions and responsibilities of a CIT include the following:

- studying a process to understand its current performance
- identifying the major problem areas of poor quality, long lead time, and poor reliability
- selecting one specific project to work on
- determining what approach or course of action to employ
- collecting data as required to identify symptoms and specific causes
- preparing solutions, recommendations, or both to the process
- implementing necessary changes in the process to affect needed improvements
- installing process controls for holding the gains

STEPS IN STRUCTURING AND IMPLEMENTING

A continuous improvement team should exist for each process in the PSS. In some cases, two or more processes are so closely related in the PSS that a common crossover team is more desirable than two or three separate

---

* (Coopers & Lybrand 1988)

teams. This should be done carefully, however, as the team may become so large or cover so many different processes that it becomes ineffective. The executive committee defines and initiates the CITs and identifies team leaders who should work with the organizations involved in the chosen process to determine the appropriate team structure. As processes, problems, or both change, so can the structure of the teams.

The CITs typically consist of first-line managers and employees who work the process being studied, product/process engineers, quality engineers, and other support staff assigned to a given area. Other employees (e.g., from maintenance, laboratory, product development, and cost accounting) may become either temporary or permanent team members. This decision is made by the team as various problems are encountered.

DUTIES OF THE TEAM LEADER

Team leadership means sharing leadership responsibility with all team members and guiding the team to the achievement of the goal. The power of the team comes from the active participation and interaction of its members. As the team works toward its goal, a collaborative team effort is essential. The team leader must assume many responsibilities during this process, including:

- scheduling meetings (choosing the meeting room, notifying members of time and place, and inviting management and other team leaders that may have input or interest)

- publishing and distributing agenda and minutes

- using resources (being aware of training available, using team member expertise, interfacing with other CITs, and acquiring other available technical assistance)

- guiding the team to become an effective problem-solving unit

- reporting on team performance by publishing results and notifying the executive committee of team efforts and achievements

In addition, the team leader's most critical responsibility is to lead and facilitate the team to the successful attainment of the CIT goals. This requirement is a very difficult and important one, and it is often misunderstood and underestimated in terms of complexity and difficulty.

Successfully leading teams begins with an understanding of the four stages of team development (Scholtes 1988).

1. *Forming* involves creating the team as people go from being individuals to team members. They typically move cautiously as they try to find their role and feel their way around for acceptable behavior.

2. *Storming* is when the team experiences the difficulties of group problem solving. They become impatient about the lack of progress, and argue, challenge, and resist against using a systematic approach to improving processes. This is the most difficult and frustrating stage for the team.

3. *Norming* is when team members begin to reconcile differences and competing personal agendas to come together. Conflict starts to give way to cooperation as team members accept the team purpose, their roles, and the common group objectives.

4. *Performing* is the stage where the team members become productive. They begin collecting data, diagnosing problems, and generating solutions. Team members better understand each other at this stage and work together as an effective, cohesive unit.

Managing the team through the treacherous four stages of development is the team leader's role. This involves a delicate mix of cajoling, confronting, coddling, and asserting. A poorly led CIT will get equally poor results. Selection of CIT leaders should be taken very seriously and should only include the organization's best people. In many ways, CIT leaders form the engine that drives the TBM organization.

TEAM MEETINGS

The team should meet regularly once each week, or every other week, depending upon conditions of the job. Meetings should be more frequent in the early stages of the effort while the process is being closely studied. It is seldom necessary to meet more often than twice a week. It is not advisable, even on a well-controlled process, to have meetings less often than once every other week.

A well-organized agenda is vital to meeting effectiveness. A prepared agenda helps the team avoid unnecessary time lags during the course of the meeting. When provided to the attending members in advance, it serves to notify each member of their role during the meeting. The effective agenda will function to:

- visually and clearly depict the goals and content of the next meeting

- provide awareness to each team member and visitors of their responsibility during the meeting

- present a visual means of communicating the meeting purpose to other CITs and members of management

- effectively direct team efforts toward the completion of critical tasks both during and between meetings

- help the team to keep the meeting brief (ideally one hour or less) and to the point

The keeping of accurate and correct minutes is a vital link in an effective functioning CIT. While the agenda functions as a guide to where the team is going, the minutes show where the team has been. The minutes show the team's achievements by providing a record of what used to be, what is, and what is going to be. This comparison of team progress is very difficult if accurate records are not kept as the team moves toward its goal. CIT minutes should contain the following:

- who attended the meeting
- what items were covered
- the current status of each item
- what actions are to be taken on the item
- who has responsibility for each action item
- when action is expected to be taken

The minutes of each meeting should be distributed to those affected by and interested in the team progress. Items being acted upon by the team should be assigned target dates and reviewed each week until resolved. At the start of each meeting, the minutes from the previous meeting should be reviewed. Based on what has transpired since the last meeting, action items should be closed or updated. After the item is resolved, it should appear on the minutes one more time and show completed or closed as the status.

PROBLEM-SOLVING TOOLS

As the CIT goes through the steps of process improvement, it should use several proven problem-solving tools. These tools, presented in Chapter 6, are the basic quality tools and they enable the CIT to visualize the process, detect problems and their causes, and find solutions. The first tool, the flow chart, is a diagram of the step-by-step progression of a process. Two types of flow charts that prove effective in solving problems are process flow-charts and work-flow diagrams. The process flow chart details all the steps in a process. The CIT should be able to use this flow chart to see where the process gets off track. The work-flow diagram is a picture that shows the movements of people, material, and information in a process. The CIT can generate these flow charts by tracing the movements onto a floor plan sketch. The pictorial presentation is effective in uncovering problems in the process.

Another effective tool is the fish bone diagram which provides the CIT with a structured method of performing cause-and-effect analysis. The fish bone diagram has a problem listed on the right side of the diagram and a large horizontal arrow that points to it. Branches fan out from this main arrow and represent groups of causes for the problem. Typical groupings are materials, methods, people, equipment, and environment. The CIT may choose different groups, however, depending on the problem. Sub-branches fan out from these main branches representing additional supporting causes. The CIT then asks questions about these causes. For example, how do the materials used cause slow response time to service calls? Are the right parts available? Are the right tools available? Furthermore, why are the right parts not available? Have they arrived from the vendor yet? Has manufacturing produced them yet? By asking questions about each of the groups, the CIT identifies the causes of the problem and works to eliminate them.

Finally, the Pareto chart, is useful for illustrating the biggest causes of a problem. A Pareto chart is a prioritized histogram; the Y-axis of the chart shows the impact of the causes, and the X-axis lists the causes in descending order of impact. The measure of the impact could be frequency, dollar value, or whatever variable the CIT feels appropriate. By showing the impact in descending order, the largest problems become obvious. Pareto charts are valuable throughout the life of the project. Early on they highlight the most critical problems, later they identify which causes of a problem to address. Other tools available include check sheets, control charts, histograms, and scatter diagrams.

CONTINUOUS IMPROVEMENT THROUGH THE TEAM APPROACH*

There are many different team methodologies that companies use today. While each of these is slightly different, they all contain the same tools, components, and basic work steps. The CIT approach uses a nine-step problem-solving method that contains these same tools and components (see Figure 8-4).

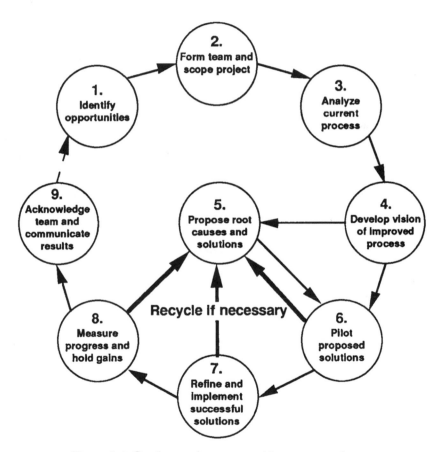

Figure 8-4. Continuous improvement team approach.

---

* Coopers & Lybrand 1988.

STEP 1: IDENTIFY OPPORTUNITIES

Continuous improvement team projects should integrate tightly into the statistical process control approach outlined in Chapter 6 (see Figure 8-5). Process improvement priorities are driven by PSS opportunities to improve performance in lead time reduction and quality. CITs should work to improve processes that:

• have a positive impact on customers
• have a high probability for success
• contribute significantly to overall PSS performance improvement
• have high visibility (especially early on)
• are measurable and controllable
• have a clear starting and ending point

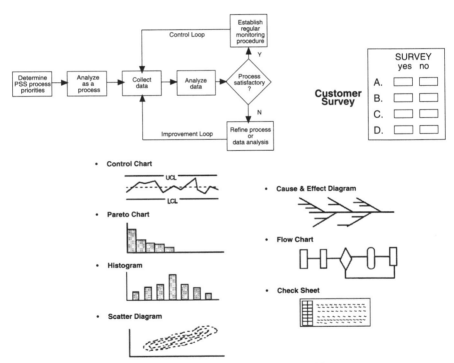

Figure 8-5. Step 1: identify opportunities.

STEP 2: FORM A TEAM AND SCOPE PROJECT

Once a project is identified, the CIT should determine and involve the appropriate people who can contribute to process improvements. The team should develop a simple and concise mission statement. This mission statement should include an understanding of the beginning and ending activities of the process under study, who the customer is, who the suppliers are, how progress will be measured, and timing (see Figure 8-6).

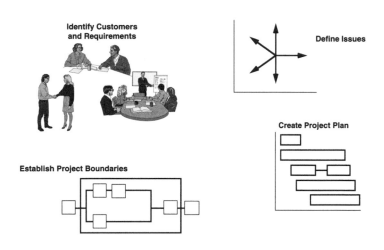

Figure 8-6. Step 2: Form a team and scope project.

STEP 3: ANALYZE THE CURRENT PROCESS

Analyzing the current process forces the CIT to understand how the process actually works versus the common perception. Often, this step highlights glaring problems that are fairly easy to correct. The CIT should create a process map to define process boundaries, flowchart the process, and diagram its physical and information workflow. Additionally, the team must understand how the process should work (see Figure 8-7). By comparing the "as is" to the "should be," the CIT can determine where the process goes wrong and often make quick and simple improvements.

The first step to process improvement is understanding whether or not the process is in control. Process control can be measured in the following way:

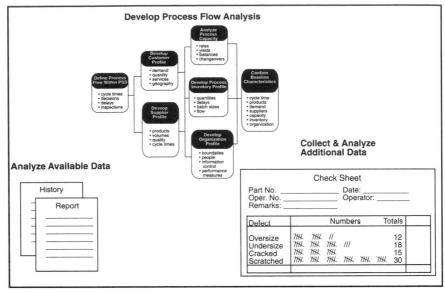

Figure 8-7. Step 3: Analyze the current process.

1. define the process
2. determine the process parameters (reliability, control charts, yields, etc.)
3. collect the appropriate process data
4. conduct SPC studies

Once the process is in control, the team is responsible for process improvement to assure reduced lead times and optimum quality and reliability at minimum costs. This involves continually evaluating all phases of the process and obtaining answers to the following questions:

• Is the process operating in the most effective manner?
• Is redundancy a problem somewhere in the process?
• Are unnecessary jobs being done?
• Is there a better way to perform the existing job(s)?
• Where in the process are wasted efforts or unnecessary costs?

All team decisions and actions must be supported by accurate and relevant data. Accurate and reliable on-the-job data collection is necessary to monitor, evaluate, and control the process. The team's purpose for collecting data may vary with the area and the process being examined. The aim of data collection should be:

- to assist in understanding the process—how much variation exists from product-to-product and how many products are good or bad
- for analysis—to determine the relationship between a defect and its cause.
- for throughput—to understand the process rate, reliability, and volume of inputs and demand for outputs
- for process control—to monitor the process to determine whether or not it is in statistical control

The data must pertain to the process. Since processes vary in nature, the team may need to collect several types of data. Data types include:
- measurement data: enumerate data (resistance, length, etc.)
- countable data: enumerate data (number of defects, percent defective)
- data on relative merits: good, better, best

Data will reveal the facts about the process; therefore, data collection's purpose should be to resolve one particular problem, or to monitor one particular process characteristic.

Random samples of a product provide data that can be considered representative of the total product. Sampling is useful when data are to be collected on a large population of items. Examining the entire population is not usually desirable or necessary. In many cases, it becomes time consuming and costly. In addition, some products cannot be examined or tested without being destroyed.

The team should take samples from the process to determine the conditions of the process (monitor the process), to determine the ability and capacity of the process (process capability), and to obtain data for action (data to help locate and solve a problem). Before the sampling can take place, the team must determine that they know the purpose of the sample, select the most representative samples from the population, and establish what characteristics (type of defect, shift, operator, etc.) will be examined and recorded.

When the data type and sampling method have been established, the next step is data collection. The data collection itself should be done in a way that simplifies later analysis. When collecting data, the reason and nature of the data should be recorded. The data should be classified into defect groups and should include a list of key characteristics of the item and time the observation was made. Many tabulation devices are available to assist in data collection. The methods of collecting data most often used are check sheets, concentration diagrams, and computerized data entry devices.

The current process analysis should result in the complete team understanding of the following process characteristics:

• total activities, including value-added versus nonvalue-added steps
• lead time
• first run yield
• reliability
• level of process control and process capability
• customer requirements
• supplier capabilities
• process demand profile and capacity requirements
• inventory
• cost

STEP 4: DEVELOP VISION OF IMPROVED PROCESS

Once the CIT understands the current situation, it can develop a vision of the new process and set goals for improvement (see Figure 8-8). This vision comes from the development of a "to be" process map that addresses the opportunities discovered through the current process analysis. The key to generating the "to be" vision is in understanding the key process drivers that have the greatest leverage for improvement of that process. Each process will have different key drivers that contribute to breakthroughs. Improvement goals set by the "to be" vision must support the process performance levels necessary to achieve the PSS requirements for throughput, reliability, first run yield, and process capability.

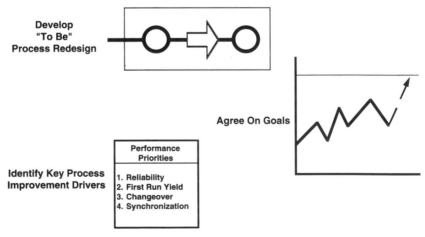

Figure 8-8. Step 4: Develop vision of improved process.

STEP 5: PROPOSE ROOT CAUSES AND SOLUTIONS

Complex and ineffective processes are error prone. The CIT must initially isolate where errors are occurring in the process and determine their root causes. This is achieved by using the seven basic quality tools discussed in Chapter 6. The CIT must then propose to either change the current method and procedure or develop new ones that reduce the likelihood for error. Stopping at this point, however, would not promote continuous improvement. The CIT must promote a mindset that constantly detects errors and eliminates them immediately (see Figure 8-9).

The CIT also seeks to eliminate waste in the process. Waste is costly and often covers other problems. The CIT should scrutinize the value of each step in the process and its level of performance. Are the steps necessary or are they the result of other performance problems in the process? If the step does not add value, then it likely exists because of some upstream problem. The CIT must determine the root cause of this performance problem and seek to improve it.

Finally, the CIT seeks to reduce variation in the process. The more variable a process is, the more inefficient it is likely to be. Therefore, employees either take extra time or add extra steps to address these inefficiencies. By reducing variation, the CIT can reduce the time or number of steps in a process and simplify it. To reduce variation, its sources must be located and analyzed. Then the CIT should identify and separate

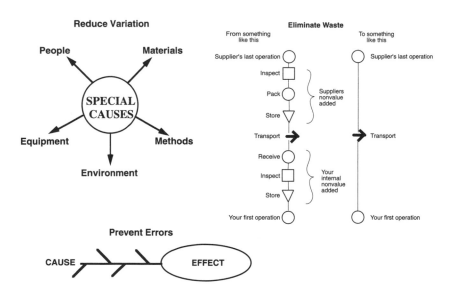

Figure 8-9. Step 5: Propose root causes and solutions.

common cause and special cause variation, eliminating the special causes of variation first.

STEP 6: PILOT PROPOSED SOLUTIONS

After theorizing solutions, the CIT must pilot those solutions that the team feels are most likely to improve the process. This is a step of testing the waters to see if team recommendations yield the expected results. Piloting is a method used to implement a proposed change on a small scale to study results before attempting a broader scale implementation (see Figure 8-10). By piloting change, a CIT can evaluate whether a solution yields the expected results , what the likely causes are if results are different, and the extent to which a solution should be adopted on a broader scale. Piloting a solution is also an effective method to facilitate positive change, as demonstrable results are always more powerful than yet unrealized expectations. The idea here is to think of decisions as experiments; piloting is the method of experimenting to achieve improvement.

STEP 7: REFINE AND IMPLEMENT SUCCESSFUL SOLUTIONS

As the CIT pilots solutions, it moves toward making continuous improvement a part of the new process. It implements changes using the plan-do-check-act philosophy (Deming 1982) as shown in Figure 8-11. In the *plan* phase, the CIT must consider who the change will affect, when to imple-

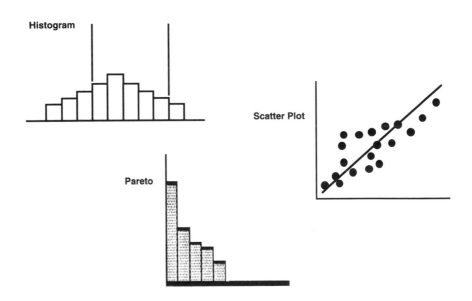

Figure 8-10. Step 6: Pilot proposed solutions.

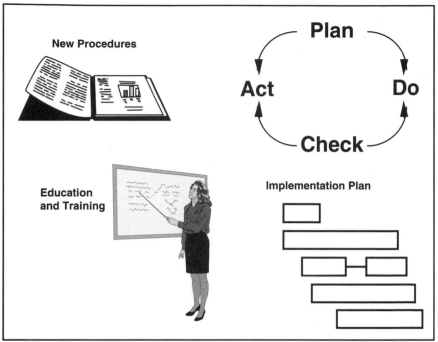

Figure 8-11. Step 7: Refine and implement successful solutions.

ment, how to measure, etc. In the *do* phase, the CIT must train the right people and then implement the change. During the *check* phase, the CIT monitors the impact of the change and checks for any side effects or differences from the plan. In the *act* phase, the CIT fine-tunes the changes according to the data collected, adopts the solution, and standardizes the new methods and procedures into new operating practices.

STEP 8: MEASURE PROGRESS AND HOLD GAINS

As the CIT progresses through the improvement process, it should constantly evaluate gains made relative to the original team goals set in Step 4 and the level of improvement necessary to support PSS performance objectives. The measures used to evaluate process improvement should be standard across the entire CIT organization structure. These measures should include the following (see Figure 8-12).
• lead time
• first run yield
• process control and capability
• reliability
• cost
• inventory

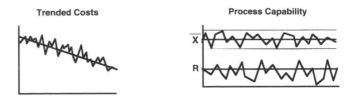

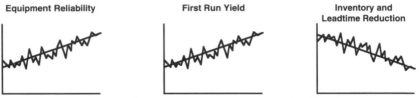

Figure 8-12. Step 8: Measure progress and hold gains.

By using standard CIT measures, the TBM organization can create a common understanding of what is important to the overall organization success. Teams members can also move across different team activities and quickly understand the various levels of process performance in the PSS.

STEP 9: ACKNOWLEDGE THE TEAM AND COMMUNICATE RESULTS

Providing the right consequences (i.e., positive reinforcement) is an absolute must to CIT successes in the TBM organization. A great solution not installed is worthless (Scharf 1983). The TBM company, therefore, must reward, celebrate, and communicate positive team accomplishments. Celebrating CIT successes involves addressing four questions (Dingus and Justice 1989):

1. What has been achieved?
2. Why is it important?
3. How did the team do it?
4. What is the best way to positively reinforce these improvements to sustain and even accelerate improvement?

Fueling the team fire is the method for continued success of the TBM initiative. Time-based manufacturing leadership absolutely cannot communicate progress too often or too loudly (see Figure 8-13). Staying close to the people on the front line by hearing their voices, meeting their needs, and rewarding their successes is truly the road map to the new TBM paradigm.

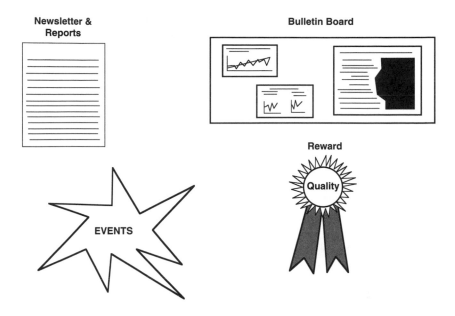

Figure 8-13. Step 9: Acknowledge the team and communicate results.

REFERENCES

Barker, J. 1992. *Future Edge.* New York: William Morrow and Co.

Chu, E. K. M. 1990. Worker requirements for just-in-time production. *International IE Conference Proceedings.* Norcross, GA: Institute of Industrial Engineers. 411-16.

Coopers & Lybrand. 1988. *Integrated Quality: Quality Improvement Teams.* New York: Coopers & Lybrand.

Cotter, J. J. 1991. Improving employee performance at work. *The Work Design News.* 1(March): 1.

Deming, W. E. 1982. *Out of the Crisis.* Cambridge, MA: Massachusetts Institute of Technology.

Dingus, V. R. and R. E. Justice. 1989. Celebrating quality. *Quality Progress.* November: 74-75.

Pearson, A. E. 1987. Muscle-build the organization. *Harvard Business Review*. July-August: 49-55.

Scharf, A. 1983. Making workshop teams effective. *International IE Conference Proceedings*. Norcross, GA: Institute of Industrial Engineers. 373-81.

Scholtes, Peter. 1988. *The Team Handbook*. Madison, WI: Joiner Associates Inc.

Weisbord, Marvin R. 1987. *Productive Workplaces*. San Francisco: Jossey Bass Inc.

Wiggenhorn, William. 1990. Motorola U: When training becomes an education. *Harvard Business Review*. July-August: 71-83.

Information Management and Time-Based Manufacturing 9

INFORMATION is the time-based manufacturing (TBM) integrator. Time-based manufacturing requires the availability throughout the organization of information that is relevant, accurate, and timely. This information "boost" can lead the TBM company to a sustainable competitive advantage. The information revolution is affecting competition in three vital ways (Porter and Miller 1985).

1. It changes industry structure and, in so doing, alters the rules of competition.
2. It creates competitive advantage by giving companies new ways to outperform their rivals.
3. It spawns whole new businesses, often from within a company's existing operations.

An organization's capabilities are greatly enhanced by a computerized management information system (MIS). For TBM, an effective MIS is an absolute requirement. Every work activity in TBM has both information and physical components that must be linked together. A broad TBM initiative cannot be implemented without a MIS focused on specific, breakthrough time compression elements. In general, the MIS is an automated system that presents information, both internal and external to the business, that aids in making a defined and specific set of decisions. The purpose of the MIS is to aid decision making and not just to automate the decision making process (Martin and Shell 1988).

Several incorrect assumptions are commonly made that often account for the failure of MIS projects, including those associated with TBM. The first incorrect assumption is that most managers and workers suffer from a lack of relevant information. Although there is some truth to this, it is more common that they suffer from too much irrelevant information. In the TBM environment, it is important to initially eliminate the overwhelming irrelevant information and then focus on providing relevant, necessary information. The second assumption is that the MIS should be based on information that managers and workers perceive they need. Many people do not understand the "vital" information needed for decision-making situations and often ask for more information than necessary. By doing this, they play it safe. Any analysis to develop the information system required for TBM should start with the decision process, and the MIS should be a support system specifically focused on that process. A third incorrect assumption is that if a manager or worker has all the information needed, decision making will improve. This assumption has been proven incorrect many times, as individuals often misuse valid data. The last erroneous assumption is that people do not have to understand how the information system works before using it. If this is true, they will probably lack confidence in the system and it will provide little real value to them (Martin and Shell 1988).

A few fundamental management decisions must be considered when designing and developing an MIS for TBM. First, the best systems design approach is one that specifies only the needed results. This provides flexibility for people working together to design and implement a system to achieve those desired results. The second consideration is to identify only the most vital information and data needs for the organization. Finally, the MIS must be cost-justified and cost-effective. The information system design and implementation must be completed by competent MIS managers and users who are well informed in the organization's TBM policies along with the appropriate use of computer technology to support the total system (Martin and Shell 1988).

MANAGEMENT INFORMATION SYSTEMS IN A TBM ORGANIZATION

High-quality information systems can provide a strong infrastructure for the competitive TBM organization. The design of these systems largely dictates how the organization operates. Because information is one of the most influential sources of power in a company, cultures frequently grow up around the MIS as managers learn to take the available information and use it to further career success. Information systems reflect what top management sees as most important to the organization's performance. This can be seen in the management reports generated, the data that are captured, and in the use of available information in management decision making. The design of an MIS can greatly facilitate an organization's achievement of its vision and goals, or it can literally make that achievement impossible. Understanding this point is critical to achieving breakthrough performance improvement.

How MIS Differ in TBM

Information systems play a vital role in the TBM company. However, the TBM company's use of information systems differs from the traditional manufacturing organization and its use of information.

Information systems are simpler. The TBM company relies heavily on the idea of process simplification first, automation second. This comes from experience with information systems over the past twenty years. A complex process usually requires a sophisticated, computerized solution. A highly sophisticated solution usually does not work well with large groups of people. Simple is manageable. Simple is better. Simple works. For example, in the traditional manufacturing resource planning (MRPII) implementation, it is not unusual to create a bill of material structure that contains six to ten levels. The many levels are necessary to coincide with the functional plant layouts and disintegrated product flows. In this case, the information system simply mirrors the physical flow. The typical TBM company has streamlined its product flows such that only one to three levels are usually needed in the bill of material structure. The fewer levels needed, the simpler the product structure is to manage. The simpler the product structure, the more basic are the information systems required to support it.

Information systems are focused on the key leverage processes in the PSS. When undergoing the TBM transformation, different areas of importance come forward as the key leverage processes for overall PSS performance improvement. This is in sharp contrast to the traditional view, which is functional and departmental. By looking at total cycle time and its relation to information flow and physical flow, the need for information systems improvement moves dramatically forward in certain areas and takes a back seat in others. For example, in traditional manufacturing, detailed shop floor data collection systems for labor reporting and cost accounting are highly valued for the depth of information and control they provide. These systems are also usually considered very difficult to implement. This difficulty comes from the complexity and added efforts required to achieve system integrity due to the high volume of data and transactions. Many companies have implemented bar code systems to manage these high transaction volumes.

In contrast to the situation above, in TBM the need for detailed capturing of labor data goes away. In fact, the bar code system, so highly valued in a traditional environment, could get in the way of performance improvement in the TBM company. How could this happen? By bar coding every material move and transaction, workers can spend more time using the bar code system (nonvalue-adding) than making product. Instead of labor reporting, the TBM company would likely invest the same information system efforts in first run yield measurement, or in improving equipment reliability.

Better still, the TBM company could invest those resources to improve customer order management by reducing order lead time. Both of these focus areas represent a large departure from the traditional mindset.

Information systems are used to create speed. In another major departure from tradition, the TBM company views the information system as a means of compressing cycle times versus the traditional view of improving productivity. In taking this view, system priorities frequently change for the overall PSS. We have seen several companies where material flowed through the PSS faster than information did. For example, many companies use manufacturing work orders that are entered into the information system once per day and updated overnight. Using this method guarantees that the overall lead time will not be shorter in days than the number of work centers that the product must pass through. By holding up the product to the progression of a single work center per day, the "sophisticated" information system actually slows down product throughput. Time and again, companies have seen information systems negatively affect cycle times.

Information systems supply a few key elements of information. Much of the wait time created by information systems comes from the timing of transaction updates to the host computer. This delay is most often found in the area of customer order management and inventory management. Companies have often invested millions of dollars in information systems technology, only to offer inventory status information to its managers and workers that is between two and five days out of date. Managing in a TBM environment is nearly impossible when critical information needs, such as customer order visibility and inventory status, go unmet through outdated information flows. Time-based manufacturing companies need only a few key elements of information, but they need them to be accurate and available in real time.

Information systems use integrated data. A key element to the successful implementation of TBM is the visibility of the same information up and down the PSS. The more information available to each component of the PSS, the less filtering there is by each level to "interpret" customer needs for the next stage in the PSS flow. The elimination of these "interpretation" filters allows the entire PSS to synchronize and supply products to the same customer requirements. In this way, taking out complexity (i.e., PSS filtering) allows the entire PSS to operate in a greatly streamlined manner. An integrated database of key information is the building block for supply system improvement.

Information systems are built around a process/system orientation. Most organizations have "functional silos," where communication and information barriers exist between departments. As a major element to breaking down these silos, information systems in the TBM company are reconfigured to manage across organizational boundaries through process flows. Ultimately this process flow orientation comes together to form the overall PSS flow. The reorganization of information is a major contributor to the breaking down of barriers and to the management of a whole new set of organizational initiatives. To achieve this, information systems are used as enabling technologies to link across organizational boundaries and to support product and process flows by working toward the key PSS performance improvements.

THREE IMPORTANT FLOWS IN ANY PSS

When evaluating the cycle time of a PSS, three interconnected, and usually not well understood, flows determine the overall cycle time performance of the system.

Customer order flow. The customer order flow cycle time is the time beginning with the placement of the customer's order with the company and ending with the receipt of the ordered product at the customer's location. This is the time typically seen by the customer as the company's ability to deliver product.

Material flow. The material flow cycle time begins with the placement of a company purchase order with the raw material supplier and ends with the receipt of the finished product shipped to the customer. This is the actual time required by a company to move material through the entire product supply system continuum.

PSS information flow. The PSS information flow cycle time begins with the development of the high-level production plan (usually twelve months out) and ends with the receipt of finished product shipped to the customer. This flow of information moves alongside activities through the PSS. The PSS information flow can have a substantial impact—both positive and negative—on the timing of material flow.

Examples. Each of these flows plays an important role in the lead time of the PSS. For example, if the company produces in a make-to-stock finished goods inventory environment, the customer may only see lead times of five days or less (the customer order flow lead time), while material flow lead times would likely be dramatically higher. As another example, the process time for material flow through five production operations could be one hour while the PSS information system could require one day per work order transaction, which would require five days of total lead time. In this case, the PSS information lead time would control the material flow lead time and dictate the overall lead time.

Summary

As previously stated, the goal of TBM is to execute the PSS lead time (a combination of material flow and PSS information flow) in less time than the expected customer order flow lead time. Doing this allows the PSS to supply all products directly to customer order without finished goods inventory. The three PSS flows are compared graphically in Figure 9-1.

THE ROLE OF MRPII IN TBM

Manufacturing resource planning is a computerized method of planning a company's resources to manufacture products, including scheduling of people, production equipment, vendors, and inventory. It is a computer-driven planning and control system that uses the "push" system to plan and execute production based on forecasted demand. Conversely, TBM relies heavily on the use of the "pull" system, which initiates production as a reaction to actual demand (Karmarker 1989).

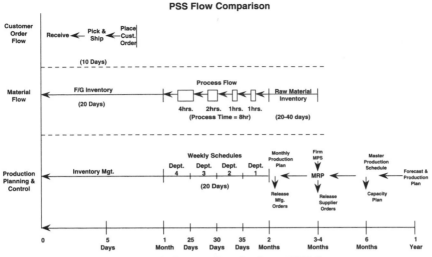

Figure 9-1. Understanding the three PSS flows.

The basic objectives of MRPII stress organization, planning, discipline, and control usually in the form of extensive planning, monitoring, and feedback systems. When answering the basic TBM question as to whether an activity adds value or cost, MRPII systems are technically not necessary. In fact, some TBM purists have been known to recommend that MRPII systems should be thrown out and not used at all. Purists assume that products and corresponding processes can be simplified to knowing the overall demand, calculating the PSS throughput rate, rationalizing people with activities, and making product. If all manufacturing planning and control processes were that simple, MRPII would never have been justified (Edwards and Wheeler 1987).

In reality, no TBM company is ever completely managed by the pull system. MRPII almost always plays a role in manufacturing, especially where lead times are long and process flows are complex. When looking at MRPII's push philosophy versus TBM's pull, the following statement may best sum it up: "A little push, a little pull ... we'll get there."

THE MRPII/TBM STRATEGY*

The best information system for TBM is a hybrid consisting of MRPII and pull scheduling. In general, MRPII is best suited for long-term planning while pull scheduling should be used for executing daily operations (Karmarker 1989, Bose and Welch 1991).

---

*The remaining sections in this chapter are adapted from Edwards and Wheeler 1987.

With the dramatic reduction in lead times and batch sizes that a time-based manufacturer delivers, the role of MRPII is altered significantly as a planning and execution tool. In TBM, the planning effort becomes more oriented to capacity and resource planning, rather than product availability. Furthermore, due to the customer order visibility of a TBM environment, many MRPII functions are no longer necessary. Specific examples of what can happen follow.

Traditionally, the approach in an MRPII environment is to create a production plan for a family of products, a master schedule for individual items within this family, and department production schedules (including final assembly) to produce what is desired. The final assembly schedule is often a part of the master schedule.

In a pure TBM environment, the master scheduling function may not be needed. Because of short manufacturing lead times, the customer schedule is driven directly by customer orders, thereby eliminating the need for a master schedule. The entire planning process can be handled by a combination of production planning for PSS capacity and a daily schedule for customer orders. With extremely short supply lead times, both manufacturing scheduling and material withdrawal can be handled by pull signals. Shop floor control systems used by MRPII become unnecessary within this TBM environment because of increased visibility, short lead times, focused flow, and the built-in priority of pull signals.

The TBM goal is to streamline MRPII planning and execution to the absolute minimum, eliminating as much paperwork and corresponding delay as possible. As a point of comparison, the following two flow diagrams highlight the shift in emphasis between an MRPII environment and a TBM environment.

Figure 9-2 shows the traditional MRPII planning and control system flow where an extensive demand management system is interfaced with the supply management system through successive levels of production planning, master scheduling, material requirements planning (MRP) and shop floor scheduling. The figure implies that finished goods inventory is used to buffer demand and supply.

In Figure 9-2, MRPII functions are shown as a matrix. The matrix is divided horizontally into planning and execution activities, and further divided vertically into demand, supply, and capacity elements. The planning elements of MRPII are all vital to the success of any manufacturing strategy. In fact, U.S. efforts started in the late 1950s to provide computer-based information support have developed highly sophisticated computerized functions such as order entry, forecasting, production planning, distribution planning, capacity planning, and master scheduling.

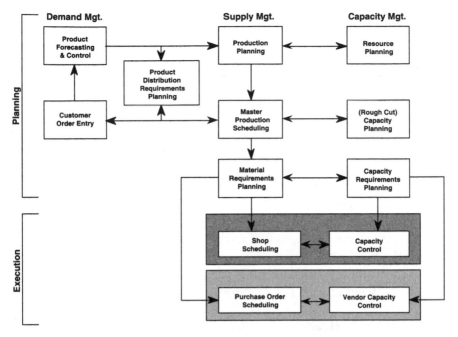

Figure 9-2. MRP II planning and control.

Those systems initially came from MRP efforts in the early 1960s, where many companies attempted on their own to find a better way to plan parts. They realized that order point systems or the project control methods previously used were not sufficient for inventory management. With mushrooming computer capabilities, many companies independently installed material planning systems to plan material at all levels of a product by using bills of material to create requirements in an "explosion" process. At each level, requirements were netted against inventory both on-hand and on-order to plan new supply orders (manufactured or purchased). This evolved into an order launching process. In time, this was refined to include "pegging" to give visibility to the source of the requirements. This provided better priority planning capabilities so that manufacturing worked on the most important jobs first.

The next advance of MRP included the incorporation of master production scheduling (MPS) to drive it. MPS planned end items or key option level components, first for availability and then for capacity impact. This resulted in MRP systems that were expanded to include capacity or resource planning and shop floor management systems. As part of this enhanced process, MRP was renamed MRPII, which was intended to provide total control for manufacturing from initial planning to the latest priority in shop floor control.

The MRPII systems of the 1980s were refined to support many characteristics including multiplant environments, single- and multi-level pegging, "as planned" and "as-built" configuration control, product control on a project-by-project basis, and repetitive manufacturing control, in which material is controlled by schedules instead of job lots. However, the original thrust of MRPII has remained the planning of material by part for how much and when needed.

In a TBM environment, demand and supply are considered to be one and the same (see Figure 9-3). Therefore, the emphasis is on planning for needed PSS resources and using customer orders to determine what needs to be manufactured or purchased. This is a much simpler approach to material control.

A key part of the simplification process is pull scheduling, a concept that works on the principle that each feeding activity replaces what is consumed by the next succeeding operation—no more, no less. While MRPII need not be eliminated by this approach (it performs a capacity and high level material planning function), it is no longer required for individual part number planning or priority scheduling. It may be an oversimplification, but MRPII deals with planning while pull scheduling deals with execution. The portion of Figure 9-3 showing the execution phase is drastically simplified and quite different under TBM. For a company evolving to TBM, the key connecting link can be MRP and scheduling.

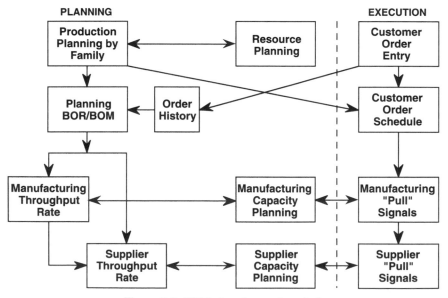

Figure 9-3. TBM planning and control.

This is especially useful until TBM changes and improvements are sufficiently advanced to allow the "pull" system, with its negative feedback principles, to execute the detail scheduling.

The TBM direction of process simplification is in contrast to the MRPII approach where the emphasis is on predefining the manufacturing process and then attempting to manage the process with a computer system. This MRPII task is accomplished by first quantifying a base data (e.g., bills of material and inventory balances), and then using a series of logic rules (explosions, planned orders, etc.) to present information to manage the process to closer tolerances.

INTEGRATING MRPII INTO TBM

The information systems used in any organization must support the operating philosophy and not vice versa. In other words, MRPII is not an end in itself, but rather a means to better manage the PSS. The system is not the solution; it exists to support the management of the PSS.

With the dramatic reductions in lead times and lot sizes that the TBM environment creates, the operation of MRP should be significantly altered as a planning tool. In practice, the TBM goal is to have the combined PSS lead times shorter than customer delivery lead times.

With short manufacturing lead times, it becomes practical to manufacture to real demand. This facilitates the need to improve "forecasting" with suppliers, because their capacity loads will be more accurate as the total internal manufacturing lead times are in hours and days, as opposed to weeks or months.

The three major areas of change caused by integrating MRPII into TBM are material flow and functions, demand management, and material planning and control. They are discussed in detail in the following sections.

MATERIAL FLOW AND FUNCTIONS
A fundamental concept of TBM is that the flow of material through the PSS is always moving. Also, the inventory amount at any point in time is so small that elaborate tracking systems are both impractical and unnecessary. Because activities are linked closely together through synchronization, space, and timing, the product is visible and PSS control is simplified.

Material flow. To gain an overview of the manufacturing process, the first step is to develop a picture that shows the current manufacturing flow through existing stockrooms and manufacturing areas. Figure 9-4 shows a typical manufacturing environment using MRPII. Figure 9-5 shows a

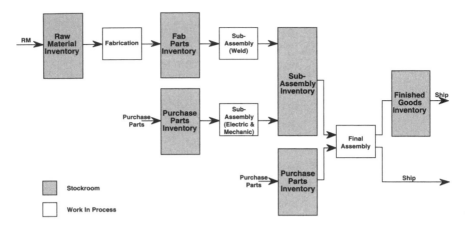

Figure 9-4. Material flow with MRP II.

conceptual design of how material would flow differently under TBM, integrating all activities and using the customer schedule as the driving element. Manufacturing resource planning must adapt to these process improvements.

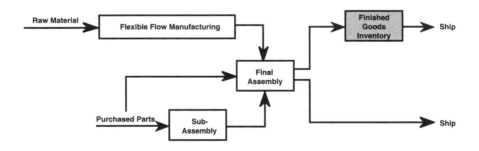

Figure 9-5. Material flow with TBM.

Material tracking. Theoretically, material tracking in a TBM environment is not needed because the pull signal is the only authorization for material to be moved. However, to migrate to this environment a plan must be developed to change from work order control to a rate or flow control environment.

In an MRPII-scheduled environment, material tracking includes the timing of when a job is opened and material is allocated, how and when material is issued, when material is "converted" to a higher level, and finally, when a job or a schedule is closed out. This is called a push environment where detail schedules and pick lists "push" material to the floor.

As the company migrates into TBM with synchronized activities, a shift to a pull environment occurs where the "using" activity gets or "pulls" material from a feeding activity, thus authorizing the feeding activity to make more material. This simpler pull environment does not require schedules, priority lists, or pick lists, because the authority to make material is generated from the material's consumer with its pull signal. Therefore, before a company achieves a pure TBM environment, it most likely will operate a modified MRPII environment where there may be at least three methods of tracking material. Table 9-1 compares tracking methods.

Table 9-1. Tracking methods in different manufacturing environments.

Manufacturing Environment	WIP Tracking Method
Job Shop MRP II	Work Orders
Repetitive MRP II	1. Work orders (as lots)
	2. Schedules (as gateways)
	3. Floor-on-hand (schedules are not netted)
TBM	Floor-on-hand "Four-wall" inventory

The traditional order approach (using requirements for shortages) is well understood. The repetitive manufacturing approach may use either work orders or schedules to track material on the floor, where schedules are effectively work orders for a defined period of time, e.g., a week. Unfortunately, in some repetitive environments work orders are still used to batch material, which is contradictory to the flow concept. Either way, netting is done against the work orders or schedules. As part of the material tracking approach, the process of transacting individual material issues to a job may be replaced by "backflushing" work-in-process (WIP) inventory to reduce transaction volumes. Backflushing is the process where component material is "consumed" or "issued" upon completion of a job. A second, more preferable, repetitive tracking of WIP is to use floor-on-hand balances along with backflushing as completed material passes a "gateway" count point. These floor-on-hand balances represent the quantity of a component on the floor regardless of whether this component is now part of a subassembly. This means that work orders, schedules, or both are not recognized in the netting process, only the floor-on-hand balances of components and assemblies.

In a TBM environment, material is pulled through the PSS and the role of material tracking is theoretically not necessary. However, material tracking is a valuable audit assist in highlighting potential imbalances and bill of material problems. In either case, the amount of transactions are significantly reduced.

Finally, the shop floor control function in a TBM environment is not needed to track material since visibility of material is key to TBM, making shop move transactions and paperwork unnecessary.

Material delivery. The key change in MRPII for TBM is in the delivery of material to the next-higher operation. In an MRPII push mode, pick or kit lists are the usual method of getting and delivering material to the shop floor. Quite often this material is "pushed" to a staging area whether or not material is required since the schedule instructs that the items be picked. This push is also used by many companies to assure adequate stock on hand, which adds no value.

In a pull environment, material is not "delivered." Instead, the using activity retrieves (pulls) material from the supplying activity. This "pull" then becomes the authorization for the supplying activity to make a predefined quantity of the same item just pulled. It should be noted that in a job shop environment where the same item rarely is repeated, the pull signal becomes the authorization to manufacture the next predetermined block of work (usually in standard hours).

DEMAND MANAGEMENT

Effective demand management is key to the success of either a traditional MRPII or TBM operating environment. In order to get an overall perspective on the planning process, it is first necessary to discuss what is necessary for TBM planning and control and then progress to a mixed environment where both MRPII and pull scheduling are involved.

Using the MRPII planning and control chart (Figure 9-2) as a reference, the demand management functions are primarily for distribution activities. The supply and capacity management functions are more significantly altered. The production planning function may be the only capacity or resource planning function in a TBM environment especially if planning is by major product groups. When the entire materials continuum is synchronized to a daily customer order schedule, customer orders (or finished goods stock replenishment orders for seasonality management) become the only people-managed schedule for the factory.

TBM planning and control. In both the traditional and TBM environments, MRPII has the same starting point in the manufacturing planning process: a production plan by product group. In a traditional MRPII environment, the production planning process balances the market forecast along with the customer order backlog, the finished goods inventory, or both to achieve a production plan. In a TBM environment, the production planning process is altered to balance the production plan to the market forecast by managing PSS capacity.

The production plan becomes the input source to both PSS capacity planning and customer order scheduling (Figure 9-3). The purpose of the production plan is to develop the required PSS capacity using a combined bill of resource and bill of material. Capacity calculations begin by determining the time frequency that a product comes off a given line; this is expressed as the demand rate. The demand rate along with lead time become the basis for the required PSS calculations such as PSS staffing, supplier demand rates, and capacity required.

The daily customer order schedule in TBM effectively replaces the master production scheduling process in traditional MRPII. The role of the master production schedule in MRPII serves two functions: it checks for availability of product and it checks for load. In the TBM environment, the purposes of the daily customer schedule are primarily to check for capacity by ensuring that customer orders do not exceed the production plan from the "planning" perspective and to sequence the customer schedule. The "availability" requirement, which balances supply schedules and on-hand balances against demands, is secondary, for the TBM goal is to manufacture all products to the customer order as needed. The emphasis is on planning and execution as opposed to demand and supply, because we plan products in groups for capacity purposes and execute with specific end products. This effectively eliminates the need to develop "planned" manufacturing orders as in traditional MRPII. In addition, if purchase lead times are short enough, then the supplier can deliver material through pull signals without using planned purchase orders.

MATERIAL PLANNING

The third major area affecting MRPII in a TBM environment is material planning. In a pure sense, material planning in TBM is done from the pull signals as actual lead times are reduced. The only planning needed is for resources and raw material product group availability. In an MRP environment, material planning is done with planned orders so that dependent demand on components can be developed through the bill of material explosion process. The critical requirement becomes the process of moving from planned orders to pull signals while still satisfying the existing materials systems function.

MRPII MIGRATION TO TBM

For the MRPII migration toward pull scheduling, a means must be developed that eliminates the need for planned orders. The first step is enhancing the MRPII system to recognize schedules instead of using work orders. When a schedule approach is used, the MRPII planning process nets against floor-on-hand balances at specific gateways. When an item "crosses" a gateway as a "completion," it adds to the on-hand quantity at the higher level and reduces the on-hand quantity of the lower-level component. This allows for planning without using planned orders, yet still retains the MRPII planning environment with a net requirements explosion.

Next, the material planning portion of MRPII needs to be altered to highlight capacity or resource issues for TBM. Intermediate levels are not stocked and material planning under TBM is done at execution time with pull signals. Detailed capacity requirements planning is not required for TBM, so the other need for planned orders is eliminated.

As discussed previously, material planning by part number through the use of planned orders does not occur in TBM. The order release function of MRPII is eliminated as an execution function because in a TBM environment work is both authorized and prioritized by using the pull system. In those situations where the manufacture of a product is not repetitive, the pull signal authorizes when to manufacture product and the gross explosion of the daily customer schedule determines what is to be manufactured or delivered by a supplier in sequence to the customer schedule (see Figure 9-6).

For many MRPII purchasing systems, the planned purchase orders and released open orders are tracked on an order-by-order basis. Co-op contracting needs to plan on a product group basis for capacity and demand rate purposes only. The execution again is handled by the pull system. Additionally, TBM purchasing systems must have the capability of planning raw material product group demand for capacity purposes.

Many MRPII practitioners originally thought that a TBM environment could be closely approximated in MRPII by planning with small lot quantities. They learned, however, that doing so makes the TBM environment more complicated. Specifically, if material is to flow in daily or hourly quantities, the normal MRPII approach would attempt to plan in daily or hourly discrete quantities. This may be impractical due to the long computer run times and mounds of paperwork and reports. Therefore, a longer planning interval of a week or so is usually used.

This creates the need to develop a subsidiary daily scheduling system under MRPII for the daily or hourly quantities which is difficult to maintain.

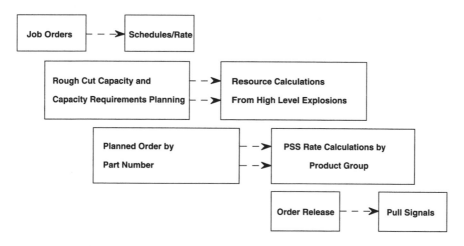

Figure 9-6. Material planning and control migration steps.

SUMMARY

Pull scheduling and MRPII and are synergistic. Many production planning and control activities require closer attention in TBM, even though they may or may not require extra effort. Some examples are:

- the production planning and customer order scheduling functions— these are the only formal resource planning and scheduling activities in a TBM environment.

- the interface between the order entry and customer order scheduling— especially if administrative lead times are to be kept to a minimum.

- the interface between engineering, materials, and the shop floor on engineering changes and process improvements.

- managing resources and identifying product groups that have an impact on those resources—for example, maintaining the bill of resources and the planning bills of materials may require a significant review of the new booking mix and process changes that have an impact on the resources required.

- the pull scheduling process—it should be monitored to generate new pull signals when the production plan changes and to handle exceptions. This means letting the shop floor know what to make when the pull signal gives the authorization that something should be made.

A number of principles that should guide the MRP transition follow:

1. MRPII is the planning tool; pull scheduling is the execution tool.

2. Significant changes must be made to existing MRPII systems.

3. MRPII must migrate with TBM implementation.

4. Computer systems should enhance, not deter, lead time, space reductions, and productivity improvement.

5. System improvements in and of themselves do not improve productivity; it is process simplification that realizes significant improvement.

The merging of MRPII into TBM will result in significant gains in customer service as well as reduced inventories and operating costs (see Figure 9-7).

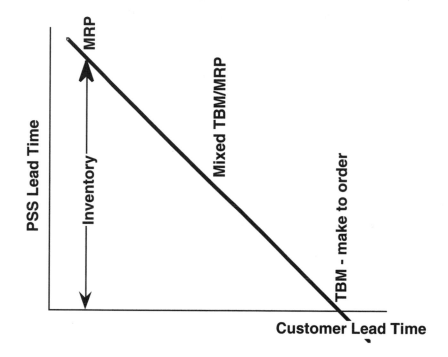

- MRP - make to forecast
- Mixed TBM/MRP - make to forecast or order
- TBM - make to order

Figure 9-7. Information system stages to support TBM.

REFERENCES

Bose, G. J. and J. A. Welch. 1991. Sales and operations planning: Just in the nick of time. *International Industrial Engineering Conference Proceedings.* Norcross, GA: Institute of Industrial Engineers. 117-21.

Edwards, J. N. and W. A. Wheeler. 1987. *Integrating MRPII with JIT.* New York: Coopers & Lybrand.

Karmarker, U. 1989. Getting control of just-in-time. *Harvard Business Review.* September-October: 122-31.

Martin, D. D., and R. L. Shell. 1988. *Management of Professionals.* New York: Marcel Dekker.

Porter, M. E. and V. E. Millar. 1985. How information gives you competitive advantage. *Harvard Business Review.* July-August: 149-60.

Performance Measures and Rewards   10

PERFORMANCE measures and rewards must support time-based manufacturing (TBM). Understanding measurements and rewards can perhaps best be explained by the following story told by Michael LeBoeuf (1985):

> A weekend fisherman looked over the side of his boat and saw a snake with a frog in its mouth. Feeling sorry for the frog, he reached down, gently removed the frog from the snake's mouth, and let the frog go free. But now he felt sorry for the hungry snake. Having no food, he took out a flask of bourbon and poured a few drops into the snake's mouth. The snake swam away happy, the frog was happy, and the man was happy for having performed such good deeds. He thought all was well until a few minutes passed and he heard something knock against the side of his boat and looked down. With stunned disbelief, the fisherman saw the snake was back—with two frogs!

This story carries two important lessons. First, we get more of the behavior that we reward—not what we hope for or expect people to do, but what people see as the right actions to take to get rewarded. Second, people often unknowingly or inadvertently reward the wrong behavior. In trying to get behavior A, we unwittingly reward B and wonder what went wrong when B happens.

The snake and frog story is easily applicable to most company situations. Matching the proper performance measures and rewards must drive the organization behavior necessary to achieve TBM.

Lord Kelvin in 1883 said the following about measurements. "I often say that when you can measure what you are speaking about, and express it in numbers, you know something about it; but when you cannot measure it, when you cannot express it in numbers, your knowledge is a meager and unsatisfactory kind; it may be the beginning of knowledge, but you have scarcely, in your thoughts, advanced to the stage of science, whatever the matter may be." Performance measures must be carefully linked to the fundamental goals of the organization . In times past, measurements have often had little or no effect on goal attainment. Some common criticisms of performance measures include unclear purpose, too vague, not linked or even opposed to the business strategy, not fair or consistent, and used mostly for "punishing" people.

How many times have you heard a manager or supervisor say, "I know the performance measurement system doesn't support this, but I really want you to concentrate on doing more of behavior A. Don't worry about the performance measure; trust me that you won't be punished if the measure's results look bad." It is futile to ask for behavior A, reward B, and expect A. No wonder companies struggle to motivate their work forces.

It is reassuring to know that the strong majority of workers are not lazy but instead want to contribute to the goals of the organization. They may be confused and misled by companies who do not provide clear visions, goals, measurements, and rewards that are consistent with the behaviors required to successfully compete. Remember the saying, "If you don't know where you are, you can't get to where you want to be." The bottom line is that workers at all levels in the organization provide more of the behavior that they are measured and rewarded to achieve: what gets measured and rewarded gets done.

The purpose of performance measurement in TBM is to ensure the same focused improvement throughout the entire organization and to balance resources in all work areas for the required PSS output capacity. The measures must encourage all personnel to identify and implement desirable changes to improve performance.

The trend of highly competitive manufacturing has been to focus on increasing customer satisfaction through improved quality, product variety, customer service, and short lead times. These performance characteristics can be improved through TBM with focused, supportive performance measures and rewards.

THE ACCOUNTING PERSPECTIVE

For years managers have relied on accounting information to assess manufacturing performance. The common view is that costs, revenues, assets, liabilities, and other accounts act as an integrated database containing the cause-and-effect relationships that determine the financial outcome of operating activities. During recent years, however, there has been increasing doubt about managing business operations with traditional accounting information. Progressive businesses today organize their operations quite differently than in years past when management accounting systems had their origin. Using information from these systems to evaluate and measure operating performance unwittingly causes companies to make decisions that impair competitiveness. They do not monitor critical aspects of the business such as quality, flexibility, dependability, timeliness of delivery, and overall customer responsiveness. At best, costs are imperfect signals that a problem exists; they provide no clues as to what the problem is, or how to treat it (Kaplan 1984).

THE BREAKDOWN OF TRADITIONAL COST ACCOUNTING

Traditional cost accounting systems typically focus on a standard costing approach that develops annual standards for factory labor, material, and overhead. These factors produce a standard product cost that represents the expected cost to manufacture a product. Standard cost accounting systems provide input for company pricing policies and for evaluating product line profitability.

Traditional cost accounting systems emphasize the following:

1. measuring direct labor using industrial engineering techniques, such as time study or predetermined time systems, such as Methods Time Measurement (MTM). Changeover time, material handling, and other support tasks are unmeasured and classified as indirect labor. Labor standards are averaged from a variety of working conditions and job methods to develop a single standard for a process or product.

2. estimating a standard vendor price for purchased parts. This cost is often rolled over from the material cost at the end of a year into the new year's standard cost for each purchased item.

3. combining all other manufacturing costs into overhead, which is typically applied as a flat rate(s) or a percentage. It is absorbed in a manner proportional to the labor content of a product.

4. emphasizing the management of variance between standard and actual cost for direct labor, material, and overhead. Management reports generate information to measure labor efficiency, purchase price variance, and overhead expenditures to budget.

5. frequently using individual incentive pay systems as the improvement of direct labor efficiency assumes the overall improvement of product costs and the manufacturing process.

As manufacturing methods have changed, traditional cost accounting approaches have exhibited several shortcomings, including the following:

1. The improvement of direct labor efficiency is overemphasized. Direct labor typically represents less than twenty percent of total product costs. Many manufacturers report less than ten percent. In addition, with the rapid advancement of factory automation, direct labor costs as a percentage of total product costs will decline steadily. Labor efficiency improvement does not always correlate to overall productivity improvement.

2. Raw material is analyzed and managed for purchase price only. Quality, timeliness of delivery, reliability, and other important factors are not commonly considered.

3. Overhead components of product costs go largely unmanaged. For example, machine changeover costs are assumed to be fixed and are grouped into the aggregate overhead rate. This eliminates any incentive to improve the changeover process.

4. Standards cause waste to be institutionalized. Where budgets for scrap exist, scrap will continue. Where incentive rates exist for rework operations, rework will continue. The emphasis is on meeting the standard, which does not contribute to improving the manufacturing process.

NEW AGE COST ACCOUNTING REQUIREMENTS

Cost accounting's new role is to supply the management information necessary to improve total performance and to establish manufacturing as a competitive weapon in the marketplace (Kaplan 1984). Several key areas discussed in this section must be considered.

To excel as a competitive manufacturer, a company must commit to a level of quality that at least meets customer requirements. The cost associated with quality problems in many manufacturing companies are as high as ten percent of sales. These costs include material scrap, inspection, rework labor, and customer returns. Most manufacturers do not know their true level of quality and the associated costs.

The longer the time required to ship a product, the greater the uncertainty of sales forecasting for market demand and production requirements. While long lead times were accepted in the past, today's time-based manufacturer is finding a strategic advantage in shorter delivery times and quicker response to customer demands. The lead time measurement includes the time required to process an order, engineer the product, purchase materials, and manufacture and ship the product to the customer.

Measuring total productivity is important to managing the entire product supply system (PSS). It includes an analysis of all factors of production and goes beyond the traditional view of units produced per direct labor hour. For example, the time required for machine changeover, traditionally viewed as indirect, is an important factor for a total labor productivity measure. Other inputs including energy, capital, facility requirements, and distribution costs are also important to total productivity.

The requirement to maintain inventory is due to a company's inability to purchase materials and manufacture a product within the customer-expected delivery lead time. This condition creates the need to stock inventory to accommodate the uncertainty of customer demand. As companies implement TBM, direct inventory measures such as lot sizes, work in process, and raw material inventory levels are necessary.

A customer buys a finished product, which results from the value added by a manufacturer to its purchased materials. Value-added activities are those activities that transform purchased items into finished products. Typically, value-added activities are less than five percent of the total activities performed to produce a product. Measuring the ratio of value-added activities to the total activities provides a benchmark for eliminating waste.

The manufacturing methods and techniques presented above require the work force to have increased knowledge, skills, and flexibility. Multi-task workers will become increasingly necessary to compete effectively. The implication of this shift is that group incentive schemes, employee involvement, and profit-sharing plans will continue to replace individual incentive systems and specialized jobs for driving manufacturing performance improvement and profitability.

SUMMARY

Cost accounting must change as manufacturing companies implement improved TBM methods. These changes must focus and support management activities in the critical areas where performance improvement is necessary to succeed.

ADVANCED COST MANAGEMENT

To make TBM a success, the cost management system must provide the right information on a timely basis to measure the improvement process. Manufacturing management should focus on eliminating nonvalue-added activities. This includes eliminating cost accounting reports that are redundant or are not being used to manage the business. For advanced cost management (ACM) to work effectively, the system should adhere to the five basic principles that follow.

1. The system must be *simple* and easy to use, providing only relevant and human engineered information that aids in day-to-day decision making and performance improvement.

2. The system must provide *visibility* to nonvalue-added activities. These activities represent opportunities for corrective action and improvement.

3. The system must provide *rapid feedback*. In an environment where problems are corrected as they occur, monthly financial assessments, generated after the fact, offer little value to problem-solving teams on the shop floor.

4. The system must provide *compatible performance measures* with the continuous improvement philosophy. For example, individual performance measures that direct behavior toward unnecessary machine use and excess inventory do not support manufacturing improvement principles.

5. The system should provide *meaningful trend information* to illustrate achievement of continuous, goal-driven improvement.

There are six major factors that are integral to ACM: cost drivers, product costing, cost control, performance measures, inventory valuation, and product continuum management.

Cost Drivers

Cost drivers are those activities and transactions that cause costs to occur, or result in increased costs. All cost drivers do not necessarily add value. They are used to assign the costs of service department activities to product costs, reflecting the resources consumed to support the product. These drivers should reflect factors that are critical for competitiveness, supporting a philosophy based on continuous improvement and waste elimination. Cost drivers should be monitored and targeted for improvement and elimination. When used properly, cost-driver unit costs are the basis for evaluating key activity performance.

Product Costing

Product costing in ACM avoids cost distortions by directly reflecting the impact of service department cost drivers. This reduces allocations by directly assigning costs to focused factories or cells wherever possible. Product costs distinguish between value-added and nonvalue-added cost elements, thereby giving visibility to opportunities for improvement. Advanced cost management uses the activity-based costing (ABC) method presented in Chapter 4 to avoid the traditional allocation of costs to products from aggregated overhead pools based on traditional labor absorption techniques.

Cost Control

Advanced cost management provides cost control through the rapid reporting of those costs that are directly related to the PSS. Actual cost per unit is compared to historical performance—but only for those cost elements assignable to the PSS. Costs that cannot be directly attributed to the PSS and controlled within the PSS are excluded or controlled at a higher organization level. Allocated overhead, for example, can obscure the information needed to monitor operations. Services and other overhead costs not attributable to the PSS should be controlled through functional reporting and cost-driver monitoring.

Performance Measures

Performance measures that reflect TBM objectives such as continuous improvement and elimination of waste are a critical component of ACM. Cost control and cost-driver monitoring are essential and common elements of any advanced system. Performance measures relating to quality, lead time, productivity, and service provide a framework that ties all business goals together.

Inventory Valuation

Advanced cost management simplifies inventory valuation and supports continuous lead time reduction to increase throughput and reduce work-in-process inventory (WIP). Consequently, the need for transactions to track paperwork, material, and WIP status are eliminated. Backflushing methods are used to relieve in-process and raw material inventories based on reported production. Extensive data reporting for valuation of inventory is not emphasized in general, while other value-added decision support activities are encouraged.

Product Continuum Management

Product continuum management links expenses incurred across an organization's entire PSS for the life of the product. Traditional cost accounting focuses on material costs and the manufacturing conversion costs, usually exclusive of other costs associated with the product. These may not always be the largest cost elements. Advanced cost management includes not only factory costs but also the costs of the distribution channel, sales and service, and product development and support.

Summary

The limitations of traditional accounting measures encourage the use of new systems that track quality, flexibility, dependability, timeliness of delivery, and overall customer satisfaction. Feedback in the form of standard cost variances generally has been counterproductive. Other financial reports such as profit and loss statements, budgets, and margin analysis have been too aggregated, too late, and too one-dimensional to be useful. Managers require clear, relevant, and timely signals from their internal information systems to understand root causes of problems, to initiate corrective action, and to support decisions at all levels of the organization. The following recommendations are offered to improve accounting systems (McNair, Lynch, and Cross 1990):

- provide strategic cost information on products and resource allocation decisions
- quantify productivity improvement proposals
- suppress meaningless variances
- get management accountants to focus on the vital few
- modify the accounting system to bring it in line with operational realities
- mitigate the potential for mixed signals
- help accountants and operations personnel agree on what constitutes continuous improvement

MEASURES OF PERFORMANCE FOR THE TBM ORGANIZATION

What's wrong with performance measures today? Answering this question gets at the root cause of what is wrong with many organizations. Most companies' performance measures and rewards drive organization behavior in two counterproductive directions. The first direction is that of a short-term, results-only orientation. It does not matter what you are doing, management only wants to hear about results and how quickly they can be attained. The message is that shortcuts are okay, and people should do whatever it takes to make the "numbers" look good. The second direction is that of departmentalization, causing strong functional silos. The message here is that each department should have its own measures of success, independent of what it takes for others to succeed. This situation causes suboptimization of the organization's capabilities.

The following are several guidelines for setting proper performance measures.

1. Measures must be process/system based, not departmental. Processes flow through the organization. Measures should recognize and support this fact.

2. Measures should be managed on the front lines. People at the source should collect, analyze, and report their own performance.

3. The measures chosen should be relatively few and simple. Companies should pick the vital few that also accommodate the trivial many.

4. Measures must be timely and managed as close to the transactions as possible.

5. Measures should measure group performance, seldom individual performance.

The TBM guideline for developing performance measures in any organization should be to use the fewest measures needed to manage those processes whose improvement is most important to the success of the organization. Therefore, performance measurement design begins with defining the major PSS processes along with their output characteristics. Obviously, processes and output characteristics vary from organization to organization; consequently, the key measures of performance should also vary.

Remember, the performance measures must assist in realizing continuous improvement and establishing behavior consistent with TBM, as follows:
• synchronize supply to demand
• make only what you need when you need it
• do the right activities right the first time
• compress system lead time
• eliminate waste
• delight the customer
• reduce variation
• solve problems through teamwork
• offer the optimum variety of products
• improve reliability and capability
• manage the entire supply system

There are many good measures of performance that progressive manufacturers monitor today. These include:
• on-time and complete shipments
• return on assets
• inventory turnover
• number of parts per finished product
• number of suppliers certified
• productivity (product output versus resources consumed)
• product returns as a percentage of sales
• percent defects

In addition, some simple measures have proven to be very successful drivers of TBM behavior to increase quality, reduce lead time, lower costs, and improve customer service.

OVERALL PSS MEASURES

Lead time. Lead time is a measure of the speed to execute an input through a process into a delivered output. It is the linchpin of TBM. Lead time can be measured in a variety of ways for different processes. For the overall PSS lead time, we recommend the following lead time ratio.

PSS lead time ratio—The time stretching from the placement of the purchase request with the supplier to the delivery of finished product to the customer should be equal to or less than the customer's expected replenishment lead time.

$$\text{PSS lead time ratio} = \frac{\text{total actual supply lead time}}{\text{customer's expected replenishment lead time}}$$

where
PSS lead time ratio goal ≤ 1

This definition measures a multiple of internal lead time over customer lead time. The goal of the lead time measure is a value less than one, meaning the PSS can supply product to the customer's order without the need for forecasts or excess inventory.

For companies that produce custom products to customer orders and therefore quote lead times in weeks or months, the denominator can be modified to be either the customer-desired replenishment lead time or the best industry-competitor lead time.

Value-added. The value-added measure is an indicator of the effectiveness of a process relative to its potential. Value-added time is the "processing" time where activities are being performed on the product that the customer (if it were known they were being done) would be willing to pay for. The value-added definition, formula, and goal follows.

Value-added ratio—Value-added time is the time spent directly on activities that develop, produce, convert, and deliver products to the customer. The goal is to add value to the product the entire time it is within the PSS.

$$\text{Value-added ratio} = \frac{\text{total system value-added time}}{\text{total actual supply lead time}}$$

where
Value-added ratio goal = 1

First run yield. First run yield (FRY) is a measure of the ability of a process to deliver high-quality products effectively. It measures the product loss at all relevant points in the PSS versus the total product delivered by the PSS. The FRY definition, goal, and formula follows.

First run yield ratio—First run yield is the ratio of good units delivered by the PSS versus the total products started into the PSS. The goal of FRY is to produce one hundred percent of the targeted product the first time without fallout.

$$\text{First run yield ratio} = \frac{\text{actual good units output first time}}{\text{total quantity input}}$$

where
First run yield ratio goal = 1

Linearity. Linearity measures the ability of a process to produce and deliver precisely what the customer wants without shortfall or excess. It is a key indicator of the matching between supply and demand. The linearity definition, goal, and formula follow:

Linearity—Linearity is the daily matching of what the PSS is producing versus what customers have ordered. The linearity goal is to produce only the products and quantities ordered by customers, no more or less. It is expressed as a percentage. In measuring linearity, too much supply is considered just as bad as too little.

$$\text{Linearity percent} = \left(1 - \left|\frac{\text{yesterday's orders} - \text{today's actual production}}{\text{yesterday's orders}}\right|\right)(100)$$

where
Linearity percent goal = 100

Total product linearity can be computed by using a weighted average. An example follows:

Products	Yesterday's customer orders	Today's Actual Production
A	11,232	11,001
B	8,927	9,327
Total	20,159	20,328

$$\text{Linearity percent (A)} = \left(1 - \left|\frac{11232 - 11001}{11232}\right|\right)(100)$$
$$= (1 - 0.021)\,100$$
$$= 97.9\%$$

$$\text{Linearity percent (B)} = \left(1 - \left|\frac{8927 - 9327}{8927}\right|\right)(100)$$
$$= (1 - 0.045)\ 100$$
$$= 95.5\%$$

Using a weighted average,

$$\text{Total linearity percent} = \left(\frac{11232}{20159}\right)(97.9\%) + \left(\frac{8927}{20159}\right)(95.5\%)$$
$$= 54.5\% + 42.3\%$$
$$= 96.8\%$$

Activity level measures. In addition to the overall PSS performance measures, the following three performance measures are appropriate for the major activities within a process.

Reliability. Reliability measures the effectiveness of an asset to perform relative to its capability. It comprises three submeasures: uptime, which is a measure of utilization; dependability, which is a measure of activity efficiency; and yield, which is a measure of activity quality.

$$\text{Reliability} = (\text{uptime})(\text{dependability})(\text{yield})$$

Changeover time. Changeover time measures the time to perform a changeover to a different product on a given asset. In many manufacturing companies, changeover times are a major barrier to the TBM strategy. Managing this indicator with a heavy focus will often pave the way for dramatic improvements.

$$\text{Changeover time} = \text{Last good unit produced to first}$$
$$\text{good unit produced at target run rates}$$

Process capability. Process capability measures the ability of an asset to produce product within the customer specification. It is a good predictor of the level of quality being produced by the asset. The higher the process capability ratio, the better the product quality relative to a given specification.

$$\text{Process capability (Cpr)} = \text{Min} \left| \frac{\text{USL} - \bar{x}}{3\sigma} \right| \text{ or } \left| \frac{\text{LSL} - \bar{x}}{3\sigma} \right|$$

where
Process capability goal $\geq$ 1.33

THE ROLE OF WORK MEASUREMENT AND ITS APPLICATION IN TBM

Work measurement is an important tool for developing a successful TBM design and maintaining a balanced PSS. It is useful in determining the correct resource allocation for all activities in the total cycle (customer order to delivery) and for synchronizing and configuring the PSS to the customer's daily demand profile.

OVERVIEW
Work measurement is applying techniques designed to estimate the time for a qualified worker to conduct a specified task at a defined level of performance to produce high-quality output. Properly practiced, the field of work measurement encompasses a proper methods definition that specifies the human interface with all necessary tools and equipment to perform a cycle of work. In addition to determining how and with what to perform the task, it is important that the workplace meets acceptable standards of ergonomic design and occupational safety and health. A final requirement of professional work measurement is to ensure worker cooperation in the measurement process and involvement in the creation of the total job environment. The importance of applying interpersonal skills by the work measurement analyst cannot be overvalued; labor standards are not psychologically limiting if workers are involved and motivated (Martin and Shell 1988).

The use of work measurement substantially changes context in the TBM company. Work measurement in the TBM company is not to measure and closely manage individual labor, but to understand and match the output capability of a process with the demand requirement. This is a quite different perspective than the historical usage of work measurement.

THE TECHNIQUES
There are five categories of work measurement techniques available for use in TBM. Each has certain application advantages and are discussed in the following paragraphs (Shell 1992b).

1. predetermined time systems
2. direct observation timing with performance rating (stopwatch time study)
3. work sampling
4. historical data (includes accounting records and self-logging)
5. judgment estimating

The first three are considered engineered work measurement techniques. The last two, historical data and judgment estimating, are often used to approximate standard time values. However, these two techniques have decreased accuracy and little underlying theory or standardized procedures, and consequently, are not considered engineered work measurement practice. An additional technique, standard data development, is also useful in establishing work standards for TBM. The engineer must be aware of the accuracy required for a given activity standard when using any of these techniques.

To varying degrees, all of these techniques may be used for TBM work activities, depending primarily on accuracy requirements, the availability of human resources, the time needed to determine the activity standard, and management objectives. Knowing the strengths and limitations of each technique is useful when evaluating the cost of establishing activity standards versus the cost of having inaccurate or no standards (see Figures 10-1 and 10-2).

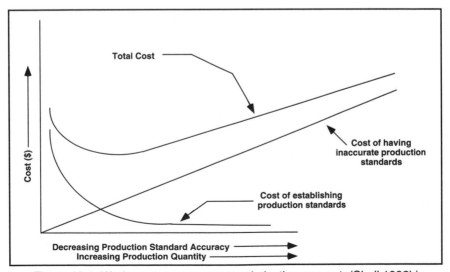

Figure 10-1. Work measurement cost optimization concept. (Shell 1992b)

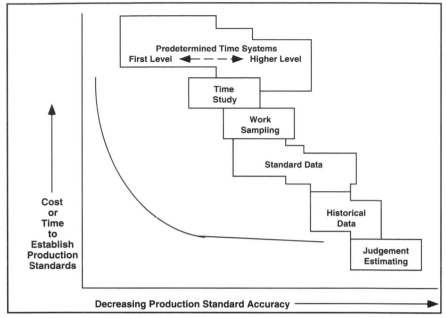

Figure 10-2. Work measurement techniques as related to cost, time, and accuracy. (Shell 1992b)

Predetermined time systems (Shell 1992a, b). By definition, a predetermined time system is "an organized body of information, procedures, techniques, and motion times employed in the study and evaluation of manual work elements. The system is expressed in terms of the motions used, their general and specific nature, the conditions under which they occur, and their previously determined performance times" (Institute of Industrial Engineers 1990).

Predetermined time systems are classified as generic, functional, or application specific. Generic systems are not restricted in any way and are widely used by many types of organizations. Functional systems are adapted for a specific activity type, e.g., machining, clerical, or micro-assembly. Application-specific systems are designed for the operational needs of a particular industry or organization, e.g., aircraft engines, banking, health care, or individual companies.

Numerous predetermined time systems have been developed over the years. Examples include Methods Time Measurement (MTM) and its many variations, Work Factor, Modular Arrangement of Predetermined Time Standards (MODAPTS), and Master Standard Data (MSD). While each has certain features, most of the systems are similar in their structure.

Outgrowths of MTM include Micro-Matic Methods and Measurement (4M) and Maynard Operational Sequence Technique (MOST). A computerized work measurement system developed at Westinghouse, 4M retains MTM-1 accuracy and element description while providing a faster speed of analysis. The MOST system uses a larger number of motions in elements than MTM and therefore requires less time for analysis, especially in its computerized version. Both 4M and MOST represent excellent examples of the positive effects of computerizing a predetermined time system. They are both well suited for TBM work applications.

Stopwatch time study and performance rating (Shell 1986). Direct observation timing (time study) has been one of the most commonly used techniques for setting activity standards. Even though predetermined time systems have been growing in popularity in recent years, direct time measurement is still used by many organizations. Direct observation timing is defined as a technique to determine the time required by a qualified and well-trained person working at a normal (average) pace to perform a specified task under standard environmental conditions. The *Industrial Engineering Terminology* ANSI standard Z94.11 defines *time study* as "a work measurement technique consisting of careful time measurement of the task with a time measuring instrument, adjusted for any observed variance from normal effort or pace and to allow adequate time for such items as foreign elements, unavoidable or machine delays, rest to overcome fatigue, and personal needs. Learning or progress effects may also be considered. If the task is of sufficient length, it is normally broken down into short, relatively homogenous work elements, each of which is treated separately as well as in combination with the rest" (Institute of Industrial Engineers 1990).

Three specified conditions must be followed for the time study to be valid. First, the individual in the study must be qualified and well-trained. He or she must be instructed in the proper method and have had sufficient time to practice the job. Second, the worker should be performing at a rate or effort level that would be expected of a conscientious, self-paced employee when working neither fast nor slow and giving due consideration to the physical and mental requirements of the specific job. Third, the task must have a well-defined beginning and end. Fourth, the task should not be measured at times when atypical environmental conditions are present. Finally, it is important that all personnel including the operator, the manager, and the bargaining unit representative (if unionized) be informed of the study, thus allowing all parties to prepare for it properly. If any of these prerequisites are not met, the results will probably not be representative of the true time required for the task.

Work sampling (Shell 1986). Work sampling is a technique used to investigate the proportions of total time devoted to various activities that make up a job or work situation. *Industrial Engineering Terminology* defines work sampling as "an application of random sampling techniques to the study of work activities so that the proportions of time devoted to different elements of work can be estimated with a given degree of statistical validity" (Institute of Industrial Engineers 1990). This technique can be applied to humans, machines, or any observable state or condition of an operation. The underlying assumption of work sampling is that the sampling percentage of any observed state of nature estimates the actual time spent in that condition.

Advantages of work sampling in a TBM organization include the following:

- Activities that are impractical or costly to measure by time study or predetermined time systems can be easily and cost-effectively measured by work sampling.
- A simultaneous work sampling study of several workers (teams) or machines can be made by a single observer.
- Work sampling requires fewer analyst hours and costs less than time study or the application of predetermined time systems.
- Work sampling may be interrupted at any time during the study without affecting the results.
- Work sampling studies are less fatiguing and less tedious to make on the part of the observer than time study or predetermined time systems.
- In work sampling, the degree of accuracy can be changed by varying the number of observations.
- Work sampling is impersonal and group oriented, and because there is no direct timing, workers usually feel positive about the study.
- Work sampling is often the only suitable work measurement technique to be applied to professional or knowledge workers.

Some of the disadvantages associated with work sampling include the following:

- Work sampling is usually uneconomical for studying a single operator or machine, or for studying operators or machines located over widely dispersed areas. Other work measurement techniques, e.g., time study or predetermined time systems, are preferred for highly repetitive operations.

- Time study provides a more detailed breakdown of activities and delays.
- Management and workers may not understand statistically based work sampling as readily as they do direct observation time study.

Historical data (Shell 1992b). While not an engineered work measurement technique, historical data in many TBM work situations are very cost effective for developing production standards and staffing requirements. Historical data are a special, less accurate form of standard data. Times are developed for work activities from previous actual recorded times (job accounting records). Task times may also be developed by workers self-logging times for activities. This time data can be averaged, evaluated, and computerized in a database.

Historical databased activity standards can be used in any work environment: manufacturing, service organizations, or government. The time and cost to develop standards with this technique are generally minimal compared with other work measurement techniques (see Figure 10-2). The obvious limitation is accuracy of the resulting standards.

Judgment estimating (Shell 1992b). As with historical data, judgment estimating is not an engineered work measurement technique. It is the least accurate but requires the least amount of time to establish activity standards and staffing requirements. Many practitioners dismiss judgment estimating because of its accuracy limitations. Experience has shown that activity standards established with judgment commonly deviate from the true standard by at least twenty-five to fifty percent. There is, however, a useful methodology for improving judgment estimating.

The recommended five-step procedure for developing a judgment estimate is listed below:

1. Subdivide the total job into major activities. This helps define what has to be done and enhances the estimating process.

2. Clearly understand the physical setting of each activity to be performed, e.g., the workplace, tools, equipment to be used, and the job environment.

3. Think in terms of producing one unit of output, i.e., an activity cycle following any changeover or get-ready activities. As with all work measurement activity standard setting, changeover or get-ready activities should be estimated independently.

4. Assume the activity will be performed by an average or normal operator.

5. Complete the activity time estimate. This can best be accomplished with a process commonly used in critical path scheduling models such as program evaluation and review technique (PERT). These models commonly use judgment estimating to determine the time values for each activity identified within the network. In place of just estimating one value for the total task, three estimates are completed: an optimistic time, a pessimistic time, and a most likely time. The optimistic and pessimistic time estimates require the engineer to mentally establish minimum and maximum time boundaries considering the major factors that could cause variation in activity completion. The activity time estimate can then be calculated with the following equation:

$$T_e = \frac{\left(t_o + 4t_m + t_p\right)}{6}$$

where
T_e = mean time estimate for the activity
t_o = optimistic time estimate
t_m = most likely time estimate
t_p = pessimistic time estimate

Standard data. In MIL-STD-1567A (U. S. Government Printing Office 1975) standard data are defined as "a compilation of all the elements that are used for performing a given class of work with normal elemental time values for each element. The data are used as a basis for determining time standards on work similar to that from which the data were determined without making actual time studies." Standard data can have several levels of refinement much like predetermined time systems. The fundamental level provides times for specific motions. Higher-level standard data provide times for elements of work and the highest level for complete activities. In practice, standard data can be constructed from any of the five categories of work measurement previously discussed. Work measurement categories most suited for lowest level (more refinement and more accuracy) to highest level (less refinement and less accuracy) data are (in order): predetermined time systems, stopwatch time study, work sampling, historical data, and judgment estimating. Most commonly, standard data are developed from time studies, particularly for higher volume work.

Standard data also includes the development of normal times through the use of mathematical equations and tabulated element or tasks times (Shell 1992a) .

INCENTIVES AND REWARDS

Experience has confirmed that workers will perform better to their capabilities with some form of incentive. Time-based manufacturing requires balancing all processes in the total cycle from initial product requirement through the final distribution and later billing and customer service functions. The work measurement question is, "Balance at what level of human and equipment performance?" People make an important contribution to the operation and output of any process, even in automated processes. Therefore, if employees are motivated through appropriate incentives, the balance for individual sequential processes can be made at a higher level of performance; that is, a shorter cycle time for a unit of work. There are three classifications of incentive plans: direct financial, indirect financial, and intangible (nonfinancial).

DIRECT FINANCIAL

Direct financial plans are those that proportionally link an employee's earnings to his or her output as measured against an activity standard. The standard may be applied to an individual or work group. It has been observed consistently that sustained high levels of output for individual incentives exceed that of group incentives. This has been the main rationale for the traditional individual incentive plans found in manufacturing. Individual incentives also:

- initially increase individual worker output.
- tie pay directly to performance.
- improve worker efficiency.
- are appropriate for completely independent jobs.
- work well in environments that do not need employee teamwork/ cooperation.

Disadvantages of individual incentives are that they:

- are difficult and costly to administer.
- are inappropriate and harmful as work changes.
- promote individuality/worker dishonesty.
- increase machine downtime, i.e. on standard time.
- cause interdepartmental conflicts and peer pressure.
- encourage production whether product is needed or not.

Conflicts between traditional incentives and TBM are given in Table 10-1.

Table 10-1. Individual/TBM incentive conflicts.

Individual Incentives	TBM
• No need to know demand	• Synchronize production to demand
• Produce all you can	• Make only what you need when you need it
• Don't change method, because standard will be raised	• Continually improve
• Each person out only for themselves	•Involve people in teams
• Functional skills specialty	• Organize around product lines
• Bigger lot sizes mean more pay	• Reduce lot sizes

INDIRECT FINANCIAL

Indirect financial plans are those that stimulate employee motivation and result in increased productivity but do not directly relate individual or group output to regular earnings. Examples of indirect financial plans include special fringe benefits, suggestion system rewards, year-end discretionary bonuses, profit sharing, and gainsharing. In our experiences, gainsharing is the best incentive system for TBM.

Profit sharing has proven to be an effective motivator in several companies but lacks the direct linkage between output performance and incentive earnings. Profit sharing is the most widely used group reward plan in the United States. Profits are distributed in annual cash bonuses or may be deferred and made a part of the retirement program. Profit sharing plans have the following advantages:
• motivate top management
• compatible with gainsharing plans
• cover entire organization
• easy to administer

Profit sharing plans have the following disadvantages:

- worker performance not directly tied to profit
- difficult to relate individual or small group performance to profit
- annual cash payout ineffective for weekly/monthly motivation (no weekly/monthly performance feedback)
- the larger the organization, the less individual or small group motivation
- often recognized as a benefit, not an improvement tool

One of the most successful profit sharing plans ever developed exists at the Lincoln Electric Company in Cleveland, Ohio. The plan was conceived by James F. Lincoln, past president and founder of the company, in 1934. Since that time, Lincoln Electric has paid more in annual bonuses than regular wages. The following suggestions are offered to organizations considering profit sharing (Lincoln 1946):

1. Determine that the system is going to be adopted and decide that whatever needs to be done to install it will be done.

2. Determine what plan and products the company will make that will carry out the philosophy of "more and more for less and less."

3. Get the complete acceptance of the board of directors and all management involved in the plan, together with their assurance that they will continue to take whatever steps are necessary for successful application of it.

4. Arrange a means by which management can talk to the people and the people can talk back. That means full discussion by all.

5. Make sure of cooperative action on the agreed plan of operation. This will include the plan for progressively better manufacturing by all people in the organization and the proper distribution of the savings that result from it.

6. Set your sights high enough. Do not try to get just a little better efficiency with the expectation that such gain will be to the good and expect to leave the matter there.

7. Remember, this plan for industry is a fundamental change in philosophy. From it new satisfactions will flow to all involved. Not only is there more money for all concerned, there is also the much more important reward—the satisfaction of doing a better job. The greatest satisfaction of all is becoming a more useful person.

It would be difficult to determine when these suggestions were written; however, many are as valid today as they were in the 1940s.

INTANGIBLE (NONFINANCIAL)

Intangible incentive plans include rewards that do not have any (or very little) influence on employee wages. These plans, when viewed as desirable by employees, can favorably affect performance. Examples of nonfinancial plans include posting of work output results, job rotation, job enlargement, and time off from work without any reduction in pay.

GAINSHARING

Gainsharing plans are incentive reward systems designed to share the benefits of improved productivity, cost reductions, and quality. The principles of gainsharing require that group-based regular cash bonuses be given and that the plan supplements, rather than replaces, the existing compensation system. Gainsharing evolved from:
- declining productivity growth rates
- rising manufacturing costs exceeding productivity improvements
- loss of world market share
- no increase in real earnings
- the need to improve productivity, and tie earnings to performance
- changing employee job attitudes and the need to improve the quality of work life
- the need to apply group incentives to the service or indirect personnel (critical for TBM)

There are two main principles behind the development and use of gainsharing. First, workers want to make a contribution to the business. Second, workers have skills and ideas that are not being used or communicated. The advantages of gainsharing include:
- productivity improvement
- quality of work life improvement
- increase in number of cost-saving ideas
- teamwork and cooperation encouragement
- product quality improvement
- easy to administer
- supports TBM philosophy
- leads to greater creativity and commitment
- improves communication
- promotes partnership between employee and company for ongoing continuous improvement

Several variations of gainsharing plans exist. Three of the plans—Scanlon®, developed in the mid-1930s; Rucker®, since the 1940s; and Improshare®, since 1974—illustrate most of the common variations and explain the fundamental concepts of how gainsharing works.

SCANLON PLAN®

The Scanlon Plan®, developed by Joe Scanlon, then research director of the Steelworkers Union, is the most widely known plan in the United States. The term "Scanlon Plan" is often used generically, referring in general to productivity sharing. After Scanlon's death in 1956, several associates carried on his work; Frederick Lesieur and Carl Frost were the most prominent. The Scanlon Plan® measures productivity improvement by a change in the computed ratio of total payroll dollars divided by the total dollar sales value of production. Most Scanlon Plans distribute seventy-five percent of the gains to employees and twenty-five percent to the company, though the percent can be changed. Twenty-five percent of the monthly gains are usually placed into a pool to absorb loss months; at the end of the year the entire pool is distributed. Other plan details relating to how and when sharing gains are paid, the highly structured suggestion plans, and labor management committees do not significantly differentiate the plan from others (Fein 1982).

Some characteristics of the Scanlon Plan® include:

- Management must share proprietary information.
- Portions of employee bonuses may be reserved for deficit months.
- Calculation can be modified to include allowed payroll costs by product permitting changes in product mix.
- Plan can be modified to incorporate quality/warranty costs.

Table 10-2 provides an example calculation of the Scanlon Plan® bonus earnings.

Table 10-2. Scanlon Plan® bonus earnings.

Net sales	$1,000,000
Add increase in inventory	100,000
Sales value of production	1,100,000
Allowed payroll costs (value of production) (base ratio)	220,000
Actual payroll costs	180,000
Bonus pool	40,000
Company share of bonus pool (25%)	10,000
Employee share of bonus pool (75%)	$30,000
Bonus percentage ($30,000/$180,000)(100)	16.6

RUCKER PLAN®

The Rucker Plan® was developed by Allan W. Rucker of the Eddy Rucker-Nickels Company in Cambridge, Massachusetts. Measuring productivity change as a change in the ratio between dollar payroll and dollar value added provides a different measure than the Scanlon measure of payroll dollars per dollar sales value; under value added, all purchased materials are excluded. The calculations are similar to Scanlon, except that instead of sales dollars, the figures used are sales less all purchased materials. Productivity measurement under Rucker with a single ratio presents the same problems as under Scanlon (Fein 1982).

Characteristics of the Rucker Plan® include the following:

- designed for use in manufacturing
- varying degrees of employee involvement
- employs a long-term average of the company's production value as a base
- guarantees workers bonuses based on a percentage of the production value
- no limit to size of bonus paid
- distribution formulas vary
- can be modified to include all employees
- can be modified to incorporate quality/warranty costs
- management must share proprietary information
- portion of employee bonus may be reserved for deficit months

Table 10-3. Rucker Plan® bonus earnings.

Value of Production (sales ± various adjustments)		$1,500,000
less Outside Purchases material and supplies	$750,000	
other outside purchases	240,000	
Nonlabor costs		990,000
Value added		510,000
Allowed employee labor costs (from diagnostic historical analysis: 41.17%)		210,000
Actual labor (employee costs)		180,000
Bonus pool		30,000
Company share (50%)		15,000
Employee share (50%)		15,000
Participating payroll		150,000
Bonus percentage (15,000÷150,000)		10

Table 10-3 provides an example calculation for the Rucker Plan® bonus earnings.

IMPROSHARE®

Improshare® is derived from "improved productivity through sharing." The plan was developed by Mitchell Fein and was first used in 1974. Parts of the plan were used by Fein since the 1950s. Improshare® productivity measurements use traditional work measurement standards and practices modified to a selected base period. Productivity measurement with Improshare® is different from Scanlon or Rucker. Productivity gains are shared fifty-fifty between employees and company (Fein 1982).

Characteristics of Improshare® include the following:

- Formal improvement ceiling is agreed upon between workers and management. Gains in excess of ceiling are bought back by the company and new standards developed.

- Gains are distributed fifty-fifty between workers and company.

- The number of finished products that a work group produces is measured.

- Plan can be modified to include all employees.

- Plan can be modified to incorporate quality/warranty costs.

- No proprietary information is shared.

- A portion of employee bonus may be reserved for deficit months.

- Plan does not distinguish between direct and indirect workers.

- Standards changed only when new equipment/technology is introduced.

Table 10-4 provides an example calculation for Improshare® bonus earnings.

Table 10-4. Improshare® bonus earnings.

Base Productivity Factor (BPF) =	$\dfrac{\text{Actual Hours Worked}}{\text{(Product output)(Standards)}}$ =2.00
Base Productivity Factor (BPF)	2.00
Period Productivity Factor	- 1.50
Equals	.50
Divided by Base Productivity Factor (BPF)	2.00
Equals Period Productivity Improvement	25%
Period Productivity 50/50 Sharing: Employee Period Bonus Percentage	12.5%

THE CUSTOM PLAN

Our experience shows that gainsharing provides the best motivation and reward system for TBM. Most companies today are designing custom gainsharing plans that meet their specific needs. A gainsharing plan divides productivity gains between employees and the company when productivity exceeds the level of the base period. Customizing the gainsharing plan allows companies to include nontraditional measures in the plan including quality, safety, and lead time. A prime objective of sharing is to create conditions under which workers and management benefit by moving on parallel paths to a common goal: more units of good product output made with fewer manufacturing costs; only sold finished good units are counted. (The entire plant or company works together to achieve this goal.)

Gainsharing is not just an incentive plan, it is a philosophy of managing that encourages employees to become involved in productivity improvement. Gainsharing creates a work environment in which employees see improved productivity as beneficial to them. Under the philosophy of gainsharing, worker productivity goals and management goals become congruent (Fein 1982).

The following are important considerations for developing a customized gainsharing plan for TBM:

- Who will the plan cover?
  - Direct/indirect?
  - Departments/plant?

- What formula will calculate gains?
  - Is the calculation a good measure over time?
  - Will the calculation be perceived by workers as fair?
  - Is the calculation easy to understand?
  - Is the calculation easy to administer?
  - Will the calculation isolate problem areas?

- How does the plan relate to continuous improvement teams?

- What type of behavior is desirable to support organization objectives? Does the intended plan drive this behavior?

- Can employees directly influence outcome of plan?

- Is the plan flexible?

Prerequisites for gainsharing in TBM include the following:
- relatively stable product lines or ability to develop stable formula
- effective production control and accounting procedures
- workable labor relations
- work environment of cooperation and team interaction
- willingness to create a more open-minded management climate

The major gainsharing plan options include the following:
- employee involvement is incorporated
- quality improvements/waste reduction included
- can measure plant-wide/departments/shifts/direct/indirect/support groups
- distribution formulas can vary (e.g., 80/20, 50/50)
- gainsharing calculations can be weekly or monthly
- reserves should be held for deficit months
- should incorporate matching production to sales so that excess product is not produced for finished goods inventory

GAINSHARING IMPLEMENTATION

Four steps are recommended to implement a gainsharing plan: diagnosis, design, execution, and evaluation and monitoring. These steps are outlined below.

Diagnose plan.
• Set long-range objectives (management commitment)

• Evaluate problems and opportunities
  - conduct interviews
  - visit plants

• Diagnose attitudes, behaviors, economics
  - historical productivity/quality/volume
  - historical sales/market trends
  - work measurement techniques and activity standards

Design plan.
• Set specific goals and objectives
  - top management commitment
  - involve people

• Design an appropriate gainsharing plan from generic structure
  - evaluate different gainsharing alternatives and features
  - measure proposed gainsharing plan against historical data, existing production standards, or both

• Create a schedule
  - set time tables/milestones
  - compute and evaluate cost of implementation

Execute plan.
• Inform group participants, get feedback
  – meetings
  – memos
  – newsletters

• Implement gainsharing plan (educate and train group participants)

• Monitor implementation progress

Evaluate and monitor plan.
• Evaluate impact on company objectives

• Analyze measures
  – productivity
  – product quality
  – customer responsiveness (lead time)
  – quality of work life

• Evaluate and identify improvement opportunities

REFERENCES

Fein, M. 1982. Improved productivity through worker involvement. *Annual Industrial Engineering Conference Proceedings.* Norcross, GA: Institute of Industrial Engineers.

Institute of Industrial Engineers. 1990. *Industrial Engineering Terminology: A Revision of ANSI Z94.0-1982.* Norcross, GA: Institute of Industrial Engineers.

Johnson, H. T. 1990. Chapter three in *Measures for Manufacturing Excellence,* edited by R. S. Kaplan. Boston: Harvard Business School Press.

Kaplan, R. S. 1984. Yesterday's accounting undermines production. *Harvard Business Review.* July-August: 95-101.

LeBoeuf, M. 1985. *The Greatest Management Principle in the World.* New York: Berkeley Publishing Corporation.

Lincoln, J. F. 1946. *Lincoln's Incentive System.* New York: McGraw-Hill.

Martin, D. D. and R. L. Shell. 1988. *Management of Professionals.* New York: Marcel Dekker.

McNair, C. J., R. L. Lynch, and K. F. Cross. 1990. Do financial and nonfinancial performance measures have to agree? *Management Accounting.* November: 28.

Shell, R. L. 1986. *Work Measurement: Principles and Practice.* Norcross, GA: Industrial Engineering and Management Press.

Shell, R. L. 1992a. Measurement of automated processes. In: *Maynard's Industrial Engineering Handbook,* 4th edition, edited by W. Hodson. New York: McGraw-Hill.

Shell, R. L. 1992b. Measurement of low-quantity work. In: *Maynard's Industrial Engineering Handbook,* 4th edition, edited by W. Hodson. New York: McGraw-Hill.

U. S. Government Printing Office. 1975. *MIL-STD-1567A.* Washington, DC: Superintendent of Documents, U. S. Government Printing Office.

Implementation—The Payoff for Time-Based Manufacturing 11

IMPLEMENTING breakthrough performance improvement through time-based manufacturing (TBM) is challenging and exciting to a company. Opportunities abound and surface in what can seem like overwhelming numbers. Without a clear vision supported with strong focus and direction, however, the implementation effort can rapidly degenerate into a group of unrelated activities that end with limited results. The net effect may be disappointment and frustration that undermine the smaller benefits achieved.

Make no mistake, implementing TBM requires major change in all areas of the organization. A company that does not implement some change in all functions has left potential improvement opportunities unpursued. Because the change initiative is so large, carefully diagnosing, designing, and planning for successful implementation can substantially increase the probability of success.

The approach presented in this chapter will help to ease the transition and ensure that all necessary changes are implemented. This three-phase method (Figure 11-1) focuses energies and enthusiasm into an integrated initiative of significant breakthrough improvement. The first phase, diagnostic review, develops the baseline of the current situation relative to its potential. The second phase, conceptual design, provides the common TBM vision and strategy to align the company for reduced lead times. The third phase, implementation, defines an integrated series of projects to achieve the TBM vision. During the implementation stage, the organiza-

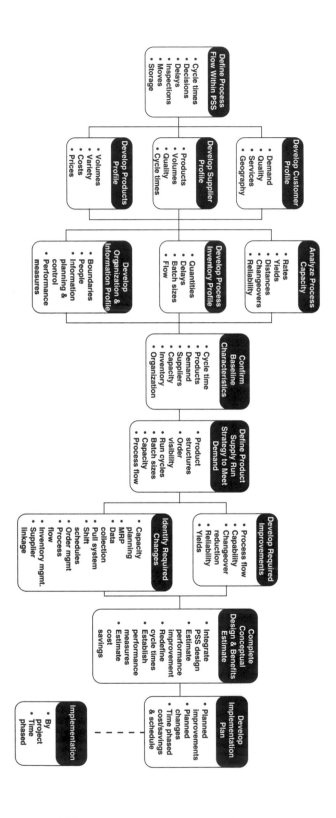

Figure 11-1. TBM implementation flow chart.

tion then begins preparing for change; it moves into implementing each defined project according to the plan and ends with the continuous monitoring of progress toward lead time reduction.

DIAGNOSTIC REVIEW

The diagnostic review begins with comprehensive data collection to form a baseline of the company's current situation that is used in assessing the TBM potential. This data collection effort follows the general work flow shown in Figure 11-2. This flow chart of the data collection is necessary to map the as-is product supply system (PSS). A brief explanation of each of the steps follows.

Identify scope of overall PSS. Correctly defining the PSS study scope is a critical step to successful data collection and analysis. The scope of study must include a common grouping of four elements: customers, suppliers, products, and the company's core converting (value-added) capabilities. These four elements combine to create a self-contained PSS for study and redesign.

Select and define process flow within PSS. Having defined the overall PSS scope of study, the next step is to further break down the overall system into a series of processes that feed each other, beginning with suppliers and ending with customers. These processes typically would include areas such as order entry, purchasing, material flow, product development, and production control. Each process contributes in some way to the overall PSS performance.

Once the processes are identified, each process should have a process map created which includes identifying and flow charting activities, decisions, delays, inspections, moves, and storage. These process maps become the PSS baseline for gathering and analyzing statistics to understand the current performance of the system.

Develop customer profile. Understanding the process begins by creating a customer profile of what the process is required to deliver. This is a major, and often overlooked, step in process mapping. The customer profile should include identifying customers, demand, quality, and geography, along with developing an understanding of additional services provided. It should include an extensive effort to study the customer demand profile and the drivers of customer behavior including marketing and selling policies and practices.

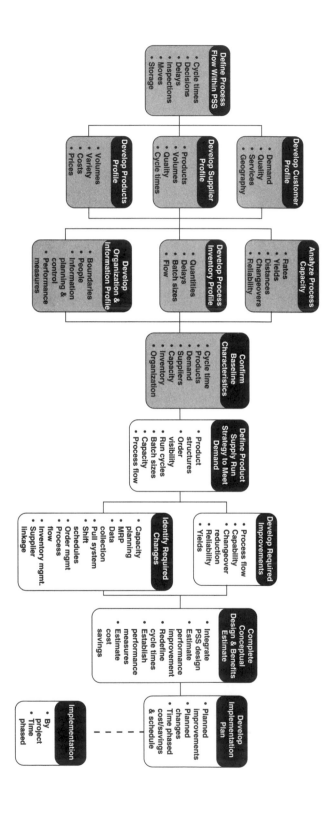

Figure 11-2. TBM diagnostic review.

Developing the customer profile also involves studying market data and customer service requirements. Initially, sales should be summarized by product group with emphasis on any demand variation and trends, such as increasing or decreasing volume levels. In addition, market perception should be assessed on price levels, product quality, service quality, etc., to determine a product group's relative standing in the market place. Demand lead time must be analyzed to understand the customer's expectation of delivery lead times relative to the PSS lead times. Finally, the company must determine the level of reduced lead time that would yield a significant competitive advantage.

Develop product profile. Along with the customer profile, a product profile should be developed to understand the product variety offered, the pricing policies, product costs, and volumes. The customer and product profiles are closely related in setting the baseline for the configuration of products and volumes that the PSS must produce and deliver.

Develop supplier profile. Converting products through the PSS generates the need to develop a supplier profile that represents the inputs into the process under study. The supplier data required includes identification of suppliers by product group and relevant information such as volumes, costs, quality, and specific products purchased.

Analyze process capacity. This step looks at the internal activities of the process and forms a baseline for a series of performance statistics to understand supply system capacity. Data collection in this step includes gathering information about reliability, changeover times, activity rates, and move distances, and matching products to activities.

Develop inventory profile. The process inventory profile is designed to understand process lead time based on the level of inventory within the process versus the demand rate. Data collection in this step should include information such as inventory quantities, delays, lead times, batch sizes, and movement. All inventory levels should be converted to their equivalent days on hand of supply based upon the demand rate.

Assess process quality. Assessing process quality begins with developing the first run yield (FRY) of the process which includes all rework activities and scrap. In addition, process capability should be measured to understand process performance relative to customer specifications.

Develop organization and information profile. This step evaluates the information system's support of the process and the organization structure through which the process passes. The organization profile determines a company's readiness to implement TBM. All companies have a distinct culture that reflects past and current management practices. Understanding this culture is critical to successful implementation. Documenting the current performance measures and cost drivers is also important to understanding the current process performance.

Any major organization change requires extensive communication efforts for successful implementation. Determining the level of past communications as well as the current vehicle for communication provides the basis for educating the organization about the new philosophy. In addition to understanding the organization, developing the information system flow and determining the level of decision-making support help to paint the overall lead time picture.

Develop the as-is baseline characteristics. This final step of the diagnostic review pulls together the data collection activities to create a baseline of current performance on several supply system characteristics, including the following:
- total PSS cycle time
- value-added time
- demand/supply match up
- process yield
- PSS costs

CONCEPTUAL DESIGN

The conceptual design phase (see Figure 11-3) is the creation of a common integrated operations strategy for the PSS. It builds upon the baseline created in the diagnostic review phase and moves the entire PSS along the continuum toward matching supply capability to demand requirements. Conceptual design elements are described below.

Define PSS run strategy to meet demand. Defining the run strategy is the major conceptual design step. The run strategy is the core operating strategy that the PSS will use as a TBM company. The limits of the conceptual design should only be constrained by physical restrictions such as equipment capability or capacity shortfall. The run strategy is defined by the five elements of synchronization: order visibility, products, cycles, batch sizes, and capacity.

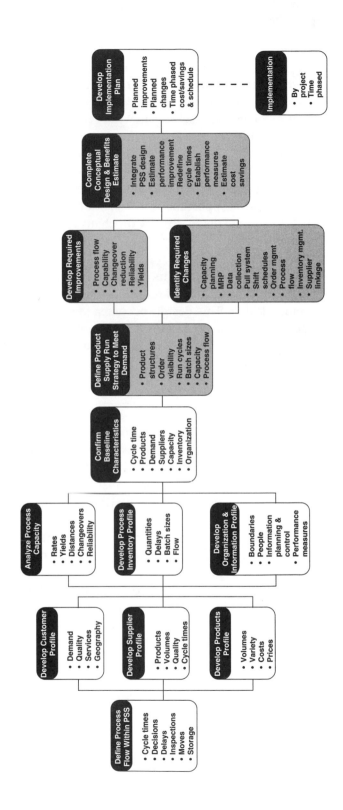

Figure 11-3. TBM conceptual design.

Design necessary improvements. Once the run strategy has been developed, a series of process improvements may be needed to support the new strategy. These include improvement in areas such as reduced changeover times, improved process capabilities, and higher reliability. Defining the necessary improvements and setting new target performance levels are completed during this step.

Determine required changes. Along with performance improvements, a variety of changes are required in policies, procedures, organization, and information systems to support the new run strategy. These changes are identified in this step, and the feasibility for change is tested to understand the opportunities.

Complete conceptual design. In this step, the run strategy is integrated with the process improvements and required changes to create the overall TBM conceptual design. This design becomes the new TBM vision and should include new performance measures, an estimate of the expected overall PSS performance improvement, and a comparison of costs savings versus investment.

IMPLEMENTATION

The implementation phase includes developing a detailed series of implementation project plans covering responsibility, work steps, resources, timing, and costs; preparing the organization for implementation; and finally, continually implementing improvements in the organization (see Figure 11-4). Implementation elements are described below:

Develop the implementation plan. Through the implementation plan, the organization essentially converts its management method from the maintenance of daily activities to a project management organization, where all initiatives, priorities, and resources are focused on achieving a single vision with multidisciplinary contributions. The implementation plan takes each conceptual design element and creates a series of project plans, containing the following elements:
• project purpose
• mission statement
• team leader and members
• work steps
• timing
• baseline performance and goals
• resources required

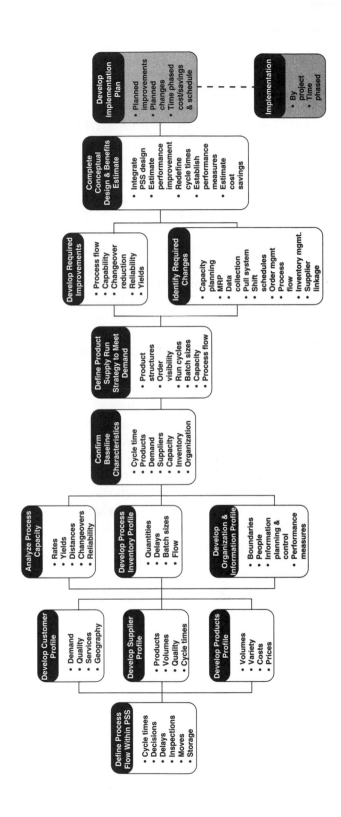

Figure 11-4. TBM implementation.

Once each project packet is completed, the company develops an overall integrated project plan through which the entire organization is managed.

Prepare for implementation. Implementation of TBM signals a new era of organization change. Preparing the organization to embrace this change is a critical component for success. Implementation preparation includes communication skills and technical training, changing organization structures, and modifying the information system. Wherever possible, infrastructure requirements should be in place before implementation.

Implement continuously. Time-based manufacturing implementation is a never-ending process. Large-scale behavior change is hard work, takes time, and causes substantial organization conflict. Confronting and managing this change process proactively is the means of ensuring the TBM competitive advantage.

A WORD OF CAUTION: WHY TBM CAN GO WRONG

Thousands of companies have embarked on some form of TBM program. Each organization has offered its own definition of what TBM is and what it means to the success of its business. In looking at these definitions, no two companies may have viewed TBM initiatives in the same way or implemented the same program. What is important is a well-defined plan and follow through by those individuals involved.

In our observations of many manufacturing organizations' TBM implementation efforts, a variety of common improvement barriers have surfaced. Summarized in the following sections are the most common TBM implementation problems.

Problem no. 1: Cellular manufacturing. When a company says it has implemented cellular manufacturing, this typically means that the company has taken existing equipment and rearranged a plant from a functional layout to a subassembly, component process, or product-line based plant layout. While this re-layout effort often benefits the company, it does not yield the breakthrough advantages seen in TBM and comes with many potential shortcomings.

In using cellular manufacturing, many companies ignore capacity planning and the principles of synchronization and balance. Synchronization requires that a cell be loaded over a period of time with the volume of work necessary to meet customer demand during that time. In addition, individual equipment rates within the cell must be balanced to the required overall output rate of the cell. So, cell staffing should be adequate to support the cell's overall demand rate. Not synchronizing a cell can result in inadequate output rates relative to customer demand. The cell may have too few of one type of machine while having too many machines of other types. When this happens, the cell will not provide the production output or productivity that management expects. The process is never under control relative to the desired performance level.

Another problem occurs in cellular manufacturing when using push-based scheduling. Push system scheduling typically involves the daily or weekly scheduling of work using machine schedules such as dispatch lists. By ignoring the pull system principle, much of the advantage of cellular manufacturing is never realized. The pull system is a fixed upper limit system of inventory replenishment that says when a unit is sold or used, an authorization (pull signal) is released to produce a replacement item. Therefore, by fixing the amount of inventory available within a cell, the cell lead time is dramatically reduced and inventory costs go down. Cellular manufacturing without the pull system will still reduce inventory in the fifteen to twenty-five percent range. However, to get the TBM breakthrough of seventy-five to eighty-five percent reduction, the use of pull scheduling within cellular manufacturing is necessary. Cellular manufacturing by itself does not embrace the encompassing nature of a TBM initiative.

Problem no. 2: Individual behavior. Successful TBM requires front-line employee involvement and teamwork. It also demands a multiskilled workforce within the PSS. Workers need to be able to work different activities throughout the PSS to support variation in demand. This situation is very different from the traditional manufacturing focus. In many companies, workers are functional specialists with relatively narrow but deep ranges of expertise. To support these specialists, individual incentive plans are often used where the employee is paid based upon his or her own production output.

To succeed in TBM, individual behavior must be changed toward group problem solving and continuous improvement teams. This requires training workers in not only new job skills, but also in team skills such as group facilitation, problem analysis, solution techniques, and presentation.

In addition, individual incentive plans must be abolished and converted to larger, group-based gainsharing plans. As discussed in Chapter 10, the gainsharing plan must be designed to provide the workforce with incentives to improve the manufacturing process in such a way that the company benefits as a whole, not as a process, for suboptimal individual reward.

Problem no. 3: Isolated focus. In a common implementation scenario, a company has started a TBM effort in one small area of opportunity. This is usually done without analyzing the bigger pipeline of opportunity, the PSS. From the customer's viewpoint, the lead time clock begins with the issue of a purchase order and ends with the receipt of a product meeting requirements. This view suggests that the TBM scope involves all facets of the organization including order entry, engineering, production planning, fabrication, final assembly, subassembly, shipment, and suppliers. By analyzing the total system, the opportunity for breakthrough improvement far exceeds the sum of the potential for each component of the system. Time-based manufacturing is not a shop floor technique, but a way to organize and manage the entire business to meet customer needs.

Problem no. 4: Making decisions without data. Many companies do not collect the type of data necessary to design a robust TBM solution. These data include detailed process flows, equipment reliability, downtimes, running rates, utilization, changeover times, and first run yields on product quality. Because of this, many TBM designs and decisions are made using only higher-level data summaries, or sometimes even without data. This can result in solutions not working as planned, and extensive frustration. Where serious problems occur, there is always a lack of understanding of some PSS component as a root cause. These problems can be avoided if detailed data are collected, analyzed, and understood.

Problem no. 5: Incremental improvement. The problem with incremental improvement in TBM is that the bigger inertia for change never takes hold. Easing into a TBM initiative by starting with a small pull signal or out-of-the-way process makes the conversion of the entire company very difficult to achieve. While continuous improvement through employee involvement is a key TBM principle, the startup of TBM should come through a conversion to a new way of doing business with all energies thrown into making it work and no old way to go back to.

Problem no. 6: Using old performance measures. As discussed extensively in Chapter 10, using old performance measures while changing to a new way of doing business will literally prevent successful implementation of the new initiative. Many companies see changing the accounting and performance measurement systems as something to be done after a successful implementation. Experience has taught us, however, that measurement systems must pull the implementation efforts toward a successful execution rather than push against the initiative through resistance. Measures must be changed before starting the new approach.

SUMMARY

Successfully implementing the TBM initiative depends on careful and comprehensive data collection and analysis, along with a thorough conceptual design and implementation plan. Spending adequate time up front to understand the PSS is paid back many times in a smoother and more successful implementation process.

Chapters 12, 13, and 14 will illustrate TBM implementation in three different manufacturing environments. These case studies represent a composite of our experiences. While they are not solely based on specific projects, they are typical examples of the application of TBM in those environments.

A Case Study in Repetitive Manufacturing 12

THIS case study is of a time-based manufacturing (TBM) implementation in a discrete repetitive manufacturer of textile consumer goods. The product supply system (PSS) includes marketing, distribution, manufacturing, and the major raw materials supplier.

Company A is a repetitive manufacturer of textile products sold in major grocery and drug store retail chains. Products are manufactured in a single plant and are sold as cases of discrete units. Approximately seven to thirty minutes are required to manufacture a dozen units, with typically one to two dozen individual units in each case.

The company has annual sales of about fifty million dollars. Products are distributed through a single distribution center, located in the Southeast. The company employs about five hundred people, including approximately three hundred union employees, who are skilled specialists in sewing, cutting, and packaging. The company produces to finished goods inventory, with customers expecting shipments within three to five days of order placement.

PRE-TBM CHARACTERISTICS

To begin the TBM initiative, Company A employed an extensive data gathering effort. The initial data collection phase allowed company management to gather and analyze baseline data to obtain an accurate picture of the environment. This information was needed to gain a complete understanding of the company's processes and to identify potential barriers to TBM. Existing programs and procedures were identified and evaluated in an effort to determine specific opportunities for improvement. The analysis was based on available historical data, more recent company trends, and supplemental data collection and analysis. The baseline data provided an understanding of pre-TBM company characteristics, as summarized in the following sections.

PRODUCT SUPPLY SYSTEM FLOW

A process flow analysis was completed for each of the eight product lines under study; moves, queues, inspections, and travel distances were identified. Based on this information, Company A completed a flow diagram for each product line, a process flow summary, and a value-added analysis of the entire area (see Table 12-1). Manufacturing lead times were found to be far greater than actual product process times (see Figure 12-1).

While manufacturing equipment was typically dedicated to product lines, materials traveled great distances, often in complicated patterns, on the shop floor. Value-added activities comprised only thirteen to sixteen percent of the production process steps required to produce the products.

UNDERSTANDING THE CUSTOMER

Company A's major customers were wholesale distributors who sell to retail drug chains and major grocery retailers. Because wholesalers were such a large component of sales, Company A often did not know the end user of their products or the major factors driving peaks in demand. Because the company accepts customer returns at any time for any reason,

Table 12-1. Summary of pre-TBM characteristics.

Product Type Number	Manufacturing Lead Time (days)	Material Move Distance (feet)	Value-Added Steps (%)	Value-Added Time (minutes/dozen)
100	13.0	360	14	10.1
200	18.2	810	13	38.2
300	10.4	750	16	31.2
400	7.2	1650	13	14.4
500	9.7	570	14	7.2
600	14.2	330	14	18.0
700	11.3	570	15	8.6

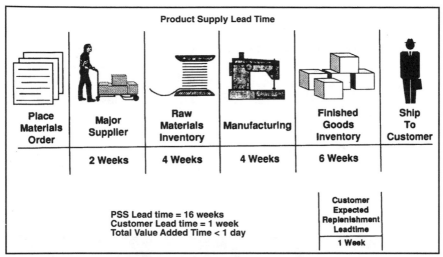

Figure 12-1. Lead time comparison.

products returned as a percent of sales revenue were very high, greater than ten percent. One product line's demand profile is shown in Figure 12-2. This profile is shown in weekly buckets because the company did not keep historical demand in daily increments.

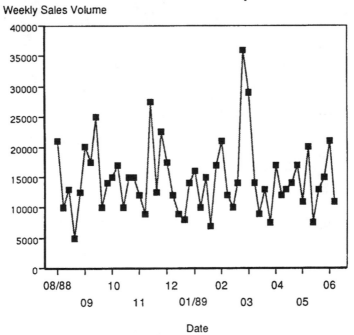

Figure 12-2. Customer demand profile.

Product Portfolio

While Company A offered a high variety of products, this variety did not present significant problems to the PSS. This was because Company A's products all used the same base materials, such as latex webbing, thread, or aluminum. Equipment was dedicated to product lines, so most of the complexity due to variety was addressed at the activity level, or in finished goods packaging.

Supply System Synchronization

Before TBM, the PSS was woefully out of balance with the customer demand profile, as shown in Table 12-2.

Table 12-2. Pre-TBM customer demand profile.

Characteristics	Customer Profile	Pre-TBM PSS
Demand profile	Weekly	6 wks F/G inventory plan
Run cycle	Daily replenishment	3-4 wks per product
Batch size	10-12 dozen	80-120 dozen
Order visibility	Actual quantity by product	Annual forecasted demand
Capacity	Varied by product and season	Didn't know, various bottlenecks existed

This was particularly significant because changeover times were very small, and adequate equipment capacity was available to meet varying demand patterns. Capacity adjustments appeared to be limited by employee capabilities because the sewing personnel were highly skilled and not easily trained.

Reliability and Capability

Plant operators had very high equipment efficiencies, due to working on a piece-rate incentive system. Although records were kept on equipment downtimes, the data were not used. There was no formal preventive maintenance program and maintenance was performed as needed or as time was available. Many dedicated machines and backups were used to offset unplanned downtime.

Although a high level of quality commitment had been demonstrated through education efforts, an ongoing quality system was not in place. Quality at Company A consisted of incoming (raw materials) and outgoing (finished goods) inspections based on attributes. No statistical quality measurements were available. Quality-related improvements came from a plant employee suggestion system and short-term corrective action teams.

SUPPLIERS

Company A directed more than sixty percent of all raw material purchasing dollars to a single supplier. This supplier provided product in monthly cycles, based on forecasts, which drove raw material inventory levels into the range of six to eight weeks supply. Inventory accuracy was also very low, about sixty to seventy percent, because inventory was spread over several unrelated locations in the raw material warehouse. Vendor quality data was not captured or analyzed. Quality problems were typically discovered during production on the shop floor, or later by customers in the field.

INFORMATION SYSTEMS

Customer order processing. Order entry required two to four working days, including executing an overnight computer batch run and printing order copies at the warehouse. Customer invoices were sent the day after order shipment.

Scheduling. Production scheduling was based on an annual forecast which was derived from a commercially available statistical forecasting software package. Production levels fluctuated greatly while end user demand was fairly constant with seasonality. Each department within the PSS had its own production schedule (see Figure 12-3), that differed from other

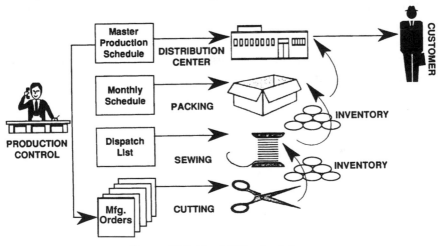

Figure 12-3. Pre-TBM scheduling.

departments. Manufacturing orders (MOs) were issued ten days before the planned start date and were used to track progress through production by bar coding each operation. The production control department reprioritized daily lists of open MOs. Backorders were not effectively included in the monthly production plan and were therefore often missed. Lot sizes were large and constant. A well-known commercial MRP II software package was used for material requirements planning. This system was configured as a standard discrete manufacturing system: that is, to produce a product, each level in the bill of material was issued its own manufacturing order for production and receipt into a central stores area. Once received into central stores the system would issue a new MO for the next-level bill of material production. This configuration demanded that a certain level of work-in-process inventory exist to support the logical system requirements. The configuration of this system drove much of the excess lead time evidenced in the PSS. Inventory inaccuracies were seen as the largest impediment to effective scheduling. Shipment performance was low because on-time shipments ranged from only seventy to eighty percent, complete shipments also ranged from seventy to eighty percent, and sixty percent of all manufacturing orders were late in the MRP II system.

SHOP FLOOR CONTROL

Manufacturing orders were bar coded upon completion of each operation in the process flow. Although considered a model implementation, the bar-code system had some apparent problems:

- Because bar codes were entered once daily, only one operation per day could be completed on a product. This situation drove a manufacturing lead time (in days) at least equal to the number of operations required to produce the product.

- Supervisors spent one to two hours a day bar coding and one hour per day editing incorrect bar code activity.

- Errors in bar coding were not immediately corrected.

- Depending on the product line, activity related to bar coding (moving to or wanding-in bar codes) made up twenty-four to thirty percent of the total production process steps.

PERFORMANCE MEASURES

Company A compensated shop employees through an individual piece-rate incentive system, which paid an average of one hundred twenty-five percent of the base wage. Individual efficiencies and highly specialized skills were considered the most important measures of worker success. No employee involvement existed. A standard cost accounting system closely tracked variance to plan. While the piece-rate structure rewarded inventory buildup, it did not penalize the production of scrap, low quality products, or rework.

SUMMARY

In summary, Company A exhibited the following pre-TBM characteristics:

- make-to-forecast system
- monthly PSS schedules
- little capacity control
- different schedules for distribution/packing/sewing/cutting/suppliers
- standard MRP II system
- large batch sizes (1000 units per batch)
- no customer order visibility
- high paperwork volume to support manufacturing orders and bar coding
- functional shop layout
- long material travel distances (average: two football fields)
- low value-added ratio thirteen to sixteen percent
- individual piece-rate pay system
- highly specialized labor skills
- quality inspection only at receiving and end of line
- total PSS lead time of about eighty days (supplier to customer)

TBM CONCEPTUAL DESIGN

Company A identified several manufacturing characteristics as the basis upon which to build TBM. For instance, recognizing that since the company sold products daily, the company could also supply products daily. The production environment had the benefit of almost no changeovers, along with primarily dedicated equipment with process times under an hour. In addition, a single supplier provided a large share of the raw materials. Building on these characteristics, while tying more directly into customer demand, formed the basis for Company A's TBM conceptual design.

Company A used a cross-organizational team approach to create the conceptual design. They identified major TBM principles applicable to their organization and formed teams to implement each principle within the overall design. Conceptual design teams were formed in the following areas:

- cell design
- production planning
- quality
- human resources
- supplier
- education and training

The teams each followed the basic sequence outlined below:

1. General education was conducted in the principles and techniques of TBM. More detailed presentations were given on quality, synchronization, reliability, pull scheduling, and gainsharing.
2. Each team developed its mission statement and goals.
3. Each team elected a chairperson.
4. Each team identified barriers to accomplishing its goals.
5. A daily meeting schedule was set to allow intensive brainstorming to address and resolve the issues identified.
6. Larger group meetings of team leaders were scheduled every two weeks to allow each chairperson to describe their team's activities and to discuss issues and recommendations.

The following sections summarize each team's charter, findings, open issues identified, and conceptual design.

THE CELL DESIGN TEAM

Charter: To create a manufacturing shop floor design (staffing, machines, processes, material) that supports TBM.

To achieve TBM capabilities, Company A's management quickly saw an opportunity to organize the PSS into eight product cells on the shop floor. These cells were organized to include products flowing through similar manufacturing equipment. This reorganization required several conceptual design considerations including capacity, material flow, employee teams, and supervision.

Using historical analysis by week of the past year's demand patterns, the team initially determined the level of production necessary to cover a minimum of eighty-four percent of all demand. This was used to derive the baseline capacity configuration for equipment in each cell. Staffing allocations per cell were based on calculations of demand at different levels. The same concept of demand was used for each to calculate cell load capacity, necessary staffing, and equipment requirements. An example of these calculations is found in Figure 12-4.

Synchronization

- Cells produce at the cell load every day.

- Cell loads are recalculated every two weeks.

- With every cell load calculation there is a cell capacity analysis based on cell reliability and first run yield.

	Weeks			
	1	2	3	4
CELL LOAD	23,000	23,000	32,000	32,000
PIECES/HOUR	575	575	804	804
NUMBER PEOPLE	7	7	10	10
NUMBER MACHINES	6	6	9	9

Figure 12-4. Cell load determination.

Material flow was simplified. Raw material was designed to enter the cells at one end and finished goods to be taken away at the other. Raw material was replenished two times per day. Finished products were pulled from the cells as needed and, because of the higher volume of movement, were placed closer to the shipping door (see Figure 12-5).

Cell team members formed continuous improvement teams. Initially, the plant manufacturing engineer was the team facilitator; ultimately, facilitation responsibility passed to cell supervisors. At initial startup, the cell teams met daily to trouble-shoot problems, and later, weekly. Substantial cross-training of workers was needed to achieve the staffing flexibility required to support various cell capacity loads.

It became immediately apparent from the cell designs that the level of shop floor supervision needed to support the previous functional layout

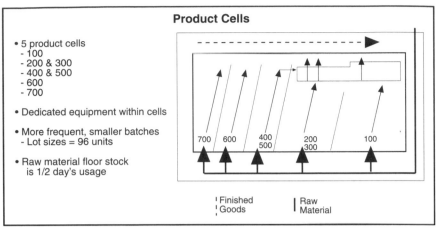

Product Cells

- 5 product cells
  - 100
  - 200 & 300
  - 400 & 500
  - 600
  - 700

- Dedicated equipment within cells

- More frequent, smaller batches
  - Lot sizes = 96 units

- Raw material floor stock
  is 1/2 day's usage

700   600   400   200   100
              500   300

Finished Goods   Raw Material

Figure 12-5. Cell layout.

would not be needed using the cellular layout. Ultimately, a third of the plant supervision moved to other areas of the organization.

THE PRODUCTION PLANNING TEAM

Charter: To design the necessary production planning and control systems to support a daily make-to-order PSS.

Manufacturing was redesigned to be driven by customer demand through a daily schedule to replenish the previous day's shipments from the distribution center. The new design is a pull-based system where manufacturing orders have been eliminated. Every day, the previous day's shipments, the current on-hand inventory, open orders, and special order demands are loaded into a daily schedule and distributed to the shop floor (see Figure 12-6). The schedule indicates the number of lots of each product to run and the sequence in which to run the lots. The lot size for all products is ninety-six units (a ninety percent reduction). Target inventory levels (including safety stocks) were initially set equal to ten days demand (a greater than fifty percent reduction). Levels were reduced further as confidence in the system grew and the company improved its response time to capacity changes.

The pull signal flow is outlined below and in Figure 12-7:

1. Cutters (the first operation) receive the daily schedule at seven o'clock each morning. A batch of pull signals (each item identified) is received with the schedule. Special orders have different color pull signals to alert the line of an unusual requirement.

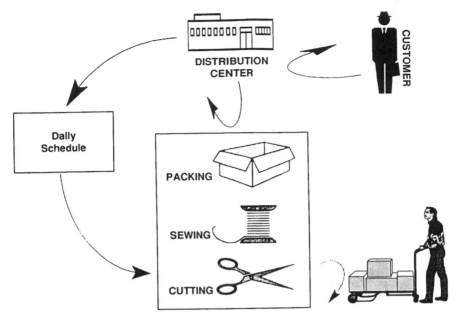

Figure 12-6. Daily integrated schedule.

2. Cutters put tickets into plastic sleeves on the sides of empty tubs. Each tub is a pull container.

3. Cutters fill tubs with cut pieces according to the schedule.

4. The next operator pulls the full tub and processes materials. Each operator has an empty tub with an empty sleeve at the station.

5. The operator fills the empty tub by working from the full tub. When finished with the tub's work, the ticket is transferred from the empty tub to the full tub.

6. The full tub goes to the queue space between operators once the queue tub is pulled by the next operator. The empty tub is kept to be filled in the next pull.

7. Each successive operator works the same way with a designated number of queue tubs between each.

8. The finished product packer pulls goods and packs according to the priority sequence set by the daily schedule. When a tub is fully packed, an inventory clerk removes the pull signal and bar codes the product into

finished goods inventory. The bar code system is not used within the cell. The pull signal (tub) is then recycled to the front of the line. The packer, pulling from the full tubs at the end of the line, signals the entire line to pull and begin work.

9. If an operator should scrap a part, a scrap ticket must be completed and given to the supervisor. The supervisor then replaces the scrapped piece from a controlled area to maintain the lot size.

PULL SCHEDULING

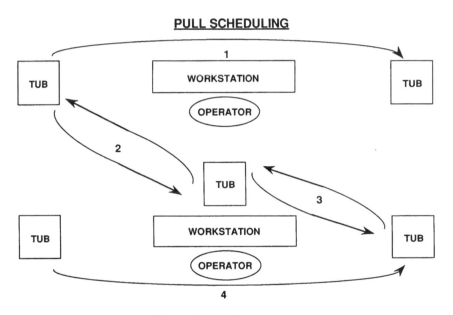

Figure 12-7. Pull system.

In support of this pull system, raw material tubs reside where needed in the line (most of them are at the cutters). Full raw material tubs contain one-half day's work. They are checked and replenished by material movers two times a day. Bar codes are only used to issue and receive raw material into and out of stock. Material movers bar code raw material as they move it.

THE QUALITY TEAM

Charter: *To design a system that measures and ensures that products are within customer specifications, produced to schedule, delivered on time, and produced with high quality.*

Stock Keeping Unit	Returns		Number Scrapped		Number Reworked		Rework Time		Cut parts	Latex	Transfer	Thread	SPI	Seam width	Press	Label	Hook	Pile	Tacks	Binding tape	Straps	Buckles	Snaps	Serge	Mat'l defects	Vulcanizing	Trim	Other
	Prior Day	Wkly Accm	Prior Day	Wkly Accm	Prior Day	Wkly Accm	Prior Day	Wkly Accm																				

DAILY CELL QUALITY REPORT — REJECT CATEGORIES

Figure 12-8. Cell quality checklist.

The quality checklist replaced quality assurance hold tags (see Figure 12-8). Quality assurance tags are used on raw material only. The quality checklist is the reporting mechanism for any quality problems. The data from the quality checklist are collected weekly and analyzed to produce a Pareto analysis of quality problems. The operator at the source of the problem completes the checklist, regardless of where in the process the problem was exposed. The checklist is a two-part form with a copy going to the area supervisor and a copy going to the quality department. Summarized reports from the checklists are distributed to the cell teams and supervisors (see Figure 12-9).

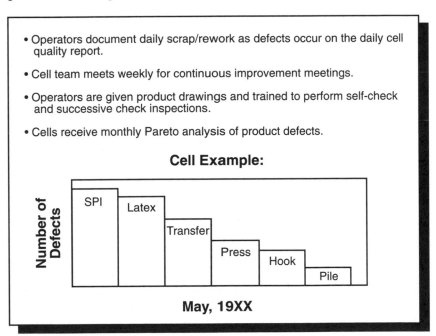

• Operators document daily scrap/rework as defects occur on the daily cell quality report.

• Cell team meets weekly for continuous improvement meetings.

• Operators are given product drawings and trained to perform self-check and successive check inspections.

• Cells receive monthly Pareto analysis of product defects.

Cell Example:

SPI, Latex, Transfer, Press, Hook, Pile (Number of Defects)

May, 19XX

Figure 12-9. Quality problem solving.

All operators perform self-checks, along with specified operators performing successive checks throughout the line. Each operator has a product design drawing with points of inspection highlighted to be used as a reference in the quality check process. The supervisor monitors the quality data collection through random spot checks. The cell teams are responsible for their own production quality.

THE HUMAN RESOURCES TEAM

> *Charter:* *To design an equitable pay scheme for all shop employees that is acceptable to both shop workers and management and that supports TBM manufacturing.*

A gainsharing program developed specifically by Company A replaced the individual piece-rate incentive system. Under this group program, any productivity gain (loss) is shared equally (fifty-fifty) between the gainsharing participants and the company in the following manner:

• Historical base productivity factor (BPF) calculated for each cell

$$\mathrm{BPF} = \frac{\text{historical actual hours}}{\text{historical finished goods produced} \times \text{IE standard}}$$

• Calculate weekly productivity factor (WPF) and compare to BPF

$$\mathrm{WPF} = \frac{\text{week's actual hours}}{\text{week's finished goods produced} \times \text{IE standard}}$$

• All weekly productivity gains (loss) shared fifty-fifty between company and gainsharing participants, paid to all members as percent of base rate

The company also developed a uniform base pay rate. Operators earning a piece-rate average above this uniform base rate were red-circled, or given their average wage. Those operators whose piece-rate average was below the uniform base were brought up to the base.

A productivity baseline was calculated based on historical data. This same formula was used to calculate weekly productivity using each week's production quantities. Weekly productivity gains or losses were determined by comparison to the baseline. Productivity gains (losses) were paid equally to all gainsharing participants as a percentage of the uniform base rate, as follows.

Example of a period bonus payout to a sewing operator

Assumptions
- Operator hourly rate (piece-work average at base rate) = $10.00
- Base rate = $8.00
- Cell period bonus percentage improvement = 10.0%
- Hours work by sewing operator = 40 hours

Payout
- Base rate × % improvement/loss = hourly differential
- $8.00 × 10% = $0.80
- Gross pay for week = $10.80 × 40 hours or $432.00

The advantages of implementing this gainsharing system are as follows:
- includes indirect workers, as well as direct
- allows work group to have stronger impact on results
- the calculation can be done daily, weekly, or monthly
- incorporates reserves for deficit months
- includes quality performance in the formula
- supports cross-training all employees

THE SUPPLIER TEAM

Charter: To integrate the major supplier's manufacturing capability into the TBM design to reduce replenishment lead time, improve quality, and lower inventory.

The supplier integration effort was driven by the opportunity to more closely match customer demand with supplier capabilities. The relationship was redesigned to be managed on a weekly pull system, where the supplier replenishes to a fixed stocking level based on weekly plant load requirements. This information is communicated each week for the next week, with daily visibility of inventory levels being available to the supplier. Batch sizes are fixed and replenished in single pallet quantities.

THE EDUCATION AND TRAINING TEAM

Charter: To develop, coordinate, and implement the TBM education and training process.

In addition to preparing and educating people about how the TBM conceptual design affects their work and responsibilities, the education program was designed to open the flow of communications. The following education program was used.

- All employees at Company A participated in one-hour kickoff meetings. Each meeting had about twenty employees and covered what TBM was, what was happening at Company A, and what was needed from the employees to support the effort.

- The initial group of employees received detailed TBM training off-site.

- The TBM team members agreed to their areas of responsibility in the implementation.

- The conceptual design teams trained employees on each component of the TBM conceptual design including findings and implementation plans. This was done in group sessions lasting from one to three hours each.

- The company conducted follow-up training as needed, including any required cross-training efforts to allow operators to perform new or different job functions.

TBM IMPLEMENTATION AND RESULTS

The TBM characteristics for Company A are summarized in the following list:
- supply linked directly to customer demand
- integrated weekly capacity control
- cellular layout
- integrated pull scheduling
- batch sizes less than one hundred units
- reconfigured MRP II system
- process flow about sixty feet
- value-added greater than fifty percent
- no shop paperwork

- multi-skilled labor teams
- cell-level quality reporting
- operator self-inspection with detailed quality specifications
- group gainsharing plan
- manufacturing lead time less than one day
- major supplier production integrated weekly
- total PSS lead time about twelve to twenty-five days

The TBM implementation plan, with major steps and timing, is shown in Figure 12-10. Within twelve months of startup, the results included the following:
- manufacturing lead times reduced eighty percent
- finished goods inventory reduced fifty percent
- work-in-process inventory reduced eighty percent
- required facility space reduced fifty percent
- total PSS lead times reduced to four weeks
- raw material inventory for major supplier reduced sixty-seven percent
- quality rework and scrap reduced more than sixty percent
- a pull-based system with manufacturing orders eliminated

	MONTH 1	MONTH 2	MONTH 3
PRODUCTION PLANNING TEAM			
1. Create daily schedule			
2. Purchase pull tubs & carts			
3. Prepare MRP system			
4. Implement cell load spreadsheet			
HUMAN RESOURCE TEAM			
1. Detail gainsharing plan design			
2. Revise IE standards			
3. Develop pay rates			
CELL DESIGN TEAM			
1. Redesign operation layouts			
2. Prepare for re-layouts			
3. Move equipment			
QUALITY TEAM			
1. Create quality reporting system			
2. Develop operator self inspection			
3. Revise product specifications			
EDUCATION/TRAINING TEAM			
1. Meet with plant personnel			
2. Conduct training (off-site)			
3. Provide targeted cell training			
4. Cross train operators			

Figure 12-10. TBM implementation plan.

A Case Study in Job Shop Manufacturing 13

COMPANY B is a custom producer of industrial equipment used in manufacturing. Products are manufactured in a single plant and sold as individually specified units. Component types are similar; however, each customer configures the product to its own needs, primarily using available options. Some products are completely custom designed and built to customer specifications. The product is shipped directly from the manufacturing plant to the customer.

The company has annual sales of approximately one hundred twenty million dollars. The company has six hundred employees, including about four hundred fifty nonunion employees on the shop floor. The time-based manufacturing (TBM) implementation in Company B includes marketing, engineering, order entry, manufacturing, and the major commodity suppliers.

PRE-TBM CHARACTERISTICS

PRODUCT SUPPLY SYSTEM FLOW

Before TBM implementation, the overall PSS lead time in Company B was about eighteen weeks, with internal lead time at about eight weeks and an additional ten weeks of lead time required in purchasing (see Figure 13-1). The internal lead time consisted of three weeks of order lead time (including order entry, engineering, and production planning) and five weeks of material flow lead time. The order process flow is shown in Figure 13-2.

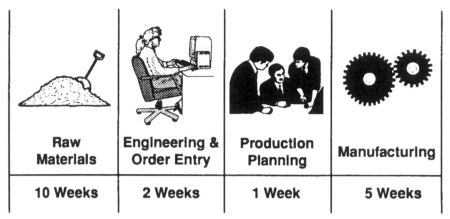

Figure 13-1. Lead time comparison.

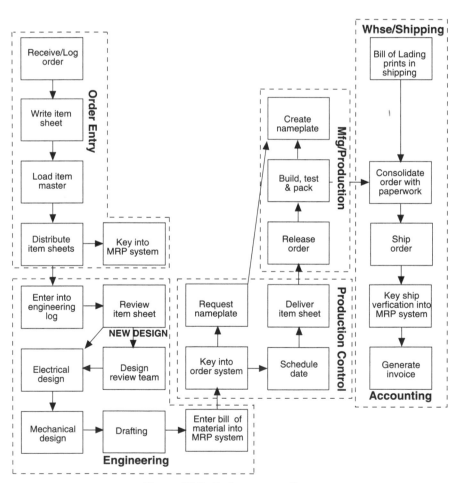

Figure 13-2. Order process flow.

The manufacturing organization was very traditional, with a functional plant layout consisting of components fabrication, welding, subassemblies, and final assembly.

A tremendous amount of data collection effort was expended initially to match company products with producing equipment in the process flow analysis. A large amount of product flow complexity existed, with many different products running across any given machine. Inventory required about forty percent of all manufacturing floor space.

The current plant setup and production processes resulted in long travel distances (about 2 miles) to produce a finished product, low value-added percent (16%), and the majority of activities (70%) being either move or store activities. The process flow summary of a typical Company B product is shown in Figure 13-3.

Component	Process Steps						Distance Traveled (feet)
	Operations	Transport	Inspect	Delay	Storage	Total	
Component A	5	20	1	12	3	41	1985
Component B	3	7	1	8	2	21	1030
Component C	4	7	1	10	2	24	870
Component D	2	5	1	4	2	14	890
Component E	6	8	1	13	2	30	1100
Component F	4	7	1	9	2	23	1070
Component G	6	17	1	10	2	36	685
Component H	4	6	1	5	2	18	670
Sub-assembly A	5	18	0	6	1	30	535
Sub-assembly B	1	6	1	2	2	12	805
Sub-assembly C	3	11	1	4	2	21	1055
Final assembly	3	11	1	2	1	18	620
Total	46	123	11	85	23	288	11,315

Figure 13-3. Process flow summary for custom product.

UNDERSTANDING THE CUSTOMER

The company studied product demand patterns to determine trends, seasonality, and other causes of variation. The demand profile used was based on weekly bookings (not shipments) that management felt would provide a truer picture of customer requirements. Company B's sales force sold directly to customers with sales volumes that tended to vary widely due to new construction and renovation. Customers tended to order in large batch sizes to minimize freight charges. Figure 13-4 shows weekly bookings for all products.

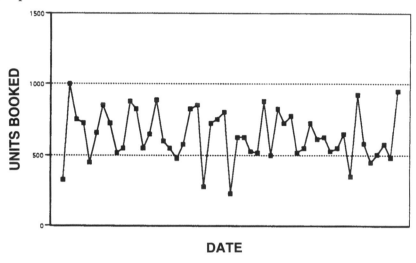

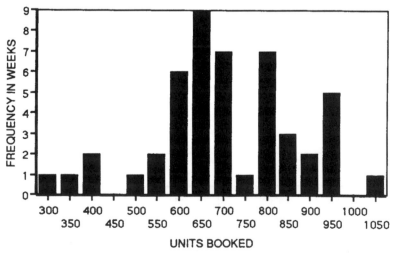

Figure 13-4. Customer demand profile (weekly bookings).

Competition for Company B had recently started promising comparable product deliveries in four weeks. Company B management felt ultimately they had to deliver product in less than four weeks (probably two weeks) to compete successfully.

PRODUCT PORTFOLIO
Because of the custom configuration requirements of Company B's products, the need for product standardization and variety reduction management was essential. The engineering group had previously implemented an effort to standardize and reduce component parts into modules for customized configurations. Therefore, Company B was well positioned in this area to move into a TBM initiative.

SUPPLY SYSTEM SYNCHRONIZATION
An analysis of PSS synchronization showed several key barriers to matching supply with demand. These are summarized in Table 13-1.

Table 13-1 Pre-TBM customer demand profile.

Characteristics	Customer Profile	Pre-TBM PSS
Demand profile	High variation within month	Eight weeks out
Run cycle	Weekly	Monthly
Batch size	By order	Very large in fabrication
Order visibility	By order	Forecasts launch components
Capacity	Fluctuating within month	Changes substantially due to batch size practices and sales practices

Changeover times substantially affected the PSS synchronization strategy, especially in the fabrication and component areas. Major changeover times fell into three categories (see Table 13-2).

RELIABILITY AND CAPABILITY
Company B did not have reporting systems in place to determine the reliability of the PSS. Intuitively, management knew this was a problem area but had no data to substantiate this belief. They had no preventive maintenance program in place. The quality system was audit based and

Table 13-2 Pre-TBM changeover times.

Number of Work Centers	Changeover Time Range (hours)
15	0.25 - 1.0
8	1.25 - 3.0
16	3.0 - 6.0

contained no statistical process control; therefore, management had no understanding of equipment process capabilities.

SUPPLIERS

A relatively small number of parts made up most of the raw materials requirements. Out of approximately seven hundred total parts, one hundred twenty comprised eighty percent of the raw material usage (see Table 13-3). These one hundred twenty products represented seven product groups. For six of the seven product groups, multiple suppliers existed (see Table 13-4). Lead times ranged from five to ten weeks.

Table 13-3. Raw material usage.

Material Class	Approximate Number of Different Part Numbers	Approximate Different Part Number		
		99% of Annual Use	90% of Annual Use	80% of Annual Use
100	82	45	25	14
200	62	35	16	11
300	27	14	7	5
400	145	84	49	35
500	126	67	37	24
600	116	50	15	9
700	106	48	28	21

Table 13-4. Purchased materials commodity analysis.

Purchase Commodity	Annual Purchases Percent of Total	Inventory Percent of Total	No. of Suppliers	Lead Time (Wks)	Reorder Point	Avg. Weeks On-hand	Inventory Turns
100	34.8	33.2	14	6	30 days	8.92	5.8
200	31.7	28.8	1	6	30 days	8.49	6.1
300	7.4	11.9	6	2	StkPgrm	15.14	3.4
400	4.3	9.6	61	6	bin min	20.68	2.5
500	15.5	7.7	2	1	bin min	4.61	11.2
600	3.3	5.2	16	4	bin min	14.89	3.5
700	3.0	3.6	21	9	bin min	11.39	4.6
Total	100.0	100.0	121				

ORDER ENTRY

Customer order processing typically required two weeks, including one week of order entry time and one week of engineering lead time to configure any custom requirements needed for the order. Customer requests requiring new product designs could take up to six months to complete including designing, prototyping, building, and testing. Company B tended to move customer orders between departments in weekly buckets.

PRODUCTION CONTROL

Production scheduling was based on a push system with one week of production planning (including rough cut capacity) and five weeks of planned manufacturing lead time. The company used a well-known commercial MRP II system with the following elements.

- The master scheduler used forecasts, an inventory status report, and customer orders to determine parent-level manufacturing orders.

- Manufacturing expeditors used the parent-level manufacturing orders to decide lower-level manufacturing orders. Orders were frequently grouped in large batches to minimize setups. As a result, lot sizes varied frequently, resource demand was inconsistent, and excessive work-in-process inventory existed.

- Production control manually calculated the work-center schedules, prepared dispatch lists, and expedited orders.

- Production schedules varied greatly across departments. They were neither frozen nor synchronized, nor were they consistently followed on the floor. Nevertheless, the system had been originally designed to use frozen schedules with standard lead times driven by the MRP II system.

- No work-in-process levels were established or controlled for lower-level component items. This practice resulted in the overproduction of components, particularly machined parts.

SUMMARY

In summary, the pre-TBM characteristics for Company B included the following:

- Product components were predominantly produced to forecast with the final product assembled to-order. MRP push scheduling was used with unlinked department schedules. Most manufacturing orders were batched together to minimize the frequency of setups.
- Capacity planning was performed on a weekly rough-cut basis.
- Lead times for finished product deliveries were planned for eight weeks.
- The plant layout and personnel resources were organized and managed functionally.
- Materials traveled excessive distances—components typically traveled a total of 2.1 miles.
- Material handling systems were labor intensive.
- The quality system was audit based with no statistical quality control.
- Lead times for key raw materials ranged from five to ten weeks.
- Key raw materials came from multiple suppliers.
- Work-in-process inventory storage used forty percent of production floor space.
- No effort was made to manage and improve reliability and capability.
- Shop-floor team initiatives did not exist.

TBM CONCEPTUAL DESIGN

Based upon the understanding of Company B's historical characteristics, several key design considerations emerged as most important to the success of TBM. These included:

- Redesigning the PSS process flow into product families to reduce the excessive travel distances. This involved heavy group technology analysis to understand product structure modularity and product/equipment relationships.

- Reducing changeover times in the fabrication area to eliminate the need for large batch sizes and to eliminate the grouping of similar manufacturing orders.

- Improving reliability and process capability was heavily emphasized. Because no data were available in these areas, the need to establish performance baselines was critical.

- Reducing the supplier base and forming co-op contracting relationships. Having multiple suppliers for each product group provided strong improvement opportunities in this area.

To complete the conceptual design, Company B formed five teams:
- cell layout
- production planning
- order processing
- quality and reliability
- supplier relations

CELL LAYOUT TEAM

Based upon the data collection and baseline review, Company B's key design concept was to synchronize the PSS by organizing the manufacturing process into cells including a base unit cell, three model size cells, and several service cells. The base unit cell performed machining operations on the components of five product model types. Each model size cell supplied two subassemblies and the final machine assembly. Service cells provided processing and services to all model size cells (e.g., clean, test, paint, and pack).

Model size cells provided clearer visibility into the progress and status of each machine being built. Work teams in the cell could better relate the effects of their actions on a component. These cells also enhanced communication among everyone associated with the production of quality machines

The overall manufacturing concept and conceptual plant flow diagram (Figure 13-5) is based on three model size cell families. To locate equipment at appropriate cells, workcenters were evaluated for functionality, commonality of use across model sizes, and redundancy (multiple machines per workcenter). Machines were preliminarily assigned to appropriate model size cells and a capacity analysis was completed to determine capacity constraints. Staffing and shifts were adjusted to minimize or eliminate over/under-capacity situations. Equipment was also adjusted between cells as appropriate. Process lead times were developed for each cell. Space savings from this concept totaled thirty-three percent.

Conceptual PSS Flow

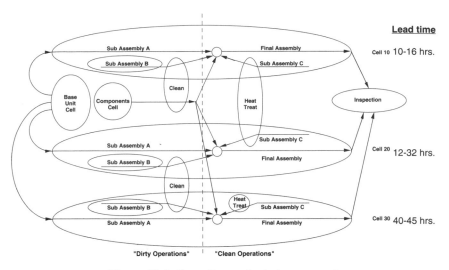

Figure 13-5. Overall manufacturing concept.

PRODUCTION PLANNING AND SCHEDULING TEAM

Demand data were restructured to correlate with the three model size cells (see Figure 13-6). The new demand profiles were used to identify demand variability and set capacity loads for each cell.

The production planning logic for the conceptual design is shown in Figure 13-7. It included heavy use of pull systems to move product through the facility. The following are cell characteristics:

- Cell loads are set weekly in capacity hours; cell resources and changeover times are the constraining factors.

- The daily sequence schedule is based on the critical path within the total process. Products can be optimally sequenced within the day as long as the daily demand and cell load are produced. When a part reaches a predetermined point in the critical path, a signal to produce companion parts is generated.

- The daily sequence of base units is supplied at the front of the subassembly subcell.

- Pull systems are used to execute movement through each cell (see Figure 13-8). First pull begins in final assembly. The daily sequence schedule is executed by FIFO.

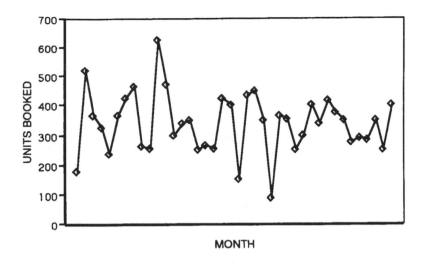

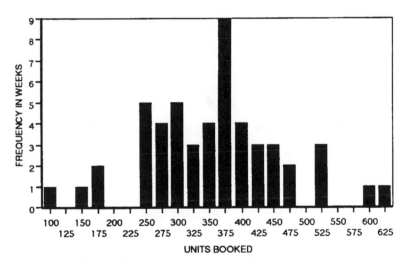

Figure 13-6. Cell A demand profile (weekly bookings).

ORDER PROCESSING TEAM

In addition to manufacturing cells, the two-week lead time to process a customer order was reduced by designing and implementing an order processing cell and a continuous improvement team. The order processing cell employed concurrent engineering techniques. The continuous improvement team identified and eliminated root problems affecting the quality and timeliness of information received from field sales. It also

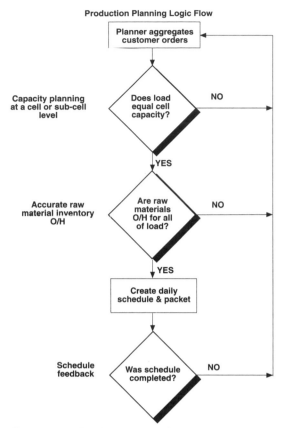

Figure 13-7. Production planning and scheduling design.

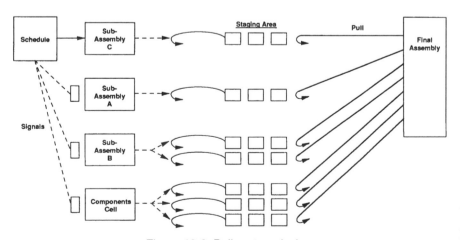

Figure 13-8. Pull system design.

worked on problems with retrieving machine information, including drawings and specifications, and problems with the ability to enter parts early for production into fabrication while final drawings for assemblies are being completed

The overall concept yielded a PSS in-house lead time of three weeks (versus eight) with the ultimate objective of two weeks (see Figure 13-9).

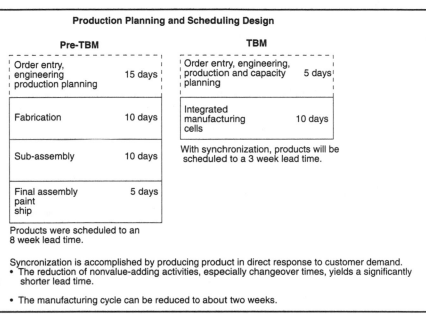

Figure 13-9. Planning system comparison.

QUALITY AND RELIABILITY TEAMS

Within each cell, continuous improvement teams were designed to address shortcomings in changeover times, quality, and reliability. These teams were led by manufacturing engineers. Each team began by establishing basic data collection and analysis, followed by implementing statistical process control to understand equipment capabilities. Primary emphasis initially was in the base unit cell where fabrication practices caused extensive downstream performance problems. Intensive improvement efforts were immediately invested in reducing changeover times, increasing reliability, and achieving process capability in the base unit cell. Improvement in these areas came from the changeover reduction and capability improvement methodologies discussed previously. These areas were critically needed short-term improvements to achieve the two-to-three week PSS in-house design lead times.

SUPPLIER RELATIONS TEAM

A co-op contracting team was implemented to develop supplier performance measures and certification. After evaluating overall suppliers effectiveness, the team formalized relations with a reduced number of suppliers. This resulted in improved raw material quality and lead times and reduced inventory. The team targeted the base units along with one additional product group because these groups represented the largest inventory dollar opportunities for improvement. The team set a goal of reduced lead times for the two groups of greater than fifty percent. Key steps toward this goal included the following:

- establishing a co-op team with representatives from quality, engineering, purchasing, manufacturing, and accounting
- establishing performance measures
- developing educational plans and training the co-op team
- establishing supplier certification procedures
- developing a procurement strategy that addressed the two major product groups
- evaluating suppliers
- constructing a matrix of supplier capabilities
- negotiating, implementing, and measuring the new procurement strategy success

SUMMARY

This conceptual design resulted in the following TBM characteristics for Company B:

- direct linkage and synchronization of the PSS to customer demand (orders)
- a product family cell for base units, three model size cells, and service cells for other processes
- implementation of pull scheduling to reduce lead times
- two to three-week manufacturing cycles with appropriate capacity planning
- changeover times reduced by greater than sixty percent
- greater flexibility to manufacture what is needed, when it is needed, in the needed batch size
- closer relationships with suppliers and customers resulting in integration of information and material flow from raw material to delivered product
- prevention-based quality management
- cell-based teams that focus on continuous improvement
- concurrent engineering through an order entry cell

TBM IMPLEMENTATION AND RESULTS

The TBM implementation plan shown in Figure 13-10 started with a pilot cell to acquire knowledge and experience and required about six months to complete. Rollout to the entire company was completed in eighteen months. The work steps for the pilot implementation are outlined below.

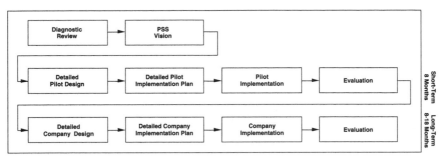

Figure 13-10. TBM implementation plan.

Detailed pilot design. The detailed pilot design consisted of plant and support system designs as outlined below.

The plant design contained:
• cell capability and reliability
• cell changeover reduction
• cell detailed layout
• cell material flow and handling
• capital and resource needs

The support systems design contained:
• order entry and engineering
• production planning, scheduling, and sequencing
• pull system rules
• capacity planning and cell loads
• inventory queues and levels

In addition, a considerable investment was made in validating pre-implementation data and training and education for the organization.

Detailed pilot implementation. The detailed pilot implementation plan consisted of the following steps:

1. defining the management structure to lead the implementation pilot
2. planning the sequence of events necessary to rearrange the physical equipment with minimum disruption to production requirements
3. time-phasing the list of activities to be undertaken, including detailed cost estimates
4. defining the activities and those responsible for completing them

Pilot evaluation. By evaluating the pilot implementation, critical success factors to be used with the TBM conceptual design could be measured. Key success factors included:

- manufacturing and supplier lead time reduction
- quality improvement
- changeover time reduction
- schedule linearity
- inventory reduction
- customer service improvement
- order entry and engineering lead time reduction

The following results were achieved by implementing the TBM design:

- PSS lead time reduction of greater than sixty-seven percent
- reduced inventory, raw, and WIP by seventy percent
- significant annual cost savings
- space reduction of thirty-three percent
- improved quality, measured by reduced yield loss, rework, and scrap of twenty percent
- improved productivity of shop labor by fifteen percent

A Case Study in Food Processing 14

COMPANY C is a national consumer goods food manufacturer providing products to major grocery retailers, convenience stores, and club stores. The product supply system (PSS) includes marketing, promotion planning, distribution, manufacturing, and raw materials suppliers. The products manufactured and sold include branded products requiring processing of powdered ingredients and product packing in cartons. Company C has a single manufacturing plant in the Midwest, along with six distribution centers located throughout the United States. The company has sales of two hundred million dollars and employs approximately seven hundred people, including about three hundred nonunion manufacturing employees. Company C produces to stock with customer orders being shipped from the plant as well as the six distribution centers.

Company C operates in the highly competitive consumer goods manufacturing industry. This industry has undergone tremendous changes during the last few years that have substantially increased pressures on manufacturers to respond. These changes include:

- increased competition and cost pressures
- higher consumer expectations
- the shift from traditional grocery retailers to alternative formats, such as club stores and discounters
- increased product variety demanded by consumers
- the need for quicker responsiveness to keep inventories low and maintain fresher products

- the recognition that traditional promotion planning practices often lower PSS performance

In response to these changes, Company C embarked on a TBM initiative to redesign the PSS to better satisfy these emerging market trends. This case study reviews a single processing/packing system to illustrate the TBM applications.

PRE-TBM CHARACTERISTICS

A substantial initial effort went into collecting and analyzing data. The analysis was made from a combination of historical data, data available to Company C but not previously analyzed, and entirely new data collection activities. The emphasis during this period was to understand the capability of the PSS to meet the customer demand profile. The baseline data identified the pre-TBM company characteristics summarized in the following sections.

PSS Flow

A process flow analysis was completed for the entire PSS. The analysis began with supplier production, went through the internal manufacturing processes including the processing/packing system, continued into the distribution organization, and finally analyzed the customer. This process analysis yielded an interesting finding relative to the previous two case studies. Company C discovered through the process flow analysis that there was little opportunity to affect the lead times of the PSS by using traditional cellular layout techniques. The equipment was simply too big and too costly to consider moving.

Company C's management perceived that TBM principles apply differently to a process business and that traditional approaches would not prove useful. As shown in Figure 14-1, however, management did discover a substantial difference in the PSS cycle time, beginning with the supplier and ending with the customer, as compared with the total processing time of a single case of finished product. While a case of product typically took less than a half-day of processing time, the overall PSS lead time was in the fifty-five day range. This meant that the value-added time of a typical case of product, when compared to the total supply system lead time, was less than one percent (four hours versus fifty-five days). The biggest share of this lead time was found in inventory because large inventories existed in several locations in the PSS, in finished goods, and in raw materials.

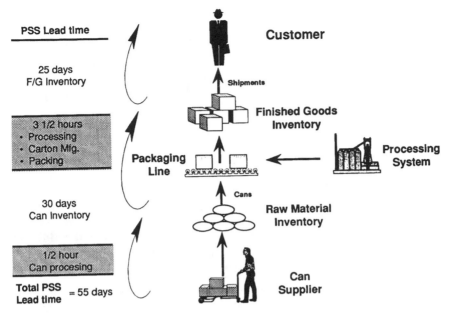

Figure 14-1. Company C product supply system.

UNDERSTANDING THE CUSTOMER

Company C's major customers were grocery retailers, club stores, and convenience stores. While sales traditionally had been dominated by the grocery retailers, recently sales were increasing from club stores. Company C ran a traditional promotion planning system, where heavy investments were made in promotion advertising and discounting to persuade both the customer and the consumer to purchase Company C's products. Promotion initiatives used by Company C generally involved giving deals in which the company offered a substantial price reduction to the customer in return for increased purchase volumes. In addition, Company C annually advertised and offered substantial price-off specials to the consumer. The biggest of these specials came during Easter.

The promotion planning process induced a substantial amount of variation into the customer demand profile. This increased variation had several interesting implications. At various times during the year, the increased promotion volume required Company C's manufacturing organization (and often a few suppliers) to work overtime to meet demand. In addition, Company C had a prebuild period for the Easter season during which they produced and stored extra product in finished goods inventory to meet the anticipated volume peak due to promotion. While the promotion plan increased volume for Company C in the short term, it also added additional PSS costs to produce and deliver the extra volume. Predictably, customer demand dropped dramatically following the end of the promotion period.

Along with the increased PSS costs due to promotion, the grocery retailer also incurred extra cost to purchase the product on deal. These costs came from the extra inventory storage costs required to hold the additional volume purchased until the consumer demand required it. While Company C felt that these promotion planning practices resulted in increased consumer spending for their products at the grocery counter, data based analysis showed a quite different story. The upswing in consumer use of the promoted product was far lower than the actual variation induced by the promotion policy on the manufacturer's demand profile.

This analysis allowed Company C to understand that it gave price-off deals to the retailer, thereby enticing the retailer to buy additional product that was stored in distribution inventory. This practice created additional costs for all components of the PSS, while minimally influencing customer demand. A customer demand profile for the Company C processing/packing system is shown in Figure 14-2.

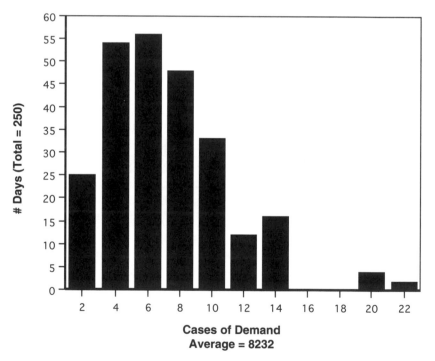

Figure 14-2. Company C daily customer demand profile.

PRODUCT PORTFOLIO

A major trend in the consumer goods industry in recent years has been the increasing product variety being offered to the consumer. This trend has driven Company C's marketing organization to substantially increase the number of products offered in its product lines. During the last three years, Company C has increased product variety by two hundred percent. This increasing variety has become a substantial issue to Company C because PSS capabilities have not kept pace with the increased complexity. The end result of this mismatch was dramatically increased inventories during this time period causing additional product costs, unneeded warehouse space, and overall lengthened supply system lead times. An analysis of the total products offered showed that fifteen percent of Company C's products yielded eighty-five percent of company sales and the bottom fifty percent of products yielded less than three percent of sales.

Table 14-1 and Figure 14-3 show a comparable example of a pre-TBM variety profile and the implication of adding products in a capacity-constrained process environment. This example illustrates how only four new products can dramatically affect the remaining products on a processing/packing system. This occurs because the increased changeover time (ten hours per week) from the new products offsets the increased run time (sixteen hours per week). Because capacity is not available to absorb the extra changeover and run hours within the week, the only alternative is to run several products on longer (two-week) run cycles instead of the previous one-week cycle. When this lengthening of run cycles is required, costs increase, inventories rise, and lead times lengthen.

SUPPLY SYSTEM SYNCHRONIZATION

As shown in Table 14-2, Company C's PSS did not match up with customer demand.

Changeover times in Company C's processing/packing system averaged about three hours, primarily due to package size changes and system cleanouts. Changeovers and system capacity were clearly significant barriers in the synchronization of PSS capability with the customer demand profile. The run cycle and batch size strategy employed by Company C are shown in Table 14-3 and illustrated in Figure 14-4.

Table 14-1. Increased product variety in a capacity-constrained environment.

Characteristics	Baseline	Increased Variety
Number of Products	10	14
Percent Volume Increase	NA	20%
Scheduled Uptime	120 hrs	120 hrs
Run Time	78 hrs	94 hrs
Available Time	42 hrs	26 hrs
One Week Cycle		
Number c/o's per week	50 (5 days * 10/day)	70 (5 days * 14/day)
Hrs per c/o	1/2	1/2
C/o hrs per week	25	35
Available time after c/o	(42 hrs-25 hrs) = 17	(26 hrs-35 hrs) = NA
Two Week Cycle		
Products @ one week cycle	NA	6
Products @ two week cycle	NA	8
Revised c/o's per week	NA	50 (5 days * 10/day)
Revised c/o hours per week	NA	25
Available time after c/o	NA	26 hrs - 25 hrs = 1 hr
c/o = changeovers NA = not applicable		

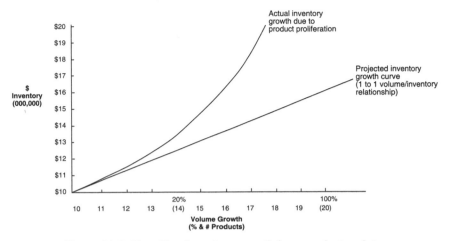

Figure 14-3. Resulting inventory growth from product variety.

Table 14-2. Pre-TBM synchronization.

Characteristics	Customer Profile	Pre-TBM PSS
Demand profile	Daily	6 wks finished goods inventory plan
Run cycle	Daily	Monthly
Batch size	Daily SKU equivalent	20 days supply
Order visibility	Daily actual quantity by product	Rolling Monthly forecast
Capacity	Promotion driven spikes	Adequate with self-induced, unplanned shortfalls

Table 14-3. Pre-TBM run cycle strategy.

MONTHLY RUN STRATEGY				
PRODUCT	SALES/DAYS	SALES/MONTH (21 DAYS)	AVG. DAYS PRODUCTION/MONTH*	AVG. RUN CYCLE LENGTH
A	2423	50479	6.2	Once/month
B	1729	36021	4.4	Once/month
C	1482	30875	3.8	Once/month
D	1235	25729	3.0	Once/month
E	576	12000	1.6	Once/month
F	247	5146	0.6	Once/2 months
G	230	4792	0.6	Once/2 months
H	190	3958	0.5	Once/2 months
I	80	1667	0.2	Once/6 months
J	40	833	0.1	Once/year
	8232	171500	21.0	

* Avg. days production/month = Sales/month ÷ 171,500 Sales/month x 21 days/month

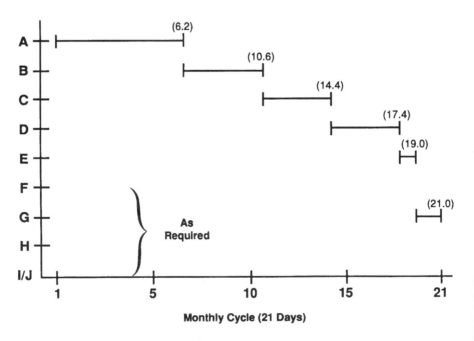

Figure 14-4. Pre-TBM run cycles strategy.

RELIABILITY AND CAPABILITY

Company C did not measure reliability and capability of the processing/packing system. To develop a reliability baseline, data were collected for a thirty-day period to document the current performance. Early on, it became apparent that system reliability was low. As shown in Table 14-4, the reliability of the overall system was measured at thirty-three percent. In addition, the first run yield on the system was ninety-six percent, as measured by actual good versus potential products produced. Statistical process control was used on the processing systems relative to product quality; however, an overall understanding of process capabilities was not available.

SUPPLIERS

Suppliers for Company C were generally classified under three material types: commodities, cans, and packaging supplies. While material commodities were relatively low in inventory—ten to fifteen days on hand—packaging materials were substantially higher—in the range of forty-five to sixty days. These levels resulted from the high proliferation

Table 14-4. Company C processing/packing system reliability.

Equipment Rated Speed	= 730 units/hr = 17520 units/24 hr day
Actual Run Rate	= 730 units/hr
Equipment Scheduled	= 100 hrs/week
Equipment Available	= 24 hrs * 7 days = 168 hrs/week
Unscheduled Equipment Downtime	= 42 hrs/week
Yield Loss	= 1520 units/week
Uptime	= 100 hrs/wk ÷ 168 hrs/wk = 60%
Dependability	= (100 hrs - 42 hrs) ÷ 100 hrs = 58%
Yield	= 40820 good units ÷ 42340 total units = 96%
Reliability	= (Uptime)(Dependability)(Yield) = (60%)(58%)(96%) = 33%

of products; substantially more packaging materials were needed on-hand to accommodate the variety that marketing required. In addition, Company C had multiple suppliers of packaging material which offered substantial opportunity to consolidate and tighten the discipline in packaging materials supply.

The can supply offered Company C the greatest opportunity for a PSS breakthrough. A single can supplier provided five different can sizes on a monthly basis. The supplier had a dedicated can line supplying Company C, which produced in monthly run cycles and had a changeover of about ten minutes between products.

INFORMATION SYSTEMS

Order entry required three days to process an order from order receipt to shipment of finished goods. Production scheduling was based on rolling monthly forecasts and product volume inputs were derived from a statistical forecasting package. Company C managed planned inventory levels of about five weeks' supply versus forecasted demands, relative to the supply system's capacity to meet that demand.

Each week, the production control department issued a production schedule for the next week's products. This schedule was revised an average of five times per week. These revisions came from a constantly changing inventory position with Company C frequently running the wrong products when shortages became known. In addition, Company C's can supplier based its production on monthly schedules, and therefore, was inflexible in responding to weekly changes in product requirements. The results of these difficulties were a low on-time shipment performance of approximately eighty percent and a low complete-shipment performance of approximately eighty-five percent. Because inventory control in Company C's PSS lagged actual material movement by two days, Company C's management always worked with two-day old product status information.

PERFORMANCE MEASURES

Performance measures at Company C were simple and straightforward. The primary performance measure was manufacturing cost for each product and the company used an actual cost accounting system. The organization's major goal was to continue decreasing product costs. To achieve this objective, the manufacturing organization's goal was to produce all possible products out of the current processing/packing equipment. Increasing output of product on this equipment allowed Company C to absorb costs into more units produced, thereby decreasing costs on an individual product basis. This, of course, resulted in high inventory levels and distribution costs, that could be seen in the six distribution centers located around the country.

The other major performance measure in Company C was that of customer satisfaction, which was derived from a combination of on-time shipments and completeness. As previously discussed, both of these indicators were relatively low, with an overall customer satisfaction level in the range of sixty-five to seventy percent.

SUMMARY

In summary Company C exhibited the following pre-TBM characteristics:

- produce to forecast
- traditional product promotions
- highly variable customer demand profile
- large run sizes
- high inventory levels
- complex production schedules
- frequent schedule changes
- long setup times
- different daily schedules for distribution, manufacturing, and suppliers
- high product variety
- low overall reliability (thirty-three percent)
- first run yield of ninety-six percent
- no formal supplier partnerships

TBM CONCEPTUAL DESIGN

As Company C embarked on its journey to develop a TBM conceptual design, company management saw that the information gathered from the data collection and analysis efforts offered the company a new understanding of the business. This new understanding opened up tremendous opportunities to redesign the business using time compression principles. The new understanding was based upon the following general characteristics:

- The company sold product daily; therefore, it should strive to redesign the PSS to supply each product daily.
- Much of the variability for Company C's demand profile was driven by internal marketing, sales, and advertising policies. This situation provided Company C with the proper knowledge to modify customer behavior so that it aligned more closely with demand within PSS capabilities.

- Company C discovered a critical need to integrate the can supplier capabilities directly into the PSS synchronization profile. This need for a tight linkage had not previously been recognized and, in itself, represented a breakthrough opportunity.
- When evaluating PSS capability versus the customer demand profile, Company C discovered that it had adequate capacity to meet daily demand. Meeting daily demand, however, would require strong changeover reduction efforts and reliability improvement on the processing/packing system (see Figure 14-5).

To complete the conceptual design, Company C created teams in the following areas:
- production planning and control
- reliability and changeover
- supplier integration
- demand management

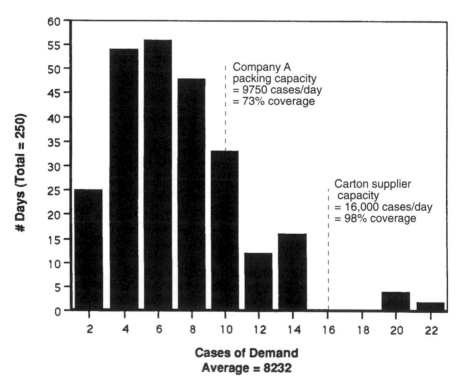

Figure 14-5. Company C capacity profile.

PRODUCTION PLANNING AND CONTROL TEAM

The production planning and control team set the overall conceptual design for Company C's TBM strategy. This design was driven by the objective to daily match the customer demand profile with the PSS capability. This is shown in Table 14-5.

Table 14-5. TBM synchronization.

Characteristics	Customer Profile	TBM PSS
Demand profile	Daily	Daily
Run cycle	Daily	Daily
Batch size	Daily SKU equivalent	Daily SKU equivalent
Order visibility	Daily actual quantity by product	Daily actual quantity
Capacity	Stable with seasonality	Buffered planned shortfalls

This run strategy (see Table 14-6 and Figure 4-6) became the integrating component of the overall conceptual design. As seen in Figure 14-6, the run strategy developed by the team had Company C running daily cycles for products A-E and three-day run cycles for products F, G, and H. This run strategy was based on an estimated minimum run length (batch size) of one hour on the processing/packing system. Based upon these same estimates, the production planning team recommended to Company C's senior management that products I and J be eliminated. These products represented about one percent of Company C's sales revenue and required significant investments in packaging materials and ingredients, along with the need to produce about one to two weeks' worth of demand based on a one-hour minimum batch size.

This run strategy also required keeping about four days of finished goods inventory to buffer those days when demand exceeded capacity. It also allowed other teams to set several PSS priorities for improvement.

RELIABILITY AND CHANGEOVER TEAM

Based upon the run strategy discussed above, the reliability and changeover team tried to accomplish several key goals. Given the run

Table 14-6. Daily run strategy.

DAILY RUN STRATEGY			
PRODUCT	SALES/DAYS	AVG. HOURS PRODUCTION PER DAY*	AVG. RUN CYCLE LENGTH
A	2423	6.0	once/day
B	1729	4.2	once/day
C	1482	3.6	once/day
D	1235	3.0	once/day
E	576	1.4	once/day
F	247	0.6	once/three days
G	230	0.6	once/three days
H	190	0.5	once/three days
I	80	0.2	out
J	40	0.1	out
	8232	20.2	

Daily Rate Per Hour = (Design Rate/Hour)(Dependability)(Yield)
= (730 Units/Hour)(58%)(96%)
= (407 Units/Hour)

Avg. Daily Processing/Packing System Capacity Required (not including c/o's)
= 8232 Units/Day ÷ 407 Units/Hour
= 20.2 Hours/Day

cycles shown in Figure 14-6, the team knew that Company C would have to make six changeovers each day with about four hours available to do them. The team then determined that the company had to execute changeovers within forty minutes elapsed time each (240 min/6 changeovers).

This forty minute changeover goal represented a seventy-eight percent reduction (180 min baseline - 40 min goal) from the baseline of three hours. While this was an aggressive goal, the team felt it was attainable and immediately began to implement the standardized changeover reduction methodology.

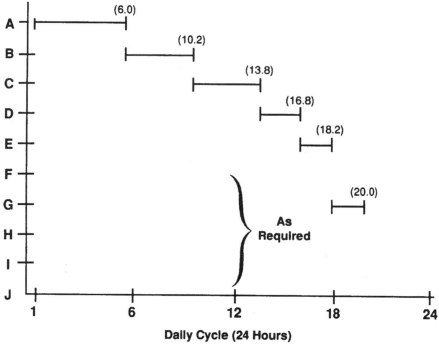

Figure 14-6. TBM daily run strategy.

Increased system reliability was also a key leverage point to the new PSS run strategy. With the previous levels of dependability and yield, the processing/filling system capacity satisfied about seventy-three percent of the daily demand profile. By increasing dependability from fifty-eight percent to seventy percent, the PSS capacity improved to a demand profile coverage of about eighty-six percent—a much higher level of coverage. This understanding sent the team into a detailed data collection effort to study unscheduled downtime for the processing/packing system. The effort included the immediate startup of a continuous improvement team on the system, thereby quickly involving operators in the much needed improvement effort.

SUPPLIER INTEGRATION TEAM

Because the run strategy required daily run cycles, the supplier integration team had to create a very tight information linkage between daily customer orders and planned supplier production. In essence, the supplier became the beginning of the daily PSS cycle by providing Company C's processing/packing system with the appropriate mix and quantity of cans to produce the required end items. Company C and the supplier's management team agreed that they would begin the run strategy with one day's supply of cans available for all five products. This quantity would buffer any uncertainties in the reliability of the system. The information flow among customer orders, the processing/packing system, and the can supplier is illustrated in Table 14.7.

Table 14-7. Run strategy information flow.

Day Shift	Monday 1 2 3	Tuesday 1 2 3	Wednesday 1 2 3
Orders received	X		
Finished goods inventory data received	X		
Production planning	X		
Can supplier production		X X X	
Packing line production		X X X	
Shipments			X X X

DEMAND MANAGEMENT TEAM

The demand management team had the goal of changing promotion and advertising practices to better smooth the customer demand profile. Initially, this process began by holding weekly meetings between marketing, operations, and the can supplier to gain a complete understanding of the company's marketing plans. This new communication immediately improved the planning ability of PSS management. Over time, the marketing department modified several promotion initiatives by providing incentives for customers to take deals over an appropriate delivery period (generally one to two weeks). They also moved several products to an everyday low price position. This provided a truer demand picture on these products without the added investment of promotion efforts and additional PSS promotion-related costs within the company.

SUMMARY

The TBM conceptual design provided a breakthrough in lead time reduction for Company C (see Figure 14-7). The TBM characteristics are as follows:

- make to demand
- almost all volume produced every day (ninety percent)
- same schedules for entire PSS
- immediate performance feedback
- pull scheduling between activities
- synchronized supply and demand
- daily supplier integration
- well-defined run strategy
- cross-organization teams

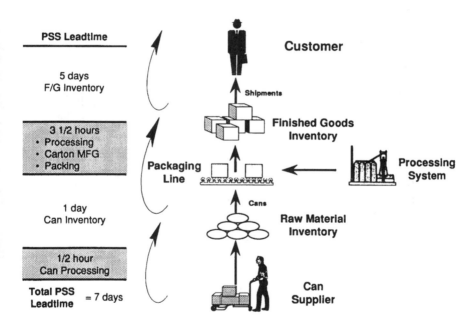

Figure 14-7. TBM PSS lead time.

TBM IMPLEMENTATION AND RESULTS

The TBM implementation took six months. The main drivers were:

1. *Improving reliability and capability of the processing/packing system*—This came through the creation of a continuous improvement team, comprised of line technicians, purchasing, and maintenance personnel.
2. *Implementing the changeover reduction methodology*—The largest share of improvements came from standardizing changeover activities and training in better procedures for these activities. In addition, a major breakthrough was achieved by redesigning packing system tooling to eliminate the need to perform a complete system changeout for each new can size. Also a new mixing tub was purchased to allow a quicker changeover of tubs when changing to a new product versus performing the cleaning out task internally.
3. *New communication procedures between inventory, production, and the can supplier*—In addition, computer program changes were implemented to allow access to inventory and customer order status daily.
4. *Personnel training*—Extensive training was needed to introduce Company C's personnel to the idea of TBM in a process manufacturing environment. This implementation represented a new application of TBM principles to a very different situation. The organization change required to accept TBM was substantial and, in the end, was the major barrier.

Within twelve months of startup, Company C's results were:
- lead time reduced more than eighty percent
- finished goods inventory reduced seventy-five percent
- raw materials inventory reduced forty percent
- quality defects improved ninety percent
- changeover time reduced ninety percent
- obsolescence reduced from twenty percent of finished goods inventory to zero
- reliability improved forty percent from baseline

Appendix

EXAMPLE VENDOR BID PACKAGE

THE CO-OP CONTRACTING PHILOSOPHY

Co-op contracting is a procurement philosophy and technique that complements the TBM objective of reducing lead time across the entire materials continuum. The focus of co-op contracting is lead time reduction and quality. Success is based on combining common products into groups and contracting with fewer suppliers for product group purchases.

The overall objective of co-op contracting on a commodity basis is to synchronize supplier capability by directly linking it to the customer output. There are several major principles for co-op contracting. They include:

• aligned capacity
• latest possible confirmation of actual product mix
• supplier output directly linked to customer requirements
• capable processes with uniform quality centered on the target value

Co-op contracting is exactly what its name implies: an interdependent cooperative effort between both parties. It is a two-way relationship between the customer and its vendors. It represents a new era of working together.

This appendix is adapted from Wheeler 1987.

321

Co-op Contracting Goals and Vendor Requirements

The following goals or vendor requirements help to facilitate co-op contracting. These goals set the new standards that a company expects for all suppliers. The company should recognize that it cannot continue to improve in the time-based manufacturing (TBM) philosophy without the full cooperation of suppliers. These standards dictate that all future suppliers have in place, or are working toward, the following:

• high product quality
• continuous total lead time reduction
• adequate production capacity
• delivery reliability
• continuous cost reduction
• financial stability
• ability to identify product cost drivers
• competitive pricing/terms
• high level of customer responsiveness

Product Specifications and Annual Usages. Product specifications and annual usages for this bid would be enclosed as a separate attachment.

Vendor Questionnaire

The following questionnaire is designed to assess a vendor's potential for a TBM partnership. Please respond to all questions thoroughly in the spaces provided. The vendor should feel free to attach any samples or additional pages required to support individual answers. If a question does not apply, please state so accordingly. Any questions left blank will be counted against you in the evaluation.

Please note that this bid package will be held in strict confidence. All contents within this bid package will be held proprietary. At no time will any bid package responses or results be disclosed outside of the customer.

The vendor questionnaire is broken down into ten categories. Questions for each category are outlined below:

1. Quality
a) Please explain in detail the quality techniques you employ to ensure defect-free products.

b) Do you have a quality assurance department? How many people work full-time in the quality assurance department? Please explain their roles.

c) To whom does the quality assurance department report?

d) What type and level of quality training has been given to your management team?

e) What type and level of quality training has been given to front-line workers?

f) Does your company have fully documented quality assurance procedures? How have they been implemented?

g) Does your company use statistical process control (SPC)? How is it used?

h) Are SPC charts available to customers upon request?

i) At what points are inspections performed and by whom?

j) Explain how you measure process capabilities.

k) Do you measure first run yield (FRY)? If so, what is your percentage of FRY? Where is it measured? How do you monitor your performance levels?

2. Lead time

a) Does you company operate in a TBM environment? If so, how long has it done so?

b) Please describe your TBM philosophy and implementation.

c) Please provide a high level process flow diagram. Explain the major activities required, beginning with order placement to your suppliers and ending with shipment of finished products to your customers. Please provide a similar flowchart for your customer order process flow.

d) What is your product supply lead time on the flow above (from the time raw material is ordered to when it is available to ship)?

e) What is your customer order lead time on the flow above (from receipt of customer order to shipment of goods)?

f) Please explain the steps you have taken to reduce the product supply lead time and the customer order lead time.

3. Supply system capacity

a) At what capacity level are you operating (e.g., 80%) by major activity? How long have you been at this capacity level?

b) Are you planning to alter capacity anytime in the next year? If so, please explain why.

c) Is your business seasonal? If so, when are the peaks?

d) To what extent do you experience wide fluctuations in customer demand? Please describe.

e) Have you experienced any work stoppages in the past five years? If so, please explain.

4. Delivery

a) What is your percentage of on-time deliveries to customers? Please explain your calculation.

b) Please explain your delivery policy on stock orders, (e.g., next day, three days, etc.).

c) Please explain your delivery policy on custom orders.

d) Do you own your own truck fleet? If not, what carriers do you use and why?

e) Is your company willing to comply to a customer designated shipping mode and firm?

f) Do you have other customers that have a TBM partnership? If so, how many customers? Would you be willing to provide references?

5. Customer service

a) Please explain your customer service practices and policies.

b) Would you be willing to make periodic visits to customers to better understand their problems and manufacturing processes?

c) Would you be willing to host periodic, informal visits and plant tours?

d) Would you be willing to commit staff to a joint vendor/customer continuous improvement team?

e) Would you be willing to share and exchange cost-savings ideas or process improvements?

f) Would the company assign a designated service representative(s) to ensure prompt response to inquiries?

g) What internal measures do you have to ensure compliance for receiving requirements? Examples include:

- carton identification
- packing slip
- invoice
- packaging
- delivery appointment

h) Please explain what makes your products and services superior to those of your competitors.

6. Financial stability

a) Please describe the recent financial history of your organization (last five years) and your current financial situation. Please support with documentation as appropriate.

b) What are your credit terms?

c) Would you be willing to jointly share financial information?

d) What level of inventory does your company carry to support your business with us (raw, WIP, and finished goods)?

7. Cost drivers

a) Are any of your major raw material purchases in a highly volatile market subject to wide pricing swings? Please describe.

b) Please note your three variable supply costs that are most uncontrollable and why.

c) Please explain what technology improvements you have implemented in the last two years in your supply system processes.

d) Please explain future plans you have to implement technology improvements in your supply system processes.

8. Pricing

a) Does your firm engage in contracts with customers? Please describe.

b) Are you willing to share your pricing formula? To what extent?

c) Are you willing to share with the customer mutually achieved cost reductions through a reduction in prices? If so, to what extent?

d) What are your credit terms?

9. Cost reduction

a) Please explain the efforts your company has in place to reduce costs. Please explain your progress in the past two years.

b) Please describe any successful cost reduction efforts with other customers. Are you willing to work with us to achieve similar cost reductions?

10. Product integration

a) Of the products in this bid, how many are you able and willing to supply? Please list.

b) What level of vertical integration does your company have for these products? Please describe.

Vendor Selection Criteria

Vendors will be evaluated by a predetermined weighted point system. Following are the ten categories that are being measured and their respective • weighted values:

Maximum Points
Allowed

1. Quality   100
2. Lead time   90
3. Supply system capacity   80
4. Delivery   70
5. Customer service   60
6. Financial stability   50
7. Cost drivers   40
8. Pricing   30
9. Cost reduction   20
10. Product integration   <u>10</u>
                                  550

REFERENCE

Wheeler, W. A. 1987. *Co-op Contracting: Just-in-Time Implementation Methodology.* New York: Coopers & Lybrand.

About the Authors

Joseph A. Bockerstette is a Manufacturing Consulting Partner in Coopers & Lybrand's Performance Improvement Division. He is responsible for management consulting engagements in manufacturing strategy planning, time-based manufacturing, and total quality management in client companies. Mr. Bockerstette has metals experience in a variety of industries including consumer goods, printing, textiles, and electronics implementing projects involving Just-In-Time manufacturing, total quality system development, Manufacturing Information Systems, and work measurement, among others. He lives in Cincinnati, Ohio with his wife Jennifer and daughter Lindsey.

Richard L. Shell, Ph.D., P.E. is Professor of Industrial Engineering and Director of Safety Engineering at the University of Cincinnati. In 1985, he was also appointed as Professor of Environmental Health in the College of Medicine. He is a consultant for business and government specializing in ergonomics/safety engineering, human performance, and manufacturing issues and also serves as a board member for several corporations. Before joining the University of Cincinnati faculty, Dr. Shell held engineering and management positions with Bourns Corporation, Ampex Corporation, and IBM. He received degrees in mechanical and industrial engineering from the University of Iowa, University of Kentucky, and the University of Illinois. His honors include being named Distinguished Engineer of the Year for 1986 by the Technical Society Council of Cincinnati and receiving the Institute of Industrial Engineers Fellow Award in 1988.

Index

ABC. *See* Activity-based costing
Accounting
    traditional cost accounting, 225-226
    new age cost accounting, 226-228
    advanced cost management, 228-230
    activity-based costing, 229
ACM. *See* Advanced cost management
Activity cost profiles, 56
Activity-based costing (ABC), 35, 55-57, 229
Advanced cost management (ACM), 228-230
    See also Accounting, Costs

Backflushing, 216, 230
Barker, Joel, 1
Batch sizes, 71-72
Bid package, 169-171, 321-327
Bottleneck, 65, 109, 130
Building block technique, 60f-61
    See also Part proliferation, Product variety, Foundation technique, Part implosion technique
Buyer-supplier relationship, 177

C chart, 148-149f, 152
    See also Statistical control charts
Capability, 107, 120-127, 150, 154
Capacity, 72-74, 107
Capacity control, 72
Category management system, 20
Cause and effect diagrams, 131-132f

Cellular manufacturing. *See* Cellular processing
Cellular processing, 94-101
    cell design, 95-96, 97-98
    cell staffing, 96-97
    layout configurations, 98-101
    as TBM implementation problem, 264-265
Central tendency, 141
    See also X bar-R chart
Champion, 178
Change
    overcoming resistance, 21
    introducing, 21
    gaining employee acceptance, 22
    managing within TBM, 177-181
Changeover reduction, 80-89, 161
    methodology, 80
    goal setting, 87-92
    calculation, 88-89
    See also Changeover time
Changeover time, 77-92
    benefits of reduced, 79
    implementation, 79-87
    equation, 88
    historic perspective, 89
    for shorter run cycles, 89-91
    See also Changeover reduction
Charting process average, 138
    See also Individuals chart
Charting process variability, 149
    See also Individuals chart
Co-op contracting, 159-163
    objectives, 160-163
    implementing, 165-173

A *t* or *f* denotes a table or figure.